With God on Their Side

With God on Their Side

William Booth, The Salvation Army and Skeleton Army Riots

James Gardner

Ⓛ
The Lutterworth Press

The Lutterworth Press

P.O. Box 60
Cambridge
CB1 2NT
United Kingdom

www.lutterworth.com
publishing@lutterworth.com

Hardback ISBN: 978 0 7188 9591 4
Paperback ISBN: 978 0 7188 9592 1
PDF ISBN: 978 0 7188 9594 5
ePUB ISBN: 978 0 7188 9593 8

British Library Cataloguing in Publication Data
A record is available from the British Library

First published by The Lutterworth Press, 2022

Contents

List of Illustrations

Copyright Information

Figures 1–7:	Salvation Army International Heritage Centre
Figure 8:	*Punch* magazine (Cartoon Library/Top Photo)
Figures 9–18:	Salvation Army International Heritage Centre
Figure 19:	British Library/British Newspaper Archives
Figures 20–25:	Salvation Army International Heritage Centre
Figure 26:	*Daily Mirror* (Mirrorpix/Reach Licensing)
Figure 27:	Salvation Army International Heritage Centre

Author's Note

In my youth I have vivid memories of Salvation Army 'soldiers' coming into pubs selling their magazine, *The War Cry*. Considering their hostility to drinking, I always wondered why they were given such a sympathetic greeting by the patrons. In town centres at Christmas their brass bands and carols warmed the hearts of shoppers. In George Bernard Shaw's play *Major Barbara* and in the Hollywood musical, *Guys and Dolls*, their 'Hallelujah lasses' were portrayed as idealistic and naïve but sincere. Later, I understood that the Salvation Army were one of the most popular charities in the country due to their fantastic support of the poor and needy and their provision of humanitarian aid. Nobody ever had a bad word to say about them. More often than not they seemed to be the main beneficiaries of charitable donations. So, it was a great shock when, whilst doing research, I came across evidence of their early persecution and the level of violence against them. Why on earth, I asked myself, would anyone want to attack an organisation that clearly did so much to try and make the world a better place? I hope this book answers that question.

To assist the reader, some idea of money value may be helpful. The Victorian History Blogspot has some very useful examples of what the poor might earn in late nineteenth century Britain:

> A matchwoman in the East End of London in 1880s would . . . be likely to have earned from six to twelve shillings a week . . . A bank clerk, a shopkeeper or a street-seller would be doing well to bring home a pound [twenty shillings] a week . . . According to Bowley [*Wages in the United Kingdom in the 19th Century* (Cambridge: Cambridge University Press, 1900)], a bricklayer might earn just slightly less than two pounds a

> week in the summer but only 36 shillings in the winter while a bricklayer's labourer would, on average earn about twelve shillings less than the bricklayer.[1]

One further point: the trust deed setting up The Salvation Army required that the definite article, with a capital T was part of its name. After using this in the title, I now revert to its common usage.

1. Bruce Rosen, 'Income vs Expenditure in Working-Class Victorian England', Victorian History Blogspot, 19 June 2014. http://vichist.blogspot.com/2014/05/income-vs-expenditure-in-working-class.html.

Acknowledgements

First and foremost, I owe an enormous debt to Chris Hare, director of History People UK. It was Chris' article on 'The Skeleton Army and the Bonfire Boys, Worthing, 1884' that first made me interested in the riots. He has been a constant source of encouragement, direction and knowledge for which I am extremely grateful.

I should like to thank the great assistance of the archivist, Steven Spencer, Chloe Wilson and staff at the Salvation Army International Heritage Centre in London. Apart from looking at their archives, Steven kept me up to date with recent articles about the riots and also gave me good advice and kindly provided me with most of the illustrations for this book. Without the assistance of the Heritage Centre, there would have been no book. As an aside, I must say I always heard laughter in the building, possibly a legacy of the wit and humour of William Booth!

I should like to thank James Kneale, Associate Professor at University College London, for kindly sending me his excellent chapter on the Torquay disturbances and, also, Dr Cronan Cronshaw, senior research associate at Lancaster University, for providing me with lots of relevant material.

I should like to thank the staff at: the National Archives, Kew; the Keep, the East Sussex Record Office; North Devon and South Devon Heritage Centres and Somerset Heritage Centre; Louise Taylor of the Jubilee Library, Brighton; Pauline Watkins of Chipping Norton Museum; and Rosie Jones from the North Somerset Studies Library. I should also like to thank the Salvation Army staff at the Congress Hall, Brighton, and at the Citadel, Eastbourne, and Major Nigel Bovey, David Crowe, Dr Peter Jackson, Mike Liardet and Amber Quatramiz for their useful comments.

Finally, many thanks to Adrian Brink, Samuel Fitzgerald and everyone at The Lutterworth Press for supporting this book and to Dorothy Luckhurst for her superb copy editing.

Prologue

Lewes, June 1891

The morning sun shone brilliantly over the nearby valleys as three blue-suited uniformed men and a woman were marched up the rugged cobblestones from the railway station towards the prison. Out of every door people came to watch, whilst excited children swaggered alongside with exaggerated steps. Some grim-faced adults, outrage and anger marring their faces, jeered and spat at the shackled, straight and stiff-backed little group with their military bearing who, strangely, appeared to be happy.

At the prison a crowd of well-wishers had gathered. The prisoners walked up the gravel path towards the big strong gates. Twice they turned and waved their caps to the crowd then fell on their knees and started to pray. Briefly, they raised their arms towards the sky, as warders looked on, before passing through a massive outer gate into a gloomy tunnel-like passage, with another inner gate at the end, then across a portion of the prison yard to the reception area. After the woman was separated, the men were unshackled, stripped naked, given a cold bath and had their hair closely cropped. In coarse jackets, trousers and pill box hats, freely stamped with broad arrows to denote crown property, they were taken to their cells. The next morning, lying on their wooden bunks, they heard the faint sound of singing and a band playing outside the prison walls. Each day of their 30-day sentence, they were to hear the same sound.

On release they were met by an enthusiastic flag-waving crowd singing songs. Later, they returned to Eastbourne railway station to a tumultuous reception from hundreds of men, women, children and brass bands. Why the welcome? Who were these soldiers and what was their crime? In the strictest sense of the word, they were not soldiers but members of the Salvation Army – soldiers of Christ – who had been imprisoned for marching and playing music on a Sunday. As such, martyrdom and the baiting of Christians marching along a dusty road was the history and symbolism which gave them strength to continue. Blind to the insults, aware of the presence of each other, finding strength and comfort from their insignificant foursome against the mob. A few against the multitude. Soldiers preaching love not hate.

Today, the Army is respected world-wide and one of the biggest and most comprehensive welfare organisations in Britain. However, in the early days they were opposed by another little-known army: the Skeleton Army. This book is about the struggle between the two, of which those Salvationists, sent to Lewes prison, were a part. The places selected illustrate different aspects of the rioting which broke out during the Salvation Army's evangelical crusade in the late nineteenth century.

Introduction

London, 29 August 1912

The morning began with a heavy downpour as dozens of special trains arrived early. Their passengers were coming to witness one of the biggest funerals[1] ever seen in the capital in living memory. They poured out of Charing Cross and Blackfriars underground stations and headed for the Embankment. By the time they were marshalled into groups, they were soaked to the skin by the drenching rain. In all, there were 40 bands and 10,000 blue uniformed men and women, strangely, not wearing black ribands but white ones. Banners and flags of every nationality flew as they marched off. It did not seem like a funeral, more a triumphal march.

At Queen Victoria Street the coffin, draped in white, of the 83-year-old man was placed on a horse-drawn hearse decorated in red and purple. Palms surrounded the simple oaken casket and a cap and well-worn bible were placed on the coffin. The mile-long funeral cortège watched by a curious, dense crowd as far as the eye could see – over a million people – wended its way on the five-mile journey to Abney Park Cemetery in Stoke Newington. It took an hour for it to pass at any one point. The pavements were black with umbrellas and mackintoshes as the bands started to play the soulful, moving 'Dead March' from Handel's *Saul*. The steady beat of thousands of feet on the sanded roads was the right accompaniment.

1. This funeral account is based on numerous contemporary newspaper reports.

The hushed multitudes who lined the route reverently saluted the coffin removing their hats as it was borne along. Everywhere people were breaking down and weeping; the majority working men and women. Black shutters were put up as a mark of respect and all shops were temporarily closed. At junctions the crowd stood 20 to 50 deep. Traffic was non-existent and the pavements were impassable. At times, there was hardly space for the procession to pass. An experienced policeman thought the crowd was twice as dense as any he had encountered during Coronation festivities.

At the Stock Exchange, flags flew at half-mast and business was suspended for an hour as its members crowded the roof of the building. Bareheaded clerks and typists flocked to the streets below to watch the spectacle. Past the Mansion House the Lord Mayor appeared on the balcony in his robes and chain and saluted the coffin as it passed. At Stoke Newington, across the High Street was stretched a large banner, with a deep border of purple, which bore the words on each side in black letters: 'The Metropolitan Boroughs of Hackney and Stoke Newington mourn the loss of a noble life'.

Nearer and nearer to the cemetery the crush became greater and ambulance men were soon busy dealing with those who had fainted. Outside the gates, mounted police rode among the vast crowd – a crowd that stretched to London's heart. Some sections sang hymns while they were waiting. Newsvendors were busy selling sixteen pages of pictures and news in a *Daily Mirror* memorial to the dead man.

After three hours the cortège arrived at the cemetery. Suddenly, the clouds parted and the sun shone, drying out those who had earlier been soaked. Inside, there was ticketed admission for 10,000. Amongst the dreadful ghostliness of tomb stones and gaunt pillars women fainted in the crush and were placed on the ground against them. As the warm sunshine bathed the cemetery, the raindrops on the grass glistened like diamonds.

The grave was in the centre of a belt of trees. Nearby, chairs were seated around the coffin on an improvised platform adorned with flowers. The air was heavy with the intoxicating fragrance of costly bouquets – apart from a small posy tied up with a piece of rag which read 'To the General with love from Joey, Jimmie and Joe, Liverpool slums'.

Messages of love and condolence from all over the world, including ones from the Royal Family and the German Kaiser, were read out for one of the greatest and most famous men of his generation. It was quite an achievement, for this was no king, politician or soldier but William Booth, a religious man from a humble background. Quite remarkably, along with his wife, Catherine, 'God's Soldier' had founded the movement known as the Salvation Army; a movement born in absolute poverty. By the time he died, it was known, loved and respected around the world. Now he was 'laying down his sword'.

His eldest son, Bramwell, led the mourners in singing 'Servant of God, Well Done!' However, 'mourners' was the wrong word for, in Army parlance, Booth was being 'promoted to glory'; his death a joyous occasion to be celebrated. As the bands played, the singers sang, smiling through their tears, occasionally crying out 'Hallelujah'. At the end, the evening shadows were drawing in and the rays of the sun fell on the coffin as it disappeared from view as it was lowered into a grave already occupied by his wife.

In the last years of his life, William Booth had supped with monarchs and presidents; so very different from his early days as a preacher when he had been pelted with stinking fish, dead cats, rotten eggs, a variety of vegetables and mud by mobs, and vilified by the religious establishment.

* * *

William Booth was born on the outskirts of Nottingham in 1829, the son of a domestic servant and a builder.[2] His early life was comfortable until his father went bankrupt. Aged thirteen, he was taken away from private school. By all accounts he led a blameless childhood although he once admitted to cheating at marbles! The following year, after his father died, he became apprenticed to a pawnbroker. Week after week, families on the verge of destitution appeared before him, desperate to avoid being forced into workhouses under the Poor Law Amendment Act of 1834, which cut outdoor relief. It was a first-hand insight into the meaning of economic distress.

In the 'hungry forties' there was a serious trade depression in the local Nottingham industries[3] and Chartism[4] was rife. One of its leaders, Fergus O'Connor, was a local Member of Parliament. According to one of Booth's childhood friends, Walter James, 'the distress was very great. Want, misery and bread riots were common in our streets. I know that

---

2. 'My father was a man given to the acquisition of wealth and indifferent to religion. . . . Mother was a woman of a religious and gentle spirit', *Sheffield Daily Telegraph*, 11 April 1889.
3. Particularly the lace market.
4. Working-class, male suffrage movement for political reform, which began in 1838 and petered out after 1848.

these things sank deeply into some of our natures and that we boys hung round the Chartist platforms, drank in their wrongs, and wished success to their remedies.'[5] Booth later admitted his sympathies had been with them.

James thought 'Will Booth' was no ordinary lad. He had once told him he intended to do something 'great' with his life. According to James, Booth's religious conversion was a gradual process rather than a dramatic experience like that of St Paul on the road to Damascus.[6] Although born into the Church of England, Booth converted, aged fifteen, to the Wesleyan Methodist chapel and soon became involved in the fervour of evangelical revivalism sweeping the country, inspired by fiery preachers like the American James Caughey, who had visited Nottingham during his tour of England. Booth refused to work on a Sunday and his employer sacked him. He was such a good worker, however, that seven days later his employer begged him to come back.

As a teenager, with other young men, he started to preach in the slums of Nottingham, despite a doctor's warning that physically he was too weak to do so. He later wrote, 'my whole turn of mind was in favour of good works, and of helping people who were in trouble. The streets were a capital school for the preacher for you had to be interesting and striking if you wished to keep your hearer's attention.'[7]

In 1858, Booth was privately ordained and became a minister of the Methodist New Connexion in Gateshead. A dynamic and magnetic preacher, his chapel was known as the 'converting shop'. However, he soon became disillusioned with Methodism and the gulf between its ministers and the poorest of its congregation. He was against charging money for the best pews and felt a church was not a welcoming place. Rather than being a place of passion, joy and celebration, it was too solemn and impersonal. Bureaucracy, too, impeded decisive action from its religious leaders.

Booth believed Methodism and the more respectable denominations were failing to attract the outcast poor – as had been originally intended – few of whom could read prayers or hymnbooks or even had

---

5. *Wakefield Herald*, 24 August 1912 (from the *Manchester Guardian*).
6. Although in George Railton's biography, *The Authoritative Life of General Booth, Founder of the Salvation Army* (New York: George H. Doran Co., 1912), Booth says his full conversion happened after one particular incident in which he owned up to another boy over an attempted deception.
7. *Wakefield Herald*, 28 April 1912.

suitable clothes to attend the service. It appeared church was only for those who prayed in their Sunday best and contributed to the collection. Those deemed 'too wicked' were not encouraged to come. (As a teenager he had taken a batch of 'ragged dirty urchins' to his local chapel. Its trustees would not let him use the front entrance and said there would have to be special sittings for them.[8]) If people would not or could not go to church or chapel, Booth argued, then the church must go to them. For him, Christianity must be dynamic, active and individual. He still accepted the central tenet of Wesleyanism that the main duty of a Christian was to save souls, which was the key to the salvation of the body and a purer life.

Booth wanted to preach where there was most sin and deprivation, which he believed went hand in hand. For years he wandered around the country barely earning enough to live on. After various postings, he ended up in the East End of London, a squalid filthy area crowded with a jungle of backstreets full of disease. In 1866, a cholera epidemic led to 573 children under five dying in one week. Half a million souls were crammed into lodgings. In his book, *How the Poor Live*, the writer, George R. Sims, describes visiting a family:

> To the particular door attached there comes a poor woman, white and thin, and sickly-looking, in her arms she carries a girl of eight or nine with a diseased spine, behind her clutching at her scanty dress, are two or three other children. We ask to see the room. What a room! The poor woman apologises for its condition. . . . Poor creature, if she had ten pairs of hands instead of one pair always full, she could not keep this room clean. The walls are damp and crumbling, the ceiling is black and peeling off showing the laths above, the floor is rotten and broken away in places, and the wind and the rain sweep in through gaps that seem everywhere. The woman, her husband, and her six children live, eat and sleep in one room, and for this they pay three shillings a week. . . . There has been no breakfast yet, and there won't be any till the husband (who has been out to try and get a job) reports progress.[9]

8. Memory of the Rev. I.E. Page, member of the same Wesleyan chapel in Nottingham. *Hexham Courant*, 18 September 1897.

9. George R. Sims, *How the Poor Live; and Horrible London* (London: Chatto & Windus, 1889) (Kindle), ch. 1.

Figure 1. William Booth in the East End in the 1860s.
Source: Twenty One Years Salvation Army (1887).

It was in the Mile End Road, Whitechapel, East London in July 1865 that William Booth, a tall, dark black-bearded man in a frock coat and wide-brimmed hat, made his way 'through ragged match-sellers, Irish flower-girls, and thrust past hulking labourers, women clad only in soiled petticoats. Children with wolfish faces foraged at his feet, gobbling up heaps of decaying plums in [the] street market's garish light'.[10] He stopped in front of the Blind Beggar pub, stood on an old chair with Bible in hand and shouted 'There is a Heaven in East London for everyone.' The patrons replied with oaths and jeers; a rotten egg hit his face. Welcome to the East End! He had found his destiny.

Along with his temperance-supporting wife, Catherine – whom he married in 1855[11] – Booth, depending on subsistence from a well-wisher, started the East London Christian Mission. With beer shops open from early morning until ten at night and every fifth shop selling gin, it was

10. Richard Collier, *The General Next to God: The Story of William Booth and the Salvation Army* (London: Collins, 1965), p. 16.

11. Their honeymoon was spent evangelising in the Channel Islands!

drinkers and the drink trade he attacked most vociferously. If people were to be saved, they had to stop drinking, which encouraged sin, as a first step. Then other 'evils': smoking, gambling, boxing and music halls – more or less the social pleasures of the working-class – could be tackled. However, as one of the early leaders of the Labour Party, Will Crooks, wrote of the East End:

> 'Can you wonder so many of our people take to drink?' And he pointed to the shabby little houses, all let out in tenements, in the street where he was born. 'Look at the homes they are forced to live in! The men can't invite their mates round, so they meet at "The Spotted Dog" of an evening. During the day the women often drift to the same place. The boys and girls cannot do their courting in these overcrowded homes. They make love in the streets, and soon they too begin to haunt the public-houses.'[12]

Sims was more forceful:

> Drink is the curse of these communities; but how is it to be wondered at? The gin-palaces flourish in the slums, and fortunes are made out of men and women who seldom know where tomorrow's meal is coming from. Can you wonder that the gaudy gin-palaces, with light and glitter, are crowded? Drink is sustenance to these people, drink gives them the Dutch courage necessary to live in such styes. The gin-palace is Heaven to them compared to the Hell of their pestilent homes. A copper or two obtained by pawning the last rag that covers the shivering children on the bare floor at home will buy enough vitriol madness to send a woman home so besotted that the wretchedness, the anguish, the degradation that await her there have lost their grip. To be drunk with these people means to be happy. Sober – God help them! – how could they be aught but wretched.[13]

12. George Haw, *From Workhouse to Westminster: The Life Story of Will Crooks, M.P.* (London: Cassell & Co., 1907), p. 25.

13. Sims, *How the Poor Live*, ch. 3.

According to Steven Spencer, 'The modern temperance movement in Britain began in the north in the 1830s and spread across the country.'[14] In a short time, those advocating total abstinence – the teetotallers – had become dominant. They believed drunkenness alone was responsible for the nation's ills and that signing 'the pledge' signified a spiritual as well as moral rebirth. Booth had signed the pledge when he was just seven years old but, by the age of thirteen, had begun to drink a little for his health's sake. By the age of 20, he was teetotal. Catherine, at the age of twelve, had been secretary of her local Juvenile Temperance Society.

Booth was preaching in one of the most irreligious places in the country. Less than two per cent of working men in London attended a church service, even fewer in the East End. His 'church' was to be the open air: on street corners and in squares. His congregation – those who needed the Gospel most but wanted it least: the working-class poor. From them he would recruit an army of reformed sinners to evangelise and convert others: 'I found that ordinary working men in their corduroys and bowler hats could command attention from their own class which was refused point-blank to me with my theological terms and superior knowledge. . . . Their message was one of hope, not condemnation.'[15]

Following conversion, they would 'save' their peers through personal testimony and dedicate themselves to their spiritual welfare. When asked where he would get his preachers from, Booth replied, 'from the public houses, from the gutters'. (His injunction was 'go for souls and go for the worst'). This new breed would have experience of poverty and the difficulty in escaping its temptations. Converts were expected to change their lifestyles radically through personal faith in Jesus. Unlike mainstream religion, Booth made no distinction between the deserving and undeserving poor. Using the analogy of a stumbling cab horse,[16] it did not concern him how it fell, it was just necessary to get it back on its feet. The message was clear: everybody could be saved. Nobody

---

14. Steven Spencer, Director of the Salvation Army International Heritage Centre in London, email to the author, 26 May 2021.

15. *West Briton & Cornwall Advertiser*, 22 August 1912.

16. Over time he developed the 'cab-horse charter': the right to shelter, food and work enjoyed by every London cab-horse but not by the poor of that city.

was beyond redemption if he or she confessed his or her sins. Heaven would welcome them all. However, the unsaved, he warned, would be condemned to the terror of Hell and eternal damnation.

With piercing grey eyes of almost frightening intensity and an Inverness (tartan) cape thrown over his shoulders, Booth started preaching in a dilapidated tent on a one-time Quaker graveyard in Whitechapel. He struck a charismatic figure. From the start he was regularly abused, ridiculed and physically assaulted (even though he had an ex-boxer as his bodyguard). On several occasions the ropes holding up his tent were cut and he and his followers were pelted with mud, stones, putrid meat, rotten eggs and fish. His wife, Catherine, remembers him coming back home every evening battered and bruised. After his first year he had made only 60 converts. Some of these were temporary and became 'backsliders' – those who went back to their wicked ways.

However, the more setbacks he suffered, the stronger his beliefs became. His hero, John Wesley – who had also taken the Gospel to the people – had been pelted with mud whilst preaching at Oxford University and the early Methodist men and women had often been violently assaulted. (In Exeter in 1745, the women had even been stripped naked, rolled in the mud and had their faces covered with boot polish, flour and dirt.) The Devil was a fierce customer who was going to put up a fierce fight. For Booth it was to be a fight between good and evil. A battle that could not be lost. This is what drove him on.

He started to use military language and spoke of 'attacking' the Devil. He encouraged abstainers to stand outside pubs – 'the Devil's Castles' – and sing 'we will throw down the bottle and never drink again' and recruited young women, 'Hallelujah lasses', to spread the message. Sometimes they would stand outside and 'pray the drunkards out' or bravely enter and distribute tracts denouncing drink and tobacco. Meetings were advertised with colourful posters imitating the rhetoric of the circus and the music hall. It was a clever ploy, for this period was the golden age of the latter; its artistes the pop stars of the day. (He also borrowed the idea of the 'Free-and-Easy' session, an unstructured entertainment with singing and audience participation.) At his earliest meeting places, he reputedly put up notices requesting 'respectable people' to stay away.

As his Mission grew and expanded outside London, and became the Christian Mission, so did the opposition. By 1869 his open-air meetings were regularly harassed by police, landlords and pub-goers. Outside

Figure 2. William Booth preaching in a tent in the East End.

London, the harassment was just as fierce. At one meeting in Harrogate, Yorkshire, local employees of Sanger's Circus pelted the missioners with clods of earth. They beat a big bass drum in front of the speaker whilst cymbals were clashed behind him. Then brought an elephant and two camels into the tent. The meeting ended in chaos.

Booth realised he needed buildings not just tents – his own was blown down in a storm – if he was to protect his followers. In any case, in winter the chilly winds drastically reduced attendances. So, he started to hire disused beer shops, warehouses, music halls and theatres for meetings. They became the Army's sacred spaces. The choice was deliberate. In urban areas they were among the best-known buildings in a neighbourhood, visited far more by the working-class than churches. Nonetheless, they were just as susceptible to sabotage as the tents and street meetings:

> For week-nights, we secured an old wool warehouse in one of the lowest parts of Bethnal Green. I remember the windows opened out into the street. When crowded it became oppressively hot; especially in summer. If we opened the windows the boys

> threw stones and mud and fireworks through, and fired trains of gunpowder laid from the door inside. But we got used to this, and we shouted 'Hallelujah!' when the crackers exploded and the powder flashed. It was an admirable training-ground for the development of the Salvation Army spirit.[17]

The War Cry described an attempted sabotage in a hall near Penge, Surrey:

> Presently a queer-looking man presented himself for admission. It wasn't his face nor the colour of his coat that attracted the 'weather-eye' of the doorkeeper, but the 'nubbly' appearance of his sides and chest.
>
> 'Can't let you in my friend. No accommodation for livestock inside,' said the doorkeeper, after having passed his hand over one of the protuberances and he quickly withdrew it.
>
> The man's coat was lined with pockets, and sewn up in each was a live rat. An attack on the gas-meter had been planned, and the rats were to be liberated when the lights were lowered. They succeeded in putting out the lights, but the rat part of the scheme did not come off, thanks to the vigilance of the doorkeeper.[18]

In 1867, for £120, the Christian Mission bought a run-down beer shop, the Eastern Star, notorious for its 'immorality' in Whitechapel Road – a road with no trees only pubs, known as 'Labour's Boulevard' where thousands passed every evening – as its first headquarters. It is not surprising that its entry into the East End ruffled the feathers of other religious groups. In 1868, the Reverend John Richard Green (later a historian) denounced it because funds intended for the relief of East Enders were being handed over to 'a single ranting revivalist of the name of William Booth':

> The breakfast and sewing classes and meetings to which people are asked to subscribe are held in his chapel, among his 'experience meetings' and his 'fellowship meetings'. We have known instances where decent and respectable poor

17. *Coventry Evening Telegraph*, 21 August 1912.

18. *The War Cry*, 23 July 1898.

> have been dragged to this place and forced from very hunger to listen to the vulgar ravings of this man and his supporters. Of course, his 'labours' are already crowned with success. He boasts of having converted a thousand people; we wonder he has not converted tens of thousands. A theatre is filled every Sunday morning with 1,500 mendicants [tramps] who are allowed a breakfast on condition that they remain to 'hear the gospel.'. . . The best comment is the plain fact that poor sufferers may be refused all assistance if they decline to listen to the doggerel parodies of Scripture, the vulgar rant, and the revivalist rhapsodies of such a person as William Booth.[19]

However, according to Booth, he had not originally intended to start a new movement:

> When I began my irregular warfare in Whitechapel in 1865, I was possessed of the idea that I could safely send my converts to join the existing churches of the locality; and, in fact, I did so. It was only when I found that my protegés were not very warmly received – to put it kindly – and that they were therefore in danger of lapsing for sheer want of comradeship and oversight that I resolved to draw them together . . .[20]

There were many missions operating in the East End, however, Booth seems to have been more successful in raising funds, even advertising for contributions in postage stamps.[21] His plans were grandiose, on one occasion asking for donations so he could take 5,000 poor people, connected to the Mission, to Southend for a break.[22]

In the spring of 1870, Booth bought the 'People's Market' in Whitechapel and changed its name to the 'People's Mission Hall'. This became the Mission's new centre of operations and for the first few years the Army's annual conference was held there. It was large enough to seat 1,500 in its main hall and had ten smaller rooms and a coffee house in its complex. On its opening Sunday night, it was overflowing with crowds locked out. Reputedly, 150 sinners confessed their sins.

---

19. *Cheltenham Examiner*, 29 August 1912.
20. *West Briton and Cornwall Advertiser*, 22 August 1912.
21. *Daily Telegraph & Courier*, 17 December 1870.
22. *East London Observer*, 25 July 1874.

By 1874, the Christian Mission was a national institution, essentially democratic, with groups of societies deciding policy at an annual conference. However, in 1877, as leader of the fastest and strongest national revivalist force in nineteenth-century England, Booth told the conference they needed a director to tell them what to do, not leadership by conference. His suggestion was accepted. The will of one man was to be supreme. Next year, with the encouragement of his eldest son, Bramwell, he changed the Mission's name to the 'Salvation Army', to reinforce the idea of a continuous war against the Devil. It was to be a militant evangelism expressed in military metaphors. The name change, in 1878, was perfectly in sync with the prevailing Victorian militaristic jingoism and the expansion of the British Empire. Appropriately, a favourite music hall ditty, MacDermott and Hunt's *War Song*, written that year, introduced the word 'jingoism' and proclaimed:

> *We don't want to fight but by Jingo if we do,*
> *We've got the ships, we've got the men, we've got the money too.*

'Yet', according to Chris Hare, 'Booth was no friend of the Victorian Establishment; his Army was to be an army of the poor and luckless, the same "dangerous classes" that respectable opinion so feared.'[23] Becoming an army would lead to enormous ridicule and uproar on the streets; streets already experiencing tension due to urban poverty[24] – caused by increasing industrialisation and the great trade recession of 1877–80 – as rural workers flooded into towns and cities looking for work. Nevertheless, the historic decision to change the name would prove to be a masterstroke. It gave the organisation a distinct identity, separate from the thousands of other 'missions' in the country, and would lead to its rapid expansion as a fully-fledged army of salvation. During the meeting which announced the change and ratified control of the movement in Booth's hands, 'roughs' outside the hall rattled cans, blew horns and placed smelly objects near the ventilators.

---

23. Chris Hare, 'The Skeleton Army and the Bonfire Boys, Worthing, 1884', *Folklore* 99, no. 2 (1988), pp. 221–31.

24. By 1851 Britain's population was, for the first time, predominantly urban.

Chapter One

The Salvation Army

William now styled himself, 'General' Booth.[1] His ministers were his 'officers', his church members/volunteers, 'soldiers'. Fashioned substantially after the model of an army, they would wear quasi-military uniforms. From now on the language would be that of a fighting army going to war against the well-drilled legions of Lucifer. It adopted the rousing 'Onward, Christian Soldiers! Marching as to War', as its battle cry. Opening a church (called a 'corps') in an area was 'opening fire' and entering places of sin became 'marching towards the sounds of gunfire'. During meetings audience 'amens' were 'volleys' towards the speaker, praying, 'knee drill', and sermons, 'bombshells'. Even reading the Bible was 'taking one's rations'.

Booth talked of 'casualties' as his soldiers were not allowed to fight back – although, under extreme provocation, some did. When Catherine, his wife, opened a new Salvation Hall in Hammersmith in October 1882, it was to 'dethrone the Devil and take his troops prisoner'.[2] A convert was a 'trophy' of war.

Brass bands were formed which played the latest music hall hits with religious words replacing the original. The word 'hymn' was dropped in favour of 'song'. Booth asked, 'why should the Devil have all the good music?' The main thing was to attract attention to their evangelising. Bands could also conveniently drown out opposition abuse. However,

---

1. He had been 'General Superintendent' of the Christian Mission so his new title was not a great change.
2. *Lloyd's Weekly*, 8 October 1882.

he did not simply see music as a way of attracting attention and recruitment. For him it had a higher purpose: to promote the glory of God to a sinful world. For his musicians he had a fundamental rule: they could only play Salvation music and only on Army service.

Joining the Salvation Army required signing its 'Articles of War' contract, similar to the symbolism of signing the temperance 'pledge'. (Junior soldiers aged between seven and fourteen signed the 'Junior Soldier Promise'). Smoking, drinking, gambling and going to the theatre or even playing football and cricket were forbidden. They were all cultural distractions to a genuine religious life. One of Booth's northern bands resigned *en masse* when told they could not smoke. Permission from the leadership was necessary to marry and you were expected to marry another member. (Marriage was to become the cornerstone of the Salvation Army's expansion.) You could be court-martialled and reduced to the ranks for breaking the rules. However, it was an easy, simple religious movement to join with no sacraments or elaborate ceremonies and which encouraged audience participation. In 1878 there were 120 paid officers, eight years later there were 3,602.

'Booth in his early years doubted[3] whether women had the intellectual capacity and other qualities necessary for preaching: the strong-minded Catherine soon revised his view for him', comments E.S. Turner in the *London Review of Books*.[4] Female officers were given equal status although not equal remuneration until the end of the Second World War.[5] The predominantly young Hallelujah lasses played a huge part in fearlessly publicising the Army, particularly in the industrial north and abroad. When it 'invaded' the United States in 1880, the Army's secretary, George Scott Railton, and seven Hallelujah lasses were sent to spread the message. By then they comprised half of all Army officers. They were sometimes spotted going out in the evening in their night

---

3. This advert appeared in the *Stamford Mercury*, 8 October 1875:
'SOUL SAVING – WANTED, in the Christian Mission, useful and devoted MEN (married or single), accustomed to open air work and able to speak acceptably to the working classes. State age, references, and all particulars. Rev. William Booth, 272 Whitechapel Rd, London East.'

4. E.S Turner, 'Hallelujah Lasses', *London Review of Books* 23, no. 10 (24 May 2001).

5. Glenn K. Horridge, *The Salvation Army: Origins and Early Days: 1865–1900* (Godalming: Ammonite, 1993), p. 70.

gowns (over their uniforms) to attract new converts. They even raided brothels in their pursuit of lost souls. Some people thought they were mad.

Catherine Booth, as well as designing the flag and the coal-scuttle female bonnets – to deflect thrown objects – was a powerful, effective speaker and her role cannot be underestimated. She had reputedly read the Bible cover to cover eight times before she was a teenager. She was a stronger supporter of the temperance movement than William and did not let him waver from the Army's total-abstinence policy, obligatory for the membership since 1877. She had grown up in a teetotal household, although her father, a Methodist lay reader, had relapsed and become a heavy drinker. She believed that 'alcohol prevented people from coming to a full saving knowledge of Christ'.[6] Huge crowds attended her meetings. Her talks centred on how to reach the masses with religion as more than 90 per cent of the working class did not go to any religious services. She encouraged audiences to shout out whenever they felt like it to express their emotions and loyalty and to wave white handkerchiefs and flags. She was frequently (and rightly) described as the 'Mother of the Salvation Army'. Her mantra was a challenging one: 'If we are to better the future, we must disturb the present.'

William Booth was already autocratic before the change in his title but now, as General Booth, he had total control – the sole possession of every Army asset – with powers to choose his successor and allocate the most important posts. (The name of the former was kept in a sealed envelope and could only be opened on his death.[7]) Increasingly, he faced public criticism for being a despot and for the lack of transparency in the movement's finances, the number of converts and for 'playing at soldiers'. Critics called him 'Pope Booth' and a 'Brazen-faced Charlatan'. *Punch* preferred 'Field-Marshall von Booth'. Some newspapers christened the bands 'tambourine bangers' and 'drum smashers'. Booth had a good sense of humour and the name-calling did not deflect him from his mission, as caricatures were free advertising. All publicity was good publicity. He used to joke that, if Noah had been compelled to form

---

6. Steven Spencer, '"The Fatal Gaze of this Moral Basilisk": The Salvation Army's War on Drink in Victorian Britain', *The Social History of Alcohol and Drugs* 33, no. 2 (September 2019), p. 237.

7. In 1904 by deed poll a special appointment could be made in case of the mental incapacity of the 'General'.

Figure 3. William and Catherine Booth circa 1850s.

a committee over the building of the Ark, it would never have been finished. Booth was a committee of one. In 1878 there was a popular music hall song:

> *General Booth sends round the hat*
> *Samson was a strong man*
> *But he wasn't up to that.*[8]

There was a suspicion that donations and collections – to defray expenses – at meetings were benefiting Booth and his family. At Exeter Hall, London, in September 1881, he demanded £1,000 'to save the world' and received over that in valuables and money from those present. Claims that Booth's followers had somehow been tricked into supporting him financially resurfaced throughout his life. Despite the accusations, Booth lived a frugal life and reputedly only wore one suit

8. Horridge, *The Salvation Army*, p. 360.

of clothes the whole year.[9] According to Bramwell, 'the slander that he enriched himself was not merely untrue, it was ridiculously untrue. It was not merely a distortion of the facts; it was an inversion of them.'[10] Rich benefactors often sent him blank cheques for his personal use. The cheques were returned.

However, Booth's patronage did strongly favour his strictly brought up family as his children took up leading positions: Emma, aged nineteen, became principal of the Officers' Training Home; Ballington, aged 23, a 'colonel'; Herbert, aged 22, head of England's Cadet Training Corp; and Bramwell, aged 25, chief of staff. Undoubtedly autocratic, he even insisted on choosing their children's Christian names. He also insisted on his sons-in-law adding 'Booth' to their own names and was accused of creating a dynasty. However, nothing angered him more than the suggestion that his family was financially benefiting from the Army. In November 1884, he told an audience in Guildford that his eight children worked twelve hours a day, seven days a week for the cause and only Bramwell received a proper salary and that was less than that of a regular army major.

Thanks to *YouTube*, we can still hear him as an old man explain his faith-in-action philosophy to an audience in his rich Nottinghamshire accent. Asking them not to forget 'the sons and daughters of misery', he declaimed:

> Brought it all on themselves, do you say? Perhaps so, but that does not excuse our assisting them! You don't demand a certificate of virtue before you drag some drowning creature out of the water. Nor the assurance of a man that he has paid his rent before you deliver him from the burning building! But what shall we do? Content ourselves by singing a hymn, offering a prayer or giving a little good advice? No! Ten thousand times, no! We will pity them. Feed them. Reclaim them. Employ them. Perhaps we shall fail with many. Quite likely. But our business is to help them all the same. And that in the most practical, economical and Christ-like manner.

---

9. At his death in 1912 he left little over £400 in his will.

10. Bramwell Booth, *Echoes and Memories* (New York: G.H. Doran Co., 1925) (Kindle), ch. 1.

> But you must help with the means. And as there is nothing like the present, who in this company will lend a hand by taking up the collection?[11]

During meetings, sinners would be expected to come forward to the 'penitent's rail' and publicly ask for forgiveness. One of Booth's close confidants, 'Colonel' Alex Nicol, described how it worked. Booth would ask:

> 'Who will be the first man or woman to leave his or her seat and walk up here and kneel down at this chair and ask God to blot out the past? We are waiting for the first – the first to surrender. Now is the time! Come! God is here. The Spirit has been striving. You are found out. Your sins are making hell in your lives. Come to my Lord, and He will turn the hell into a heaven. Come, Come!' . . . Someone comes. He is led by a sergeant along the aisle to a row of seats on the stage arranged for the penitents. . . . Shouts of 'Hallelujah!' . . . The drummer will probably whack his high-sounding instrument, and the General will rise to his feet, leap to the rail, and cry, 'I see another and another! Blessed be the Lord! The angels must be rejoicing!'[12]

Critics were sceptical about the value of penitent confessions. George Bernard Shaw for one looked on sinners' confessions as a 'nasty lying habit' and that, on the point of confession, all Salvationists wanted to be taken in. *The War Cry* repeatedly boasted about the successes: 'My poor wife gets a joint of meat now on a Saturday night instead of a black eye. Glory be to God! It is the Lord that has done it, and that landlord knows that I am converted, for he gets his rent instead of cursing and the little lambs are going to school next week.'[13] The *Saturday Review* described *The War Cry* as 'a mixture of blasphemy and buffoonery'.[14] Nevertheless, it was an attractively produced newspaper with illustrations. Nothing like the sober, dry publications of other churches. It would play a major role in the expansion and success of the Army.

---

11. https://www.youtube.com/watch?v=dSth5dpE6L4.
12. Alex M. Nicol, *General Booth and the Salvation Army* (London: Herbert & Daniel, 1910), p. 13.
13. Turner, 'Hallelujah Lasses'.
14. 26 June 1886.

Booth started organising poor relief, shelter and clothing for the poor and continued to rent or buy warehouses, disused ice rinks and former places of pleasure, such as the Eagle Tavern and Grecian Theatre in Hackney. Booth leased it in 1882 for seventeen years and changed its name to the Salvation Army Hotel. It had beds for 70, provided refreshments and could accommodate 5,000 for services. Its takeover was to cause uproar in the East End – see Chapter Five – where it was rumoured publicans offered Hallelujah lasses money to go and preach elsewhere. However, they were going nowhere.

* * *

In the early 1880s, *The Times*, an early and constant critic of the Army, regularly reported the physical attacks on its Salvationists in London, particularly in the East End. For example, in March 1881, one young labourer, who claimed he had been dragged to a meeting under a railway archway, protested in court that he had used violence in self-defence. The magistrate let him off saying, if the Army held meetings in streets, knowing fully well there would be trouble, they must accept the consequences. In Stoke Newington, outside the Shakespeare Head public house, 20 Salvationists did not have time to finish their first song before they were surrounded by roughs[15] exiting the pub. When one of them offered a can of beer to a Salvationist and started swearing, the attacks started. None of the watching crowd of hundreds tried to protect them. Although there was a police station nearby, only one constable came out to help. Three Salvationists were badly beaten up, including a young girl who had to be taken home.

In Whitechapel, Hallelujah lasses were roped together like cattle and pelted with live coals. In Chelsea, 30 or 40 Salvationists with a concertina were followed by an angry and turbulent crowd. In Oxford Street, roughs stoned the police when they tried to prevent them from attacking the Army. If arrested, they could be fined or given up to two months of hard labour. Many were young labourers under 20 and often indulged in 'horseplay' which got out of hand. Most of the attacks appeared to be unplanned and spontaneous.

To some, the Army was becoming a serious nuisance. Night-workers complained they could not sleep during the day because of the 'dismal howling of bad music'. One newspaper declared 'to anyone possessed of a fine musical ear, the torture is unspeakable, to hear morning,

15. The modern equivalent would be a 'hooligan'.

afternoon, evening'.[16] A London inhabitant was woken up early one Sunday morning by vehement preaching and singing which lasted till ten at night. The repertoire included 'Out of the Gutters We Pick Them' and 'The Devil and Me, We Can't Agree, I Hate Him and He Hates Me'. An army officer claimed a band had frightened his horse and he had been thrown off and seriously hurt.

In January 1882, *The Times* described the Salvation Army as 'a religion warped by fanaticism'. It declared:

> Men object to being treated as the spiritual booty of the bows and spears of a number of enthusiasts who have already made their own prospects comfortably sure. In working-class or lower middle-class life, variety is not so plentiful that the pleasure of masquerading under arms is an unimportant bribe at the disposal of the Salvation Army recruiting sergeants. The Salvation Army is not altogether a pleasant phenomenon. It is overbearing, conceited and unreal. The solitary weapon is gusts of spiritual intoxications.[17]

However, the *Times* editorial in the same edition believed magistrates had been too lenient with the roughs and that 'a procession, however preposterous its character and ridiculous its insignia, should be allowed to march peacefully'. On the other hand, it argued the Army should not monopolise thoroughfares or provoke riots and that the magistrates and police also needed to protect the public.

As well as verbal and physical assaults, Booth was attacked by the Church of England and Nonconformist groups. Bishops accused him of bringing religion into disrepute by indulging in emotional antics using unordained 'racy street preachers' to convert people, which would lead to no permanent good. They despised interactive services with short sermons, personal confessions, and processions led by converts walking backwards. Above all, they disapproved of female preachers; a fundamental challenge to the role of male clergy. Undoubtedly, they were jealous of Booth's success. His conversion meetings and the assaults they attracted kept the movement in the public eye as a steady stream of people appeared in court accused of attacking them.

16. *Heywood Advertiser*, 2 March 1883.

17. *The Times*, 26 January 1882.

'We were a menace to the "comfortable" worship of the day', Bramwell Booth wrote. 'Our people's zeal and joy put to shame the religion which consisted mainly in a listless rote. We aimed at definite and immediate results. This deepened some of the opposition from religious circles. We were intruders. We made religion where there was none before. Ours was a personal, practical faith. It offered a spiritual charter to the ecclesiastically disenfranchised.'[18] In fact, Booth's Army was not a church or a philosophy or a creed. It was an emotion. The only test of membership was personal purity and holiness of life. It was also probably the first Christian organisation which made a principle out of total abstinence. Although it was an 'army', there were no conscripts.

William Booth believed the brewers were behind many of the physical assaults. Nevertheless, with the Army's newspaper, *The War Cry*, selling 255,000 copies a week, his movement had become an unrivalled religious phenomenon, an evangelical bandwagon, and was undoubtedly having some success in saving people from a life of drunkenness and misery. Lives were changed and many a poor person who saw little purpose in his life was indeed reborn. Like the early trade unionists and socialists, 'the voiceless, once docile and silent, began to find a new assertiveness'.[19]

The Army's strength, however controversial, was its ability to be part of street life. Its success predicated on attracting crowds to their meetings, who came out of curiosity – to listen to life stories and enjoy free musical entertainment – as much as for religious reasons. (According to a *Times* reporter, 'the audience did not look like a group of hardened sinners but mainly consisted of single female domestic servants, sailors and petty tradesmen.'[20]) The Congress Hall in Clapton – formerly the London Orphan Asylum, bought for £15,000 in 1881 – could seat 4,500 and people often had to be turned away. It was to become the major hub of its activities. However, sometimes the Army's pugnaciousness was calculated to provoke antagonism. After it purchased the Eagle Tavern and Grecian Theatre, it put up a new sign outside: 'Under Salvation management, to do you all good'.

---

18. Booth, *Echoes and Memories*, ch. 4.para 5, (Kindle).
19. Chris Hare (ed.), "The Skeleton Army Riots" in *Worthing Village Voices*, April 2021. Available at https://worthingvillagevoices.org.uk/worthing-in-the-bad-old-days/ (accessed 11 October 2021).
20. *The Times*, 10 August 1882.

Chapter Two

Widespread Opposition and Prison

Outside London, opposition was just as widespread as the Army, in a dynamic spiritual offensive, 'invaded' areas all over Britain from Dublin to Dunfermline. Its militant evangelism often causing fury amongst those it was hoping to convert. It was, after all, attacking the most popular pastimes of the working-class. It also faced the centuries old traditional violence against anything new which seemed to challenge accepted norms. Typically, Salvationists would congregate in front of their hall before marching, with their band playing and singing songs, towards the most ungodly places. The leaders often walked backwards beating time with an umbrella in front of the 'soldiers' marching four abreast. With their singing, bonnets, uniforms, and flags, the parades resembled a carnival or a group of circus performers advertising a performance. One newspaper thought their instruments were 'instruments of torture with giddy girls and giddier old women twanging tambourines in people's faces'.[1] At times they were accused of acting like a 'Hallelujah' press gang as they overzealously sought out bystanders to come back to their hall. They gave real meaning to Catherine Booth's mantra about disturbing the present.

There were riots everywhere. When Salvationists invaded the Irish quarter of the Welsh town of Tredegar, it sparked widespread rioting and took the enrolment of 80 special constables to calm things down. (The 'Murphy Riots' of the late 1860s had already caused religious friction in

1. *Sheffield Daily Telegraph*, 9 October 1884.

some towns.[2]) At Salisbury, there was nightly violence for several months. On one occasion, a Salvationist recorded, 'the procession was literally covered from head to foot with filth, many of us with our eyes, ears and mouths blocked with mud. The mob, numbering some thousands and armed with rotten eggs, bladders of blood, fireworks, soot and ochre of three or four colours, pelted us to their heart's content. . . . Two were severely injured and many had the clothes ripped off our backs.'[3] As a result, sixteen roughs received two months' hard labour.

At Guildford seventeen men, some respectable tradesmen, were fined for attacking Salvationists. (In the 1860s the town's bonfire society, 'The Guildford Guys', had rioted so badly the Metropolitan police had to be drafted in. In future Skeleton Army riots there was often a close correlation between their members and those of bonfire societies.) When 20 flying Hallelujah lasses 'invaded' Ryde on the Isle of Wight, they were pelted with liquid manure and sewage was thrown over them. The police declined to protect them. At Cowes, after Salvationists had been pelted with flour and eggs and chased into their barracks, they retaliated by throwing flour on the crowd below. Much worse was thrown at Booth's 'soldiers'. At Bath it was fish gut and the occasional sheep's head; at Romsey it was buckets of blood from a nearby slaughterhouse.

The Army 'attacked' Chester in November 1881. At their inaugural meeting a fight broke out, the collecting box was thrown into the air and there was a mad scramble for money. More seriously, there was a huge riot when they attempted to march through the Irish quarter of the town. Miss 'Captain' Falconbridge was hit by a large stone and for a week her life was in danger. Before the arrested rioters appeared in front of the bench, the magistrates received an anonymous note: 'We the Brotherhood of Chester, solemnly vow that if you pronounce one or any of the prisoners guilty you and all your brother magistrates will answer with your lives.'[4] It was signed in blood with a coffin and

---

2. William Murphy gave a series of anti-Catholic lectures in the late 1860s that incited rioting between Protestants and Catholics. He died in 1872 after being beaten up by a 200-strong mob in Whitehaven, Cumberland, the year before. In fact, the Murphy Riots were in the first instance anti-Murphy riots. Irish Catholic attacks were invariably followed by English Protestant counter-attacks.

3. Lieutenant-Colonel Pepper, cited in *The Times*, 20 July 1882.

4. *The Times*, 1 April 1882.

cross-bones. The magistrates discharged and bound over some of the rioters but sent eight of them for trial. Six were acquitted, including, surprisingly, Falconbridge's assailant, but the other two were found guilty and sentenced to two years' hard labour.

At Sheffield, on Easter Monday 1882, the Army held a monster rally reinforced by a thousand 'troops' from Hull. The pre-publicity declared: 'Heavy fighting was expected and great victories were certain. Shot and shell would be freely thrown into the enemy's camp and great damage expected to be done to the Devil's Kingdom.'[5]

When Booth arrived, Sheffield 'Blades' poured out of the slums in their thousands to attack the parade. The police were powerless to control the mob. Stones, mud and brickbats were thrown and many were injured. Some were aimed at William and Catherine Booth's carriage. Miraculously, neither was hurt although Catherine had some mortar on her bonnet which she was reluctant to wash off before her next speech. (They had previously been pelted in Newcastle.) The General stood unflinchingly in his carriage during the entire length of the march giving out instructions and shouting, 'Take no notice, march straight on!' Of this event, in an obituary of Booth, one newspaper recorded that: 'When the hall was reached and a group of mud-bespattered, bruised and bleeding figures with bandaged heads welcomed him at the door. The General said with a twinkle in his eye, "Now is the time to get your photographs taken."'[6]

'Lieutenant' Emerson Davidson, a converted, former champion wrestler, was concussed and covered in mud and had to cling to his horse before he was rescued. A cutter, Arthur Woolen, was charged with throwing a heavy piece of wood at him. He was acquitted by a jury although Davidson had not recovered by the time of the trial. Booth commented, 'he [Davidson] has had many a fall wrestling for the Devil, but today he had a fall in wrestling for God'.[7]

* * *

Salvationists began to be prosecuted for blocking the highways and fined. Usually, encouraged by headquarters, they refused to pay and were imprisoned, although in some cases they did not have the money to

5. Ibid., 26 March 1882.

6. *Coventry Evening Standard*, 21 August 1912.

7. *Sheffield Daily Telegraph*, 17 January 1882.

pay. Louisa Lock and four of her male colleagues were the first Salvation Army prison 'martyrs'. They were sentenced to three days' hard labour for 'obstruction' in Pontypridd in South Wales in September 1879. On their release they were given a hero's welcome.

In August 1881, a Salvationist was fined ten shillings or seven days in prison for hitting a seven-year-old boy with an umbrella because he had thrown mud at him. He chose prison. More seriously, a former officer, Fred Spencer, was given eighteen months' hard labour for seducing a young woman during a meeting. There were rumours of immorality during all-night prayer meetings, begun, according to Bramwell Booth, by certain bishops of the Anglican church. 'Jumping for Jesus' or 'Creeping for Jesus' took place with the lights turned low. The 'soldiers' would be on their hands and knees simulating being lost in sin. Some critics called it 'Groping for Jesus'. One London magistrate wondered aloud how many single women in London workhouses were expecting babies after attending a Salvation Army meeting. The rumours were unfounded and an enquiry confirmed this. In reality, they were all-night prayer meetings and the gaslight was never lowered.

As disturbances grew, Salvationists were imprisoned more frequently. Thomas Maycock, the leader of the Leamington corps, was sentenced to one month for 'obstruction' after declining to pay a fine for preaching, praying and singing in the street. A large crowd of supporters went to see him taken into Warwick gaol and he shouted out to jeering bystanders that they would be 'roasted on the Devil's pitchfork'. After three days, his wife paid the fine because of his poor health. A few days later 2,000 went to a meeting to learn of his prison experience. After being sentenced, Salvationists were often led away to the court cells shouting 'Glory to God' or singing 'Anywhere with Jesus'. In the cells they would try to sing loudly non-stop which was against regulations. However, once within the harsh prison regime their spirits would sink.

Victorian prisons were notorious. After a few weeks of hard labour, prisoners were sometimes hardly recognised by their relatives when they met at the prison gates. Fortunately, few Salvationists were sentenced to more than a month. Nevertheless, they had to get used to the horrid hush at night broken by prisoners sobbing and the shrieking of someone in a nightmare. At six a.m. they were woken by the ugly voice of the prison bell which commanded prisoners to get up and dress. After washing, slopping out and cleaning the cell, the breakfast was gruel[8] and bread. They could only attend chapel by walking, single file, on landings that reeked with the stench of slops and excrement.

Hard labour was breaking stones, the treadmill or picking oakum (used to seal ships' timber and planking). The last involved sitting on a stool in your cell disentangling thick naval rope with a nail or your fingers, which was painful. The treadmill meant spending at least six hours standing within a huge wheel and making it turn with continuous steps. It was exhausting. Prison was a real test of their faith. There was no shortage of martyrs but it could be a chastening experience. On his release after a short sentence, 'Staff-Captain' Mackenzie, with a thick beard grown in prison, was interviewed by a reporter from *The War Cry* who thought he looked very ill:

> 'After my first night on a plank bed, in a stone cell, and with nothing but the two prison blankets for covering, I came out shivering and trembling from head to foot. . . . My cell was changed but I still suffered extremely from the cold, and besides my nerves being in such a disordered state, caused the strange sensation of being locked up to act upon my fancy, and a morbid idea fastened upon me that the prison would be burned down while I and my fellow prisoners remained helpless in our cells. . . . Well I could not shake off the idea, and the feelings of horror that accompanied it are beyond description. I got in such state that I could not lie upon my bed, and but for being able to get on my knees and commit myself into the hands of God, I do not know what would have become of me.'
>
> 'Did you come into contact with the other prisoners?'
>
> 'Not much, as it is against the rules of the prison to speak or to communicate with another, but I shall not forget one of the cleaners – a fellow prisoner – who came into my cell. He was a gaunt, starved fellow, and seeing some pieces of bread I could not eat, said, "What's that, bread?" pounced upon it and gnawed it, or rather tore it like a hungry wolf.'

8. Unsweetened watery oatmeal.

During exercise he caught a glimpse of his fellow prisoners:

> 'It was the most miserable crowd of human faces I had ever looked upon, and my heart went out to the poor creatures. I felt that my prison experience had done one thing for me, i.e. strengthened my determination to seek more than ever the Salvation of the lost and wretched and drunken around me in the open air or wherever I had the opportunity.'[9]

William Booth wrote to Sir Richard Cross, the Conservative secretary of state at the Home Office,[10] to complain about prison conditions and request leniency for his followers. He claimed they contracted pulmonary and other diseases in prison and that some even died as a result. Booth blamed the prison authorities for taking their 'flannels' (underwear) away, making them sleep in unheated cells on hard wooden plank beds, the poor diet and for placing them on the treadmill even if they were not sentenced to hard labour.

Cross enquired into Booth's complaints and, according to the prison governors, they were exaggerated. The governors said the prisoners had made no complaints about conditions to anybody at the time and it was unfair to complain afterwards. Nevertheless, Cross recommended that Salvationists should be allowed a mattress and bedding in lieu of the plank bed, be allowed to write letters and receive visitors frequently, have two lengthy periods of daily exercise, have access to library books and that the medical officers could be more liberal with their diets. However, they were only recommendations and conditions for Salvationists depended on the attitude of the individual prison governor and his medical officers.

* * *

After a while a pattern seemed to be emerging. The worst persistent violence against Salvationists was occurring in small to medium-sized towns where magistrates and councillors had close links to the drinks trade or were themselves publicans. A case in point was a small quiet town, 48 miles south-west of London, previously only famous for burying the same woman, Mrs Blunden, alive twice in 1674! Today, Basingstoke's population is 114,000 but in 1880 it was 6,681. It had

9. *The War Cry*, 'Look at Jail Life', 9 October 1886. Mackenzie had just been released from St Albans prison.

10. Home Secretary, 1874–80 and 1885–86.

Figure 4. Imprisoned Salvationists from Arbroath, as depicted in *The War Cry*, 29/6/1882.

50 pubs and beer houses; one for every 133 residents. There were four breweries and many of its inhabitants worked in the industry. It was an ideal target for Booth. Catherine Booth visited and told an audience the Army would use 'aggressive means of drawing those debauched classes out of the public houses, of letting them know they are going to hell'.[11]

In 1880, Booth sent 'Captain' Clara Green and 'Lieutenant' (Happy) Martha Ellis to open a spiritual offensive with posters declaring:

> *O Yes! O Yes! O Yes!*
> *To all you sinners who [sic] it may concern;*

[11] Ken Clements, *Two Feeble Women: The Early History of the Salvation Army in Basingstoke* (no publisher noted, c. 1995), quoted in Bob Clarke, *The Basingstoke Riots: Massagainians v the Salvation Army 1880–1883* (Basingstoke: Basingstoke Archaeological & Historical Society, 2010), p. 6.

Figure 5. Salvationist Charles Gardner in prison uniform.

Being a detachment of the Salvation Army
Will open fire on Sin and Satan
At the Factory, Brook Street, Basingstoke,
On Sunday, September 19th, 1880.[12]

They were immediately opposed by William Blatch, the mayor, who just happened to be the managing director of May's Brewery, the biggest in the town, and by 'Massagainians'. (The name originated from the brewers' call to arms to the local mob to 'mass again'). After their parades were attacked with sticks and stones and they had chemicals thrown in their faces, Green and Ellis left town only to be replaced by 'Captain' Lizzie Rushforth. The Massagainians immediately tried to force her into a pub. She was only saved by sympathisers.

---

12. Ibid.

During the attacks, Massagainians waved Union Jacks whilst singing 'Rule Britannia', believing they were defending their town from eccentric invaders. According to Chris Hare, 'This was the anthem of small-town rioters throughout the nineteenth century. "Britons Never Shall Be Slaves" – was the key phrase – always sung with gusto by bonfire boys and other rioting groups.'[13]

On Sunday, 20 March 1881, 'The Battle of Church Square' took place, leading to what was described as 'a reign of anarchy and disorder'. A local man, George Woodman, recorded:

> In the afternoon the mob [estimated at 2,000] assembled again. They were a drunken rabble. . . . They knocked their [the Salvationists'] heads about with sticks, kicked them and many of them being drunk would have made short work of the Army had it not been [for] the timely aid of sympathizers. I saw a man led away with his arm broken and head cut, another with his neck bleeding and another with his head cut open. There were bleeding heads and faces in all directions. On this occasion the police and the Mayor W.H. Blatch, himself a brewer, stood by and did nothing.[14]

During the struggle, Charles Elms, a Salvationist described as 'muscular', had seized the Massagainians' Union Jack. In the course of the fight to regain the flag, Elms' arm was broken. Eventually Blatch and Superintendent Hibberd, the police chief, managed to persuade the Salvationists to return to their hall. As the Army left the square, their attackers gave three cheers for the mayor. In the evening, the Salvationists stayed in. Back out on the streets, their sympathisers, if spotted, were attacked.

Booth complained to Sir William Harcourt, the Liberal home secretary (1880–85), about the lack of protection. He argued 'that [in Basingstoke] through their processions and public meetings hundreds of men and women have been reclaimed from lives of open sin . . . of course, the trade of the Publicans and Brewers has suffered very much. They are correspondingly infuriated against us'.[15] Harcourt also received

---

13. Hare, email to the author, 24 July 2021.

14. George Woodman's diary, held in the Willis Museum, Basingstoke, quoted in Clarke, *The Basingstoke Riots*, p. 28.

15. The National Archives, HO 45/9607/A2886, 'Disturbances: Salvation Army Meetings and Processions at Basingstoke'.

a petition signed by the vicar of Basingstoke and 498 others asking him to ban the processions which 'desecrates our Christian Sabbath'. A rival petition signed by five Nonconformist magistrates and 613 people asked for them to be allowed. Both petitions contained the signatures of town councillors. Harcourt replied that law and order were a matter for the magistrates and he could not interfere.

Meanwhile, after 130 Salvationists and their supporters were attacked by a mob of 3,000, Blatch was forced to read the Riot Act and call in the troops, already stationed in the town. (Under the Act, if twelve or more people remained at the scene and did not withdraw, they would be liable to penal servitude for life.) Twenty mounted horsemen and 40 foot soldiers charged down the main street, surprised to find Salvationists back in their barracks and the mob good-tempered. The Massagainians went home peacefully, singing 'Rule Britannia' in triumph.

Later, after another riot, ten Massagainians were jailed for two weeks after failing to pay sureties to keep the peace. As they were marched off to the railway station on their way to Winchester prison, they again sang 'Rule Britannia' and were cheered by flag-waving crowds. On their release, the 'Massagainian Martyrs' were treated to a banquet – organised by publicans – at the Corn Exchange and each received a silver watch. Married men were given one pound and single men ten shillings to make up for lost wages. A band played, 'Hail the Conquering Heroes Come', as 521 sat down to enjoy the feast. Afterwards their supporters smashed the windows of the police station.

After the latest attacks, the magistrates and Booth agreed on a compromise. If Salvationists were allowed to hold meetings in a meadow, they would not sing on their way there. Things gradually quietened down. The publicans realised Salvationists were not such a threat to their profits after all. Indeed, during the rioting they had benefited from the influx of curious outsiders. Moreover, the authorities knew that, if they did not quell the attacks, the continual hiring of extra policemen would become costly.

For two years the small community had been divided between pro- and anti-Salvationists. If you belonged to the former, you risked being assaulted in the street, having your windows smashed and even your house broken into. Church and chapel had found themselves on opposing sides; signing different petitions. 'As for the Massagainians', comments Bob Clarke wryly, 'what fun they must have had: parading round the town, making strange noises with a multitude of unmusical instruments, and cackling with laughter at the cacophony they were creating; carousing at the Massagainian Banquet; and listening to the satisfying sound of breaking glass.'[16]

The reading of the Riot Act in a hitherto quiet, small town had raised Basingstoke's national profile and, by the same token, that of Booth and the Salvation Army – and perhaps also provided the inspiration for the riots that followed elsewhere.

* * *

Most of the early opposition the Army faced was spontaneous and relatively disorganised. The earliest named opposition was in Whitechapel in 1880 when a group calling themselves 'The Opposition Salvation Army' or 'The Unconverted Salvation Army' paraded the streets with banners proclaiming 'Fear Not and Be Just' and marched against the Army whenever they could. However, the Basingstoke Massagainians had been the *first* fully mobilised and persistent mob supported by members of the local elite. In 1881 they were superseded by a more durable threat: groups calling themselves the 'Skeleton Army'. It became the general term for opposition to the Salvation Army. To some observers it was no surprise the Army provoked organised opposition. The *Bristol Times & Mirror* declared: 'How far a people, who call themselves an Army, who adopt a military organization, and who go out ostensibly to fight, can complain if they are taken at their word and are fought.'[17]

---

16. Clarke, *The Basingstoke Riots*, p. 123.
17. 23 September 1984.

Chapter Three

The Birth of the Skeleton Army, 1881

The name 'Skeleton' originated from the 'Skull-and-Crossbones Boys' who celebrated Guy Fawkes Night. In her book, *Pulling the Devil's Kingdom Down*, Pamela Walker comments: 'It can be read as a multiple parody. It ridiculed the Salvationists' concern with life after death and the other-worldly austerity the Salvationists practiced. It may also have alluded to the frequent accusation that the Booths bilked money from their followers to enrich themselves and left their impoverished followers to starve.'[1]

Skeletons were often portrayed as the local roughs or pre-Edwardian Teddy Boys but there was nothing stylish about them. Their uniform consisted of coloured rags, tinsel and pantomime clothing. Those who could afford it dressed in army cast-offs and brass helmets. One observer thought they had the style of 'Falstaff's Ragged Regiment' in Shakespeare's *Henry IV*. Their flags and banners were of festive skulls, skeletons – sometimes grinning – and coffins similar to those used by bonfire societies; and, occasionally, the red flag of revolution. Instead of the Salvation mantra, 'Blood and Fire', they were stamped with 'Blood and Thunder'; instead of 'Soup, Soap and Salvation', they proclaimed 'Beef, Beer and Bacca'. In fact, the Skeleton's parody of the Army banner, 'celebrated three of the central motifs of nationalism and popular Toryism'.[2]

---

1. Pamela J. Walker, *Pulling the Devil's Kingdom Down: The Salvation Army in Victorian Britain* (Berkeley: University of California Press, 2001), p. 225.
2. James Kneale, 'The Battle of Torquay: The Late Victorian Resort as Social Experiment', in Matthew Ingleby and Matthew P.M. Kerr (eds), *Coastal*

Addressing each other as 'Brother Skeleton', they had their own 'Captains' and 'Generals' who often 'swore in' recruits in pubs. Their commands mimicked the real army: 'Fall in Skeleton Army!', 'Slow March!', 'Forward' and so on. Admission to the 'Army' was easy: a commitment to getting rid of the Salvation Army as soon as possible. Sometimes there was a nominal membership fee. The Skeleton Army riots lasted from 1881 to 1893. For much of that time you could not pick up a newspaper without reading about them.

The first newspaper references to it (in a non-military sense) came in the cathedral city of Exeter in Devon in October 1881. By then its traditional industries of wool manufacturing and tanning were in decline; the Industrial Revolution had passed it by and it had become a conservative market town dependent on agriculture. Perhaps it was not surprising the Skeleton Army riots started in Exeter as there had been serious fifth of November riots there in the past. According to Roger Swift, 'the celebration of the Fifth of November was a notable feature of popular culture in many nineteenth-century towns and cities, none more so than in Exeter, where the festivities had long constituted one of the great annual events of the city'.[3] Fifth of November celebrations were 'the reflection of an intimate and paternalistic society',[4] a symbol of the Protestant Reformation, a day of high spirits for youngsters and 'an opportunity for the expression of popular sentiment on particular issues, and unpopular personalities were often lampooned during the pageantry which preceded the firing of the bonfire'.[5]

Robert Storch in his article, 'Please to Remember the Fifth of November',[6] details how in the Victorian period the day had become more riotous because of the formation of secret or semi-secret bonfire gangs, known as 'Guys' or 'Bonfire Boys' or 'Young [name of town]', who resisted local authority attempts to suppress or reform the celebration

---

Cultures of the Long Nineteenth Century (Edinburgh: Edinburgh University Press, 2018), p. 87.

3. Roger Swift, 'Guy Fawkes Celebrations in Victorian Exeter', *History Today* 31, no. 11 (1981).

4. Ibid.

5. Ibid.

6. Robert D. Storch, 'Please to Remember the Fifth of November: Conflict, Solidarity and Public Order in Southern England, 1815–1900', in Robert D. Storch (ed.), *Popular Culture and Custom in Nineteenth Century England* (Croom Helm, 1982).

because of fears that it was getting out of hand. (This was in the light of the disorder caused by the Reform Acts and Chartism.) They were mainly composed of young men.

'Young Exeters' had rioted in 1867, when the local authority tried to ban the celebrations after a serious food riot the day before. It took armed infantry to put it down. There had been further riots in 1879, when the authorities again tried to clamp down on the celebrations. According to Storch, 'in some old, stable Tory towns such as Exeter, the will to crush the popular demonstration was always feeble'[7] and effigies of the bishop had occasionally been burned and the mayor threatened. In Exeter, traditionally, the celebrations 'provided an outlet for the expression of popular attitudes towards religion in the city'.[8] The proceedings had taken on a marked anti-clerical tone because of the unpopularity of Henry Phillpotts, Bishop of Exeter from 1831 to 1869, who had voted against the Great Reform Act of 1832 and who wanted to introduce more ritual into church services. Exeter was a Protestant stronghold – every year on 4 November the Cathedral bells were rung in commemoration of the landing of the Prince of Orange at Torbay in 1688 – and new religious groups, like the Methodists, as we saw earlier, were initially ill-treated.

Although fifth of November celebrations could result in riotous behaviour, the participants saw themselves as patriots and loyalists and often sang 'Rule Britannia' or 'God Save the Queen'. This was also to become a tradition of the Skeleton Army.

In March 1881, a Methodist preacher, Ernest Stear, had written to Booth inviting Salvationists to use his chapel. On Sunday, 10 April 1881, 'Captain' Abraham Davey, a former drunkard, 'opened fire' at the Victoria Temperance Hall in the Friars. Before joining, he had been foreman of a flour mill earning £100 a year. He was accompanied by his wife, 'Private' Leigh, and their two little boys. The hall was full, with a thousand people locked out. Men even scrambled up a high fence to get in. A few young men in the gallery interrupted the service. Davey warned that, as the hall was licensed for preaching, they could suffer serious penalties.

After three weeks, Davey reported that 400 souls had been saved. *The War Cry* declared one woman had walked six miles to get to a 6.00 a.m. meeting and that Army 'detachments' were marching to outlying

7. Ibid.

8. Swift, 'Guy Fawkes Celebrations in Victorian Exeter'.

villages to spread their message. In May, two boys, Henry Hunt and Frank Miller, were fined one shilling for disorderly conduct outside the hall. By June, Davey was regularly being mobbed:

> On Friday night, about 10'clock, I found Capt. Davey and his wife surrounded by a mob of 150 youths (for so they were there not being a man amongst them), who were yelling, hissing and making a frightful noise. The Captain and his wife had just quitted the Temperance Hall, and were on their way home to Portland street, the above mob following them the whole route not only hissing but frequently throwing showers of stones and other refuse. On their home being reached, one or two police came to the rescue who quickly dispersed the mob. . . . Here is a people who are respectable, and who are doing good amongst our lower classes in dragging them from misery, and yet they are insulted in this vile manner. I do not belong to them myself; but as an Englishman I must call the way in which they are being treated 'simply disgusting'.
>
> 'A Lover of Fair Play'[9]

Davey asked the magistrates whether police could come to the hall and protect them, even offering to pay. They told him "no" but said he could take legal action against the men instead. He complained that he had asked police at a meeting to come inside and take some names and they replied: 'You have brought the mob here, you can clear them away.'[10] Captain Bent, the chief constable, had publicly declared that he had travelled the world and did not consider the Salvation Army to be religious. A letter from 'Not a Salvationist' in the *Devon Evening Express*, accused him of wanting to put down the Salvation Army so it was hardly surprising that his men did little to protect them.[11]

In August, Davey was attacked outside the hall and one 'soldier', William Cornish, a labourer, was knocked down and kicked so badly he had to spend a few days in hospital. Skeletons had scaled the outside walls and gates whilst the police looked on. As the attacks grew, more and more Salvationists and their attackers were being summonsed to court. Several cases were dismissed but one Salvationist, Ebenezer

---

9. *Devon Evening Express*, 7 June 1881.
10. *Exeter Flying Post*, 29 June 1881.
11. *Devon Evening Express*, 27 June 1881.

Rattenbury, a tailor, was fined five shillings and costs for physically stopping Daniel Allen, a labourer, from leaving a meeting. (Attendees were only allowed to leave during the singing.) Davey decided not to press charges after a couple of attackers apologised and in order to 'stop the ill feeling' even paid the fine of Henry Hartnoll, a labourer, who had grabbed the hall gatekeeper by the nose and hit him twice. He had been fined ten shillings plus costs or fourteen days' hard labour. As he did not have the money to pay, Davey saved him from going to prison.

Davey reported that many well-dressed, respectable youths were throwing flour, rotten eggs and other missiles during meetings. During one procession, they marched in front joining hands and tried to stop Salvationists from returning to their barracks. In the collision, Davey had his umbrella broken. As he headed for home, 'a number of men made a rush crying "Forward", with an intention of getting at Davey and his friends'.[12] The Skeleton Army was in the making. Davey eventually got home with a police escort. Later, a mob threw a shower of stones at his front door. Rather belatedly, Captain Bent started to put policemen in uniform and in plain clothes inside and outside the hall for the purpose of spotting offenders.

When William Booth visited in September to present the 'colours' to the Exeter corps, there were no reports of ruffianism because a large body of police was on guard outside the hall. On this occasion the Salvation Army had charged for admission in order to raise funds to buy the Temperance Hall, loaned to them by the local Methodists, and to convert it to accommodate 2,000 people. Posters on the walls declared 'War! War! War!' in bold type and in blood-red ink. One offered a £5 reward for the identification of Cornish's attacker. After Booth spoke about the Army's great expansion, Davey boasted that in six months 'hundreds' had been converted, including 'fallen' women.

The *Exeter Flying Post* reported that 'the "General" on Sunday, conducted several services, and all were well attended, the movement having, it was admitted, been greatly benefitted by the recent disturbances'.[13] Davey had not marched out for a few weeks but now, with the 'colours', organised a procession. In a tense skirmish, they were captured by a hostile crowd and then recaptured.

---

12. Ibid., 31 August 1881.

13. *Exeter Flying Post*, 7 September 1881.

On Sunday, 2 October, the Skeleton Army made their first appearance with their own 'colours'. Their banner proclaimed 'Stand like the brave' under a skull and crossbones. Their leaders were described as 'not individuals of prepossessing appearance';[14] their followers mainly youngsters keen on creating mischief. They were led by 'Major' 'Figgy' Martin, a sailor who marched around the city with a banner 'Death to the Salvationists'. They wore badges with the words 'Skeleton Army' – with the skull and cross-bones roughly drawn – on their arms or caps. Some had tickets stuck in their hat-bands inscribed: 'Skeleton Army, Death or Glory Boys. Admit one to the council of war.' The tickets were distributed by sympathetic pubs.

Cards were circulated announcing that an assembly of the Skeleton Army would be held on 7 October at the quayside where there would be a presentation of 'colours' by 'Major' Martin. After several speeches and pub stops, 3,000 Skeletons, in ranks of ten linking arms, attacked the Salvation Army barracks with fireworks and stones: '[The Skeleton Mob] took up a position outside the railings of the Temperance Hall, which they nearly all tried to scale and so enter the building. Many of them were thus able to reach the doors but not to gain admittance, the Salvationists offering a sturdy resistance to keeping them out.'[15]

The Skeletons outside were joined by hundreds of reinforcements and the scene was one of complete disorder and riot with only one policeman being present. He went and fetched a colleague but:

> it was painfully evident that the combined efforts of the two officers were insufficient to keep order. 'Captain' Davey, in the inside of the building conducting the service, was made aware of the proceedings outside and of the danger. He and his hearers ran from the stones that were being thrown through the windows, breaking the glass, pieces of which fell amongst them.[16]

Davey recalled years later that they had to sit with umbrellas up because of the broken glass showering down on them. Over the next couple of weeks, crowds obstructed the entrance to the hall and smashed

---

14. *Exeter and Plymouth Gazette Daily Telegrams*, 8 October 1881.

15. *Western Times*, 10 October 1881, quoted in Nigel Bovey, *Blood on the Flag* (London: Shield Books, 2015), p. 140.

16. Ibid., p. 141.

windows. The police, even those in plain clothes, seem to have made little effort to disperse the mob. Inside, roughs repeatedly ruined the chorus, stamping their feet and shouting out 'shut up'. They laughed and hooted at the 'captain' and tried to drag Hallelujah lasses outside. One local observer who lived opposite, claimed that not all the Skeletons were roughs and witnessed a well-dressed and apparently respectable youth take up a stone and deliberately throw it. However, a local councillor described them as 'the greatest blackguards' in the city.

The mayor, Walter Pring, a brewer, issued a proclamation saying marches by the Salvation Army or the Skeleton Army which caused a breach of the peace would not be tolerated. The advice from the home secretary, Sir William Harcourt, was that processions in themselves were not illegal but, if they caused disturbances, the magistrates had the power to prevent them. Davey agreed not to march because of the lack of police protection but said he would still have open-air meetings. The ban seems to have had an immediate impact:

> I have been a ratepayer of this city for thirty years. I live near the Hall, and it has been quite a different place since the processions have been stopped. I believe that if the city was polled on it, four fifths of the inhabitants would be against the processions. I hope the Mayor will still abide by what he has done, and that his successors will do the same.
>
> 'A Dissenter and Working Man'[17]

In November, in an unusual move the Army asked the city magistrates whether sixteen of their members could be made special constables to protect them. With the dark nights setting in, serous disturbances were feared. The request was turned down. Pring, who would soon step down as mayor, said he was willing to protect them in their hall and in front of it but not on their marches.

In a bid to boost morale, Catherine Booth came to the city and gave a speech. She was described as looking 'very weak'; perhaps showing signs of the cancer which would kill her by the end of the decade. She told her audience that it was necessary to 'thrust the Gospel down the throats of people as gentle measures have been tried before without success'.[18] She had no qualms about the fact that she wanted to compel people to come

17. *Devon Evening Express*, 23 October 1881.

18. *Express and Echo*, 24 November 1881.

to the services, particularly the working class. Neither did she have any about asking her audience for money towards the new hall. One builder even promised to contribute 1,000 bricks.

In December 1881, Davey told *The War Cry*:

> These last few weeks have been a great time in Exeter for the Salvation Army. When the rowdyism was so great, the roughs formed themselves into what they called a 'Skeleton Army', but we have shown them every kindness throughout.
>
> Three weeks ago, a young man came up the street at the same time as I did, he was drunk; and he said, 'You are Capt. Davey of the Salvation Army, I am "Major Martin", of the "Skeleton Army"', and he came to the Hall, and shouted out, 'Give "Major Martin" a hymn book.' He bought a penny hymn and sat down.[19]

Davey described how several men came up to the penitent's rail during their 'Free-and-Easy' session and recounted how the Army had saved them from drink. There followed a display of the 'trophies of war': discarded clay pipes, greasy ostrich feathers and tobacco pouches. At the end, 'Major' Martin told Davey he had been impressed by what he had seen. The following week he and four other Skeletons brought him their flag and surrendered. One of them, James Perkins, the 'standard bearer', had made the flag himself. The Skeletons were outraged and sent him a threatening letter illustrated with a skull and crossbones and a coffin. A labourer, Henry Richards, said they would torment him wherever he went and demanded the return of the Skeleton 'colours'. Perkins refused. Richards went to the hall and struck him. He was fined 20 shillings with costs or fourteen days' hard labour. According to Perkins, Richards was a 'captain' in the Skeleton Army who used to imitate Davey by parading backwards in front of the procession.

Another Skeleton, Joseph Hurford, a porter, was fined £1 7s. 6d. – or two weeks' hard labour – for assaulting 'Flag Sergeant' James Pope, a grocer, leaving the hall. He and 30 others had laughed and made rude remarks during the service. At the end they had stood on a path outside trying to prevent people leaving by grabbing their hats and placing them on tops of lampposts. Over the next few months Pope was twice

---

19. *The War Cry*, 1 December 1881.

assaulted by Skeletons with sticks but on each occasion the cases were dismissed for lack of evidence. Reputedly, his blood stains can still be seen on a fragment of the flag kept by Exeter Salvationists today.

Towards the end of the year, the Army, according to the letter below, were parading again:

> It is time for the 'Skeleton Army' to have a word to say. All they want to know is: Does the Mayor know the Salvation Army are parading the streets and making their noise again? If the Mayor cannot stop this, the 'Skeleton Army' must do like they have done before. If the out-door processions are not stopped by next Wednesday the 'Skeleton Army' will appear on the field.
>
> Captain B.G.H.[20]

One ratepayer complained of Salvationists 'bawling music as discordant as a colony of rooks'.[21] Another warned the new mayor, Thomas Andrew, that he:

> should remember the feelings of the majority of the citizens, and not show too much delicate sympathy for the 'Army'. They may be doing good, but they should keep within their place of worship. . . . The question is: if the Salvation Army march through the streets to the annoyance of the public, have not the 'Skeleton Army' the same right if they conduct themselves in a proper manner?[22]

Andrew cautioned both armies not to parade.

Davey[23] was replaced at the beginning of 1882 by 'Captain' John Trenhail, aged 34, a native of Truro. He and his wife had been in the Army for six years and had arrived in the city after placements in the East End of London and the North of England. In March, Trenhail decided to hold an open-air meeting. He and his comrades were showered with

20. *Exeter and Plymouth Gazette Daily Telegrams*, 17 December 1882.

21. *Devon Evening Express*, 3 April 1882.

22. Ibid., 21 December 1881.

23. Davey would go on to serve a sentence in Bodmin prison for disturbances at Penzance.

bags of flour and salt, knocked to the ground and forced to retreat back to their hall. As they did, Skeletons threw mud and hit them with sticks. There were only six policemen on duty. The *Western Times* reported:

> After a little time there was a move on towards the Exe Bridge. On reaching here another of the Salvationists was assaulted, and some of the roughs catching hold of a youngster, who had the Salvation 'S' on his collar, threatened to throw him into the river. . . . There was no singing by the Salvationists, and no attempt at a procession by either party . . . when about fifty yards distant from the hall, Captain Trenhail (who was closely attended by several of his followers) started the hymn – 'I'm a Pilgrim Bound for Glory' – others took up the tune. A policeman stepped up to Captain Trenhail, told him that he would be arrested unless he stopped singing, and at the same moment P.C. Sergeant Gillard stepped up and took him into custody. The event caused the utmost excitement – the crowd now numbering at the lowest estimate, 3,000.[24]

Trenhail was taken to the police station followed by a mob, shouting 'Goodbye Captain!' and 'Give him three months!' He was charged with 'being in and aiding a disorderly mob' by leading a procession and wilfully disobeying the mayor's proclamation. He insisted he had only been walking ahead of individuals. He was offered bail but refused. His wife came to visit with some tea and a blanket but was turned away.

Reaction to his arrest was swift. Many locals, even though they had no obvious sympathy for the Army, blamed the police for not protecting the Salvationists and for not arresting their attackers. They insisted a peaceful procession had been attacked by a vicious mob. A defence fund was set up by the Reverend John Cutliffe of nearby Dawlish and the Reverend W.B Read, president of the Bible Christian Conference. Sir Wilfred Lawson, MP for Carlisle, a temperance campaigner and radical Liberal, and five other MPs contributed; an indication of the national prominence given to the disturbances.

In court, Inspector Skinner, who had charged Trenhail, had a difficult time explaining how he and his force of 62 appeared not to know who the Skeleton leaders were or why none of the Skeletons had been arrested. He said he could put down the Skeleton Army if he was instructed to do so but

24. *Western Times*, 15 March 1882.

he had not been. He did not know anything about 'Major' Martin. None of the police seemed to have noticed that Salvationists had been pelted with mud and hit with sticks. In fact, in court Trenhail's clothes were still covered in mud. His defence lawyer, Simon Reeve, argued that the Army was only trying to reach the people other churches could not. It did not matter how good a preacher was if people did not come to hear him. Salvationists felt it was their duty to drag people away from sin. Reeve continued:

> The 'Queen of the West' [Exeter] as it was spoken all over England, famed as it was for its beautiful women – one would have thought that if the men of the city were worthy of them, they would like to be spoken of and known for their courage and for their chivalry. Yet see what the rising generation of these people were. They delighted in attacking men whose only object was to convert souls. The Skeleton Army would not exist for a moment were it not for the fact that these men were under a vow – they were bound to obey the orders of their superior not to strike back again when they were struck.
>
> There were brutes in some parts of the country who delighted in kicking the soft flesh of women; and so there were brutes in some of our cities who delighted in striking when they knew they would not be struck again – aye! And as sure as they were living, if the authorities once allowed this Skeleton Army to be imbued with the taste of blood, when there was no longer a Salvation Army for them to kick – if ever the time should come – they would find something else to kick if only they could be sure that nobody would kick back again.
>
> Nobody but a coward would strike a man whose hands were tied behind him – nobody but a coward would strike when he knew there was no danger attending it; and that was the course adopted by these people who called themselves the Skeleton Army.[25]

Witnesses testified that, whilst being pursued by the angry mob, Trenhail told his followers not to do anything that could be interpreted as forming a procession. The magistrates dismissed the case against him – giving him the benefit of the doubt – but warned they considered open-air meetings to be part of the ban on processions. On his release

25. *Express and Echo*, 17 March 1882.

Trenhail was hoisted onto the shoulders of brother officers and carried to a 'war chariot' – a smart carriage – and taken to breakfast wearing an imitation prison uniform.

Shortly afterwards, Davey returned and led a detachment to nearby Crediton. During the service there, a youth tried to kiss 'Lieutenant' Charlotte Hartnoll who slapped him in the face. Meanwhile, roughs were busy sabotaging their transport by saturating the seat cushions of one of their horse-drawn conveyances with water and turning a horse loose. They also loosened the wheel caps so that on their return journey the conveyance broke down in front of the White Hart Tavern. A whistle blew and Salvationists were attacked with stones and rotten eggs. Davey suffered a blow on the back of the head and most of his companions were hurt.

By June 1882, the Exeter Salvationists were marching again, this time with umbrellas up to protect themselves from broken glass. So were the Skeleton Army:

> When the Army was opposite the New London Inn the roughs joined hands and deliberately formed a line across the street to block the peaceful progress of the Army. . . . At the corner of Queen Street their opponents again 'attacked' the Army, trying to block their march in every possible way. The Salvationists say that here the first policeman along the route was seen, and he was appealed to for assistance, but stood mute and unconcerned.
>
> The last and most determined attempt to stop the Salvationists was made opposite the Council Chambers in Queen Street. The obstruction of the roughs again took the form of 'linked' hands, and a good deal of fighting occurred. Several members of the Army allege that they were beaten with sticks, kicked, and struck in the face by their opponents with their fists. In two or three instances they say blood was drawn by the roughs. . . . The members of the Army say they know the name of a cab driver who in Queen Street urged on his horse, with a fly [cab] attached to it, into the ranks of the Army, and struck at several of them with his whip. In fact, they say that all along the route from Paris Street to the Victoria Hall they were treated unmercifully, and they complain bitterly that the police were not allowed to interfere on behalf of the Army.[26]

---

26. *Western Times*, 19 June 1882.

By the end of the summer, things calmed down in Exeter although there were still sporadic disturbances and complaints about young people wandering the streets after midnight services. In December 1882, a Salvationist, David Leigh, a sawyer, who had defended himself with his brass cymbals, was fined, along with the Skeleton who had attacked him. When 'Captain' Foster took over that month, a Skeleton mob broke up the procession and a free fistfight ensued in front of the Salvationists' hall. The Army supporters petitioned the town council (for the second time) for more protection on the streets. The council agreed, although it asked the petitioners to persuade their leaders not to allow their band to play whilst passing places of worship on Sundays.

In January 1883, William Booth arrived in Exeter to hold 'a council of war'. Wearing a long overcoat with cape, he had a military rather than clerical bearing. From the station he was carried in his 'war chariot', surrounded by his entourage, to the Victoria Hall:

> The 'General' is an ingenious person. He had three ladies in his cab; this was immediately followed by two others solely occupied by ladies. It seemed like a Mormon demonstration. One might have thought Joe Smith and his wives were coming to town. . . . It was a good policy to be surrounded by ladies. Even the Skeleton Army must have a strain of chivalry in their composition.[27]

(It was a good tactic. When the Army had a grand open-air demonstration at Reading in October 1882, it was headed by eleven young girls dressed as Italian peasants carrying tambourines. Although they were followed by a yelling mob, the procession was untouched.)

A few Skeleton 'skirmishers' with 'Skeleton' papers in their hats pelted Booth and his chariot with mud. He was described in the local press as looking 'dreadfully worn'. When he got up to speak, he still had patches of mud on his coat. He told his audience that the Army was an army of deliverance. It had been going for 17½ years and now had 457 corps and 1,070 paid officers. It was spreading round the world.[28] He noted that in India – where there had been minor riots – they had not as much mud thrown at them as in Exeter! In a light-hearted speech,

27. *Exeter and Plymouth Gazette Daily Telegrams*, 23 January 1883.

28. Between 1881 and 1883, its numbers had more than quadrupled.

Booth spoke about a man who had 'fallen into their hands'. The Army sent a telegram to his wife: 'We have found your dear husband.' Quickly came back the laconic reply, 'You can keep him!' He concluded that, although his religion may not always be polite and might be vulgar, it was essentially a happy one. A chorus to one song went:

Oh! Ain't we a funny people?
Ain't we a funny crew?
You'd better come to Jesus;
We'll make you funny too![29]

In September 1883, in the small village of Woodbury, seven miles south-east of Exeter, three Skeletons, after constantly disturbing Army marches and meetings, were sent to prison for one month by the magistrates without the option of a fine. This sent out a clear message. Salvationists were also being punished severely. In January 1884, three 'soldiers' were arrested for 'assaulting the police in the execution of their duty'.[30] John Marshall was sentenced to one week's imprisonment but his fine was paid by friends. Sixteen-year-old Fred Woolway was fined £2 or one month's hard labour and Fred Gillard, a recent convert with a long criminal record, was given six weeks' hard labour,[31] without the option of a fine, for hitting a policeman with his drumsticks. Both were placed in manacles and marched off to Exeter prison, accompanied by a Salvation Army band and supporters.

'Major' Davey – now in charge of the Army in Devon and Cornwall – came to town and addressed a 'Great Protest Meeting'. He claimed that it was the police who had attacked the Salvationists. He continued:

> One complaint brought against the Army parading was that the street was too small; but he would remind them that the Army did not make the street – (laughter) – and if the street was too small for public traffic, why, instead of having a body of police, did they not make the street wider.[32]

29. *Rugby Observer*, 7 September 1912.
30. *Exeter and Plymouth Gazette*, 25 January 1884.
31. Some accounts say he received three months.
32. *The War Cry*, 2 February 1884.

Afterwards, the entire congregation, led by the band, marched to Exeter prison and paid the fine for Woolway to be released immediately. Despite sending a petition to the home secretary complaining about his unjust imprisonment, Gillard was made to serve his full sentence. On the day of his release, he was met at the prison gates by a huge crowd of Salvationists and sympathisers. He left standing up in a four-horse-drawn wagonette waving a coloured handkerchief.

In November 1884, Davey visited Exeter again and reported no more attacks as the police had been 'kept in check'. He wrote to the mayor thanking him for the police protection the Army was receiving.[33] Now their hall was so full that people were unable to gain admittance. In truth, the real reason for things quietening down in the city had been a high court ruling in respect of a growing town, population 17,500, 65 miles to the north-east in June 1882.

* * *

Weston-super-Mare was a beautiful enchanting resort on the North Somerset coastline with miles of sands and wooded slopes. In February 1881, there were reports of Salvation 'scouts' coming over from Bristol to assess the prospects of opening a corp. The *Weston Mercury* described one such scout:

> Shouting and gesticulating, he roams from street to street, to the annoyance of all peaceable citizens, asserting that he had a Divine Command to preach the gospel. He had no food or money but says the Master will provide. He approached one gentleman, 'The Lord told me to ask you for £5.' The man replied, 'Surely you have made a mistake. Go back and make further enquiries!'[34]

Army headquarters denied he had authorisation. Salvationists eventually 'invaded' the town with a parade one Sunday evening in June 1881: described as a 'procession of boys and girls, headed by an individual scraping a violin'.[35] They were criticised for forcing people off

33. *Devon Evening Express*, 6 November 1884.
34. *Weston Mercury*, 19 February 1881.
35. Ibid., 25 June 1881.

the footpaths and interfering with them going to church. The following month there were reports of individuals trying to disturb Salvationist meetings in their hall, usually full, with many attending out of curiosity.

In August 1881, the Army opened up a second corps. On one occasion, 'the soldiers continued their religious revelry until after three o'clock on Saturday morning, making night hideous with their shouts, groans and discordant sounds'.[36] 'A Quiet Loving Visitor' complained about the 'din and uproar they create in the public street' and asked for them to be suppressed.[37] There was much debate in the local press about their methods and benefit to the town but they did attract huge crowds.

The first inkling of a Skeleton Army came during fifth of November celebrations. A hundred 'Young Westons' paraded bearing a black flag with the death's head and crossbones and 'Skeleton Army' emblazoned on it. They threw effigies of two of its well-known, resident Army supporters, with bottles labelled 'gin' hanging out of their pockets, onto a bonfire. So, in little over a month, the name of the new army had spread from the south-west coast to the north coast.

In early February 1882, Catherine Booth came down to conduct a meeting at the Assembly Rooms to lecture on 'The Salvation Army: Its Measures and Aims'. Despite admission charges, the hall was full well before it began. She was described as 'a fluent speaker with a good command of the language'.[38] She quoted the American writer, Harriet Beecher Stowe, to explain her philosophy: 'If you want to bless humanity you must go down among them, and not patronise them with a long pole.'[39] She encouraged officers to be daring in their attempts to attract followers and joked they would be sent back to shoemaking if they failed.

Later that month, the new 'captain', William Beatty, a former drunkard and 'wife-beater' from Bethnal Green, was summonsed for assaulting a former drummer, James Bale. Bale had been a drummer in the Army for six months and had even collected money and contributed £1 towards the drum's acquisition. Beatty said he had dismissed him because his playing was so bad it had created amusement in the streets. Bale came to the hall to demand his money back and claimed he was spat at, had his hair pulled by Beatty's wife, and was paid in penny pieces. The magistrates gave Beatty the benefit of the doubt.

---

36. Ibid., 22 August 1881.

37. *Weston-super-Mare Gazette & General Advertiser*, 17 September 1881.

38. Ibid., 11 February 1882.

39. Ibid.

On 23 March 1882, with 2,000 people on the streets, a Skeleton Army mob, including former converts, attacked a parade starting out from its hall[40] in a narrow street. They drowned out the band with their own unharmonious playing and jumped on the Army's musical instruments until they were flattened out like tin. A free hand-to-hand fight ensued. The *Western News* reported: 'The crowd was incited by Wilcox, the shoemaker, to seize the Salvation flag, and they broke the flag-staff.'[41] The Skeleton flag was also downed. A half-drunk boy rushed at the drum and was seized. Although there were four policemen on duty, they did nothing to protect Salvationists as they themselves were helplessly carried off their feet for 50 yards by the mob. Many Westonians intervened to support the Salvationists and managed to escort them back to their barracks. There, Skeletons let loose a flock of live pigeons through the hall's shattered windows: 'Swooping and blundering in terror, the birds dislodged acrid clouds of red pepper secreted beneath their wings; eyes and nostrils on fire, the audience stumbled out to face the fury of the crowd.'[42] Both sides received injuries.

The local magistrates decided to prohibit all marching and asked Beatty to stop parading. He was happy to do so, unless he received orders from headquarters to march. He was told to march. The magistrates' order was also ignored by other marching groups, such as the Blue Ribbon Army and the Gospel Temperance Union.

At their next Sunday parade on 26 March, 40 Salvationists, led by Beatty, marched four abreast, arms linked and faces set, to their place of worship without music or singing. They were catcalled by a threatening mob. Stones were thrown. A police sergeant told Beatty to stop the march and disperse. The slight young man yelled: "Hallelujah, proceed men and sing!" They sang, 'The Publicans Are Crying Out because the Army Is Marching Out!' The mob began to shout. Police dragged Beatty and two of his lieutenants – Bowden, a carpenter, and Mullins, a plasterer – to the police station. The crowd followed, jeering, and hung about outside the station in groups. None of the Skeletons were arrested.

---

40. A former temperance hall in York street, later knocked down to make way for a cinema extension.

41. 4 April 1882.

42. Collier (1965), *The General Next to God*, p.96.

The three were charged with 'unlawfully and tumultuously assembling with others to the disturbance of the peace'. After five hours in the cells, they were bailed to appear in court. On the same day, William Booth was chased by a mob of boys and young men after holding a service in Oxford Circus, London. He had to take refuge in a restaurant until the police arrived.

In the magistrates' court, police insisted that Beatty would have been killed or seriously injured by the encircling mob if they had not arrested him. One of the prosecution witnesses, Alfred King, manager of a corn merchants, said the Skeletons, with the support of most of the town, had paraded the streets with the hope of suppressing the Salvationists. They were 'the rag tag and bobtail of the town – little boys beating pots and kettles, simply to drown the noise of the Salvationists'. If he had not been a manager, King said, he would have had no hesitation in joining them and there were many others like him. In his opinion, even a hundred police would not have managed to keep the town quiet during the parade. He had heard the Salvationist drummer was stone-deaf and could not hear the racket he made! 'Nobody objects to the Army holding meetings and having music, as they call it, in their hall, but when they parade the streets with their noise, it is altogether different and that is what inhabitants object to.'[43]

The police chief, Superintendent Henry Gillbanks, was called to the witness stand. He said he had received many complaints from 'respectable' residents about the Army in the last six months but refused to say who they were. The prosecutor, Mr J.H. Clifton, claimed the Salvation Army was an American product – full of evangelical exhibitionism – and like all American products would not last long. (According to Steven Spencer, 'So similar were the methods of Salvationists to American preachers that some early newspaper reports even assumed that William Booth himself was American.')[44] Clifton argued that the question wasn't whether the Army was a force for good or not but whether it had broken the law. The Skeleton Army had obeyed the proclamation and had not paraded, unlike the Salvationists.

The defence lawyer, Thomas Sutherst, a London barrister, blamed the police for not putting down the Skeleton attackers. He regretted that they had not been able to identify any of the stone throwers. According to witnesses, the Army had been walking peacefully before being

43. *Bristol Mercury*, 30 March 1882.

44. Spencer, (2019) p.253.

surrounded by a mob on both sides. The worshippers were only guilty of going to their place of worship and should have been protected. Instead, the police had illegally arrested and detained them. Sutherst finished by dramatically tearing up the magistrates' proclamation banning parades in front of them, ripping it in two. The court broke out into boos and applause. In a case lasting five hours, Beatty was defiant, insisting he obeyed God's law before man's law.

The Salvationists were given the choice of paying sureties to keep the peace for a year or to go to prison for three months. They did not have the money and next day were transported to HMP Shepton Mallett. William Booth had a policy of encouraging Salvationists to choose prison rather than pay any money. When three in Hereford telegraphed him which to choose, he telegraphed back: 'Go to prison; will release you.'[45] He did this by either appealing against the sentences or sometimes paying the fine or sureties once they were in prison. Many did not want their fines paid.

A great outcry followed. Some of the townspeople, led by local church leaders, believed the punishment was too harsh and petitioned Harcourt, the home secretary, for their release. The petition was signed by clergymen, medical men, army and naval officers and 'highly respectable' householders: 32 people in total. It was supported by the *Western Daily Press* which believed Salvationists should have the same rights as a friendly society accompanied by a brass band. However, one man wrote to the *Weston Mercury* to complain that he had hastily signed the petition and been misled by its contents:

> We have in Weston almost a superfluity of religious agencies and excitements, – regular services, house-to-house visitations, tract distribution, tent preaching, services on the sands etc. Surely sinners can be reached by these not by means of street processions, coloured flags, religion bawled and shouted into them in a manner that to any well-regulated mind must be simply offensive and disgusting.[46]

In fact, there had also been a counter petition, signed by over 100 people, which included members of the Local Board – forerunner to the borough council – gentry, leading professionals and tradesmen.

45. *John Bull*, 17 February 1883.
46. Letter from J. Russell Leonard, *Weston Mercury*, 8 April 1882.

They were worried the disturbances might deter visitors and bring the town into disrepute so they supported the actions of the magistrates and police. The petition also objected to the first petition's contention that it 'represented all shades of religious and political opinion'.[47] A letter from a 'tradesman' claimed three of the five ministers who had signed the original petition were Nonconformists and sixteen were Liberals.[48]

The Army decided to challenge the proclamation of Weston-super-Mare's ban on processions in the High Court in London and so Beatty was temporarily replaced by two young Hallelujah lasses, Lizzie Moors and Fanny Smart, who restarted the processions. Surrounded by crowds of up to 3,000, the police offered protection and merely cautioned them. Because of the lack of cooperation by the local magistrates, who refused to answer questions, the challenge was not heard until June. William Booth hired a leading London barrister, Edward Clarke QC (who would later represent Oscar Wilde in his disastrous prosecution of the Marquess of Queensbury), to lead the appeal. Clarke criticised the magistrates:

> For the magistrates merely to say that because the Salvation Army are likely to be assailed by roughs and ruffians that therefore they are to be suppressed by force is simply to proclaim mob rule and the abolition of law and order. The roughs and ruffians ought to be put down, not those who are lawful and peaceful.[49]

He added that the Durham Miners' Gala parades, which were much larger, were not stopped on Sundays.

After listening to the Weston magistrates' views and those of the Salvation Army, the Court of Judges in London ruled that the magistrates and police had arrested the wrong parties and should have arrested members of the Skeleton Army. They ruled that it was not unlawful to provoke unlawful acts in others, quashed the convictions and awarded the Army costs.[50] It had seemed odd to ban a procession on the grounds

47. *Somerset and Wiltshire Journal*, 6 April 1882.
48. *Weston Mercury*, 22 April 1882.
49. *The Times*, 14 June 1882.
50. *The Times*, 'Beatty v Gillbanks,' 14 June 1882.

that it would cause a disturbance and then charge the Salvation Army, when it was the Skeletons who rioted. A legal precedent was now set. Salvationists were free to march the streets.

In fact, before the hearing, the sureties on Beatty, 'Our Jail-Bird for Jesus',[51] and his men had been paid by six residents and they were released. They had been driven through the streets in a carriage and been welcomed home by a crowd of 3,000–4,000. In May, William Booth had come to open the new barracks, which could accommodate 1,600–2,000 and presented Beatty with the 'colours':

> 'I ask you, Captain Beatty, to pledge your faithfulness to the colours, to wave them in the streets of Weston, and to live and die under them.' Beatty replied, 'I am determined to fight under the colours and carry them through the streets of Weston in the face of all opposition, let the consequences be what they may.'[52]

Within days Beatty was posted with his 'Lieutenant' wife, Sausannah, and child to Devonport. At his 'Farewell', the Reverend G. Fisher declared, 'the Salvation Army had done more good in the town than all the churches in the town and now had the largest place of worship.'[53] Its increasing popularity was demonstrated when, in the same month, an anti-Salvation Army lecturer, 'Recruiting-Sergeant Walton', visited to give a lecture. On his arrival, as he was getting out of his carriage, he was surrounded by a thousand-strong mob, four of whom tried to throw him into the sea. He took some of his assailants to court but the cases were dismissed. At the 1882 fifth of November celebrations, the 'Young Westons' tried to collide with the Army parade. However, they were deterred by temperance army members carrying sticks.

Although the Army had won a great legal victory, it did not mean that the attacks would end. A year later in June 1883, Salvationists were still suffering cut heads during Skeleton assaults. In October, whilst celebrating the marriage of two 'soldiers', their hall was attacked by a large crowd who smashed all the windows. The *Western Daily Press* had advice for supporters of both 'armies':

---

51. *The War Cry*, 6 April 1882.

52. Undated newspaper source at the Weston Library Information Centre.

53. *Weston Mercury*, 6 May 1882.

Whatever bawles fills gospel halls
Peace should possess the street
Where business drives and fashion crawls
'Armies' should never meet.[54]

Disturbances in the town gradually died down. By the end of 1886, 1,000 people were attending the Sunday evening services and 100–200 were being 'saved' every year.

The bitter struggles in Exeter and Weston-super-Mare had put the Skeleton Army on the map. Despite the High Court ruling, it was not about to disappear.

54. *Western Daily Press*, 1 March 1883.

Chapter Four

Hell in Honiton, 1882–84

In July 1882, The Salvation Army 'opened fire' in the lace-making South Devon town of Honiton – population 3,358 in 1881 – by holding a service in a tent in a field at the top of it. They had been invited by a local shoemaker, Richard Thorne, who had read a copy of *The War Cry*. It was soon disrupted by 30 Skeletons, who ripped open the tent's canvas and cut the ropes. The uproar was so great the two Army 'captains' who were conducting the service closed it early. For the next two weeks, 'missiles of various descriptions were hurled at the 'captains' and the lamps which hung in the centre of the tent were smashed'.[1] Services were curtailed and the Salvation leaders left town.

In August, Henry Stone, a Salvationist and a brickmaker, took James Hann, a labourer, to the county court for assaulting him in the tent. Hann was fined 2s.6d. To put this into perspective, a few days later seven boys were fined five shillings for stealing apples. In October, two female Salvationists arrived with some followers from Exeter. As they paraded the streets they were pelted with mud, turnips and other missiles. They made their way to the house of a local farmer and toll collector, George Wood, on the outskirts of town, where they started to conduct regular meetings in a small ill-ventilated room. On each occasion, Wood's windows were smashed and attendees abused on their exit. Afterwards, several Skeletons were taken to court and fined. However, this only seemed to make matters worse, despite the fines being unduly lenient and two cases being dismissed.

---

1. *Exeter &Plymouth Gazette Daily Telegrams*, 8 August 1882.

Claiming successful recruitment, the Salvation Army decided to purchase a publican's malthouse in the town to use as a barracks. It had a capacity for 500–600. On 7 November, 'Major' Davey from Exeter arrived with supporters to open it officially. As they marched out in the afternoon, a bucket of water was thrown over them and they were covered in flour. Skeletons posted warning notices around the town soon after the purchase:

CAUTION
SKELETON ARMY AND ALL RESPECTABLE
INHABITANTS
KEEP FROM THE HALL
SALVATION PREPARE FOR DEATH

Led by a 'Lieutenant-General', the Skeletons had their own set of rules, claiming anyone found guilty of breaking windows would be court-martialled. Training consisted of throwing turnips and red paint. Their red banner bore the inscription 'Down with Fanatics' and their members could be identified by "Skeleton Army" cards in their hats. And just as the 'Salvation Army corps were mutually supportive within and between towns',[2] so too were the Skeletons, supporting attacks in Exeter, Newton Abbot and Honiton.

Soon Skeletons were attacking Army processions every Sunday, crushing and kicking their instruments around the street and showering them with flour, mud and paint. Salvationists were even attacked when they tried to take refuge in the local police station. Their parades became a focal point for popular amusement with an element of 'rough-musicking'. The historian Glenn Horridge has written how, through it, communities expressed their disapproval of the violation of community norms. Although rare in the late nineteenth century, it was 'still something to be witnessed with interest and enjoyed by some'.[3] Grievances were not settled by going to the police but by "rough-musicking": mob anger that could escalate from throwing stones to making someone leave town. During one attack, involving over 1,000 people, the new Salvation leader, 'Captain' John Lomas, received a head wound and was knocked to the ground. The policeman who picked him up at first thought he was dead. After Lomas had one Skeleton arrested,

2. Horridge, *The Salvation Army*, p.162.

3. Ibid., p.161.

he was chased by a 40-strong mob, which went through the town smashing windows and public lamps. Meanwhile, two of his comrades were taken to court in Honiton for 'loitering' after leaving a midnight meeting and 'causing a disturbance'.

In Honiton, the magistrates were the mayor, John Murch, and former mayor, Henry Hook, both well-known Skeleton supporters who were probably influenced by the stance of Pring in Exeter. Initially, they said it was not necessary to hear the defence as it was obvious the Salvationists were guilty! They had already publicly declared that the Army would get no protection in Honiton. However, they reluctantly agreed to listen to witnesses who insisted it was the Skeleton Army that had caused the disturbances. Despite this, the two magistrates – the only ones in Honiton – found the Salvationists guilty and sentenced them to a month's imprisonment. As they were taken down to the cells they sang "Anywhere with Jesus". After the court case, the Skeletons paraded the town singing 'Will You Go', and waving their hands and arms in imitation of the Salvation Army.

In a letter dated Thursday 23 November, Lomas told William Booth that the Skeletons were encouraged by leading businessmen in Honiton and had been recruited from pubs and given 30 barrels of beer. It was rumoured their 'weapons' were held in a well-known house. Employers were threatening employees with the sack if they joined the Army. Lomas added:

> 'we are entirely at the mercy of the roughs who follow us through the streets to our hall stoning us . . . they break the windows of all who sympathise with us . . . Their programme on Sunday next at a given signal is to cut open the drum end and put in the drummer, cover the processionists with red ruddle[4] and flour and keep us from the Barracks. Oh! Hallelujah, the town is on a blaze from end to end, and much spiritual awakening in every chapel, glory be to Jesus!'[5]

---

4. A pigment used for marking sheep.
5. Victor Bailey, 'Salvation Army Riots', in Victor Bailey, *Order and Disorder in Modern Britain: Essays on Riot, Crime, Policing and Punishment* (London: Breviary Stuff Publications, 2014), p.15.

He claimed that the previous Sunday evening there had not been six men in the town's 23 pubs and in the first few weeks they had made at least 70 converts. Lomas sent the letter from the Swan Temperance Hotel, which indicates he might not have found it easy to find ordinary accommodation. He had been staying with a Salvationist, John Denner, but had left his house after all his windows were smashed.

When Salvationists were assaulted, the local police sergeant had just grinned and ignored pleas for help. Often showered with turnips, even the Hallelujah lasses had their clothes smeared with cow dung. The *North Devon Journal* reported events of one meeting:

> About two o'clock a company of about 50 young men marched from Ottery St. Mary [*six miles away*] to join the Skeleton Army; these young fellows enjoyed the distinction of being known as "The Ottery Light Skirmishers." In the evening [in the Salvation Hall] powder was let off, filling the room with smoke, and then rockets and other fireworks were discharged. There was a renewal of the pelting; the door was wrenched off and thrown into the streets, and, to crown it all, there were several hand-to-hand-fights.[6]

The police took an hour to restore order and clear the hall. Outside in the street a mob of at least 1,200 shrieked and yelled at Salvationists as they were escorted out of the building. As it became clear that the magistrates would go easy on the Skeletons, it encouraged more violence:

> The news reached the surrounding towns and villages that there was to be a battle on Sunday, and the consequence was that hundreds of people arrived in Honiton to see the fight. Some drove, some rode, others came by train, while many walked. It was an amusing sight to see parties of six and more, old and young, walking into town bespattered with mud, and who had evidently come long distances to see the disturbance. The town more represented a scene at a fair than a Sabbath-day.[7]

6. 30 November 1882.

7. *Exeter and Plymouth Gazette*, 27 November 1882.

A local newspaper, the *Exeter & Plymouth Gazette Daily Telegrams,* had little sympathy and claimed that the Salvation Army had recruited only a 'mere handful' of followers and that in one meeting there were only 'half a dozen on the platform, and about a dozen adults and four or five unruly children' in the public seats:

> Already the expenses at the "barracks" are being curtailed in respect of the consumption of gas, and the "captain", although an ex-military man, does not possess enough "gas" to compensate for the dullness of light. His voice is not very strong, and often it is impossible for those at the bottom of the "barracks" to hear what he has to say, and what with the youngsters singing everything that comes into their heads, one can readily imagine oneself in a beer garden instead of a "place of worship" . . . . The uproarious behaviour which has taken place since the advent of the Army has never been equalled before . . . . It seriously disregards the feelings of all church and chapel people in the town . . . . School children are debarred from going to their Sunday School at the proper time, the inhabitants of Honiton are terrified beyond description, mothers are made anxious for the safety of their young ones and the atmosphere is full of blasphemy. All because half-a-dozen so-called salvationists are permitted by law to parade the streets and sing comic-song tunes.[8]

In the same article it was reported that the Earl of Shaftesbury, the great industrial and social reformer, had recently called the Army 'downright blasphemy' and questioned its 'so-called conversions' in a speech made to the Church Pastoral Aid Society in Windsor. A local Honiton printer, John Knight, was printing excerpts from it and circulating them locally. The editor of the *Telegrams* commented, 'much praise is due to him for this, and I trust it will be the means of bringing people to their senses'.[9]

Booth decided to suspend marching temporarily and confine meetings to their hall, which the mayor assured would be protected. The Skeletons responded by posting printed notices around the town:

8. 30 November 1882
9. Ibid.

"Skeleton Headquarters December 3rd 1882"

Skeletons: Salvationists will not parade today. Keep from the hall.

By order, Lieut-General Commanding.[10]

The Skeletons parodied *The War Cry* with their own fortnightly newspaper, *The Skeleton*[11] – see Figs. 6&7. Originally started as a joke and priced one penny, it sold hundreds of copies. It first came out on 18 November and was printed and published by Hermon C. Clarke, allegedly a porter. Its third edition declared that 'the real object of this paper is to stamp out fanaticism and [the] blasphemy of the Salvation Army, which is doing so much to bring Christian religion into ridicule'.[12] Below is an extract from one of their poems:

Salvation Army Creed

They gather their knowledge from wisdom's great tree,
All their religion is £.s.d.
Pound, shillings and pence is all that they crave,
From the first step on earth, to the brink of their grave.

Some fools may ask what they do with their money,
They may just as well ask what bees do with honey,
They will answer you all with a wink and a nod
They keep three-thirds themselves and give praise to God.

In the cold silent earth they may soon be laid low
To sleep with the blest that has gone long ago,
They will slumber in peace till the great resurrection
But the first on their legs to make the collection

Lieut. Dobson, 1st Battery Turf Shiers[13]

---

10. *Exeter & Plymouth Gazette*, 3 December 1882.
11. Reproduced copies of 2 & 16 December 1882 can be seen in Horridge, *The Salvation Army*, pp.230–35. Original copies are kept at the Salvation Army International Heritage Centre.
12. 16 December 1882.
13. 2 December 1882, in Horridge, *The Salvation Army*, p.231.

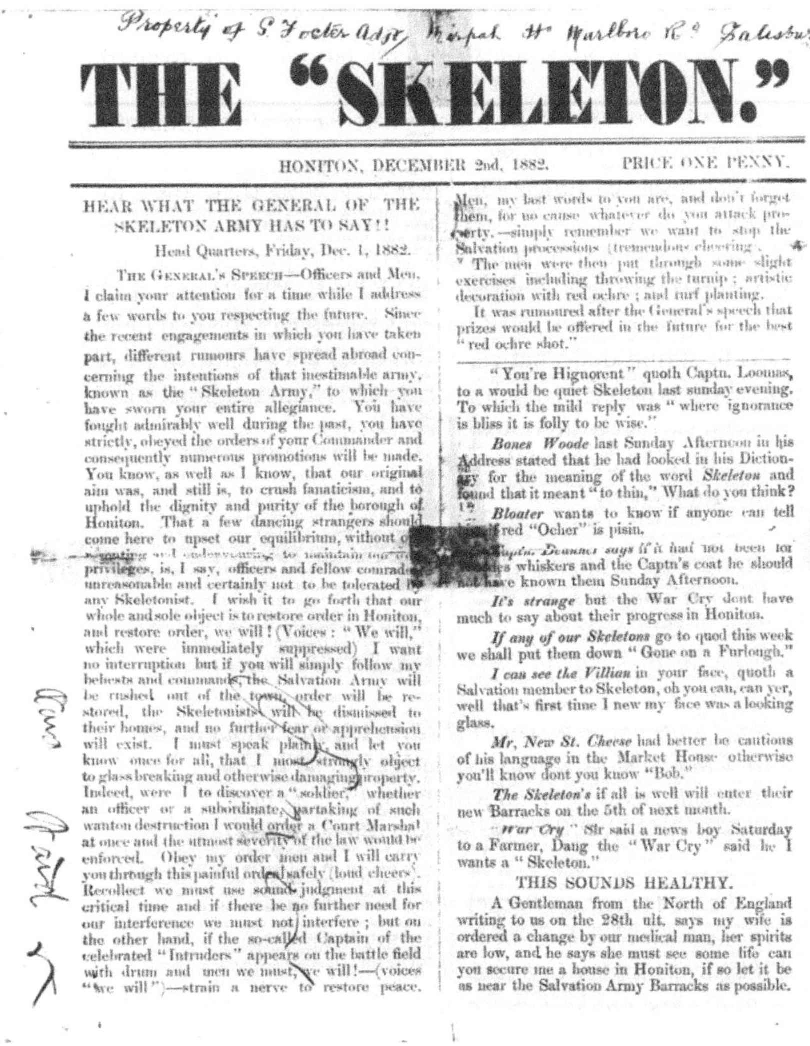

THE "SKELETON."

HONITON, DECEMBER 2nd, 1882. PRICE ONE PENNY.

HEAR WHAT THE GENERAL OF THE SKELETON ARMY HAS TO SAY!!

Head Quarters, Friday, Dec. 1, 1882.

THE GENERAL'S SPEECH—Officers and Men. I claim your attention for a time while I address a few words to you respecting the future. Since the recent engagements in which you have taken part, different rumours have spread abroad concerning the intentions of that inestimable army, known as the "Skeleton Army," to which you have sworn your entire allegiance. You have fought admirably well during the past, you have strictly, obeyed the orders of your Commander and consequently numerous promotions will be made. You know, as well as I know, that our original aim was, and still is, to crush fanaticism, and to uphold the dignity and purity of the borough of Honiton. That a few dancing strangers should come here to upset our equilibrium, without c[illegible] [illegible] and endeavouring to maintain our [illegible] privileges, is, I say, officers and fellow comrades unreasonable and certainly not to be tolerated by any Skeletonist. I wish it to go forth that our whole and sole object is to restore order in Honiton, and restore order, we will! (Voices: "We will," which were immediately suppressed) I want no interruption but if you will simply follow my behests and commands, the Salvation Army will be rushed out of the town, order will be restored, the Skeletonists will be dismissed to their homes, and no further fear or apprehension will exist. I must speak plainly, and let you know once for all, that I most strongly object to glass breaking and otherwise damaging property. Indeed, were I to discover a "soldier," whether an officer or a subordinate, partaking of such wanton destruction I would order a Court Marshal at once and the utmost severity of the law would be enforced. Obey my order men and I will carry you through this painful ordeal safely (loud cheers). Recollect we must use sound judgment at this critical time and if there be no further need for our interference we must not interfere; but on the other hand, if the so-called Captain of the celebrated "Intruders" appears on the battle field with drum and men we must, we will!—(voices "we will")—strain a nerve to restore peace. Men, my last words to you are, and don't forget them, for no cause whatever do you attack property,—simply remember we want to stop the Salvation processions (tremendous cheering).

The men were then put through some slight exercises including throwing the turnip; artistic decoration with red ochre; and turf planting.

It was rumoured after the General's speech that prizes would be offered in the future for the best "red ochre shot."

"You're Hignorent" quoth Captn. Loomas, to a would be quiet Skeleton last sunday evening. To which the mild reply was "where ignorance is bliss it is folly to be wise."

Bones Woode last Sunday Afternoon in his Address stated that he had looked in his Dictionary for the meaning of the word ***Skeleton*** and found that it meant "to thin," What do you think?

Bloater wants to know if anyone can tell [illegible] red "Ocher" is pisin.

[illegible] ***Captn. Deanne says*** if it had not been for [illegible] whiskers and the Captn's coat he should not have known them Sunday Afternoon.

It's strange but the War Cry dont have much to say about their progress in Honiton.

If any of our Skeletons go to quod this week we shall put them down "Gone on a Furlough."

I can see the Villian in your face, quoth a Salvation member to Skeleton, oh you can, can yer, well that's first time I new my face was a looking glass.

Mr, New St. Cheese had better be cautions of his language in the Market House otherwise you'll know dont you know "Bob."

The Skeleton's if all is well will enter their new Barracks on the 5th of next month.

"***War Cry***" Sir said a news boy Saturday to a Farmer, Dang the "War Cry" said he I wants a "Skeleton."

THIS SOUNDS HEALTHY.

A Gentleman from the North of England writing to us on the 28th ult. says my wife is ordered a change by our medical man, her spirits are low, and he says she must see some life can you secure me a house in Honiton, if so let it be as near the Salvation Army Barracks as possible.

Figure 6. *The Skeleton*, Honiton, 2/12/1882.

In the aftermath of the latest disturbances, the 'Lieutenant-General' of the Skeletons declared.

> Since the recent engagements in which you have taken part, different rumours have spread abroad concerning the intentions of that inestimable army known as the "Skeleton Army", to which you have sworn your entire allegiance. You have fought admirably well during the past. You have strictly

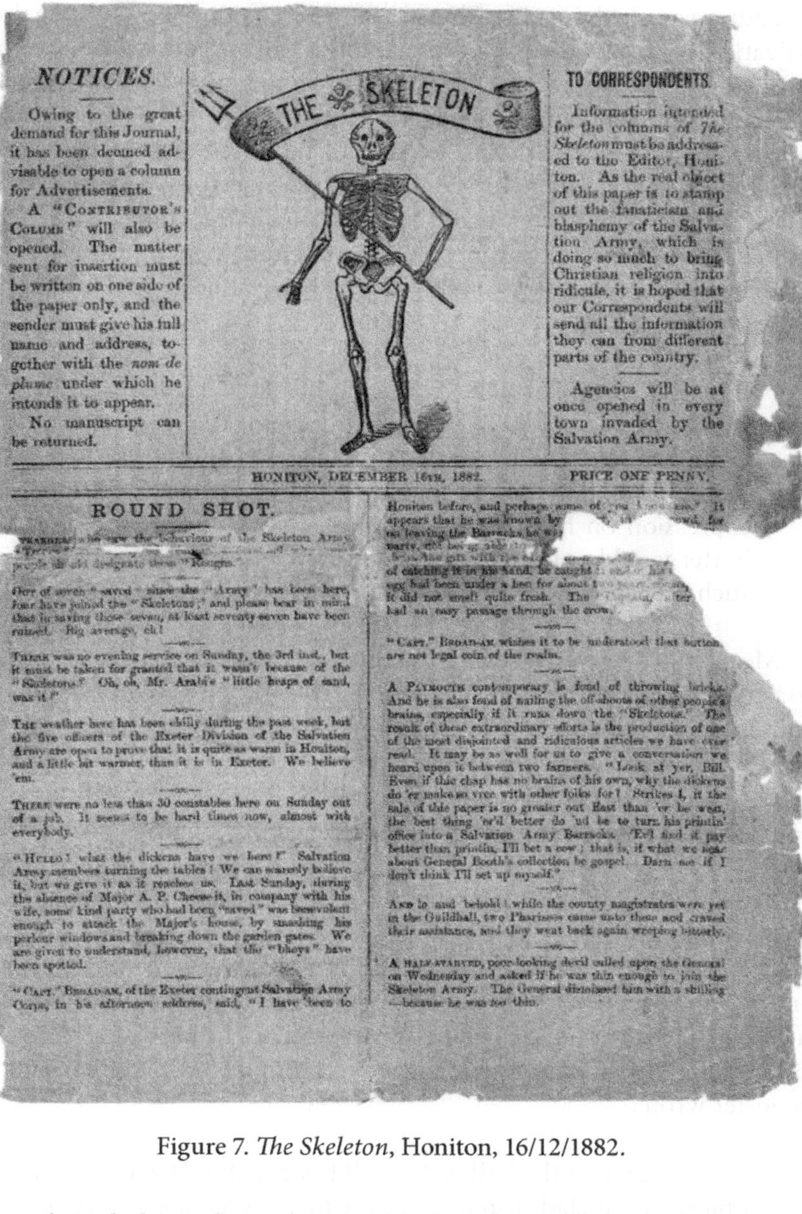

NOTICES.

Owing to the great demand for this Journal, it has been deemed advisable to open a column for Advertisements.

A "CONTRIBUTOR'S COLUMN" will also be opened. The matter sent for insertion must be written on one side of the paper only, and the sender must give his full name and address, together with the *nom de plume* under which he intends it to appear.

No manuscript can be returned.

THE SKELETON

TO CORRESPONDENTS.

Information intended for the columns of *The Skeleton* must be addressed to the Editor, Honiton. As the real object of this paper is to stamp out the fanaticism and blasphemy of the Salvation Army, which is doing so much to bring Christian religion into ridicule, it is hoped that our Correspondents will send all the information they can from different parts of the country.

Agencies will be at once opened in every town invaded by the Salvation Army.

HONITON, DECEMBER 16TH, 1882. PRICE ONE PENNY.

ROUND SHOT.

[illegible] the behaviour of the Skeleton Army [illegible] people [illegible] designate them "Roughs."

[illegible] seven "saved" since the "Army" has been here, four have joined the "Skeletons;" and please bear in mind that in saving those seven, at least seventy-seven have been ruined. Big average, eh!

THERE was no evening service on Sunday, the 3rd inst., but it must be taken for granted that it wasn't because of the "Skeletons?" Oh, oh, Mr. Arabi's "little heaps of sand," was it?

THE weather here has been chilly during the past week, but the five officers of the Exeter Division of the Salvation Army are open to prove that it is quite as warm in Honiton, and a little bit warmer, than it is in Exeter. We believe 'em.

THERE were no less than 30 constables here on Sunday out of a job. It seems to be hard times now, almost with everybody.

"HULLO! what the dickens have we here?" Salvation Army members turning the tables! We can scarcely believe it, but we give it as it reaches us. Last Sunday, during the absence of Major A. P. Cheese-it, in company with his wife, some kind party who had been "saved" was benevolent enough to attack the Major's house, by smashing his parlour windows and breaking down the garden gates. We are given to understand, however, that the "bhoys" have been spotted.

"CAPT." BROAD-AM, of the Exeter contingent Salvation Army Corps, in his afternoon address, said, "I have been to Honiton before, and perhaps some of you [illegible]." It appears that he was known by [illegible] for on leaving the Barracks he w[illegible] party, [illegible] of catching it in his hand, he caught [illegible] egg had been under a hen for about t[illegible] it did not smell quite fresh. The "Captain," after had an easy passage through the crow[illegible]

"CAPT." BROAD-AM wishes it to be understood that button[s] are not legal coin of the realm.

A PLYMOUTH contemporary is fond of throwing bricks. And he is also fond of nailing the off-shoots of other people's brains, especially if it runs down the "Skeletons." The result of these extraordinary efforts is the production of one of the most disjointed and ridiculous articles we have ever read. It may be as well for us to give a conversation we heard upon it between two farmers. "Look at yer, Bill. Even if this chap has no brains of his own, why the dickens do 'er make so vree with other folks for? Strikes I, if the sale of this paper is no greater out East than 'er be wean, the best thing 'er'd better do 'ud be to turn his printin' office into a Salvation Army Barracks. 'Er'd find it pay better than printin, I'll bet a cow; that is, if what we hear about General Booth's collection be gospel. Darn me if I don't think I'll set up myself."

AND lo and behold! while the county magistrates were yet in the Guildhall, two Pharisees came unto them and craved their assistance, and they went back again weeping bitterly.

A HALF-STARVED, poor-looking devil called upon the General on Wednesday and asked if he was thin enough to join the Skeleton Army. The General dismissed him with a shilling —because he was *too* thin.

Figure 7. *The Skeleton*, Honiton, 16/12/1882.

obeyed the orders of your Commander and consequently numerous promotions will be made. You know, as well as I do, that our original aim was, and still is, to crush fanaticism, and to uphold the dignity and purity of the borough of Honiton.[14]

14. Ibid.

Four cases involving disturbances of meetings and of assaults against Salvationists resulted in no prosecutions. On one occasion, after his counsel had failed to arrive, Lomas declined to give any more evidence in court as he thought that Henry Hook, the ex-Mayor and sitting magistrate, was not a 'proper person' to try cases of assaults against Salvationists as he was so biased. In turn, the Skeletons' defence lawyer, Merlin Fryer from Exeter, had threatened to charge Lomas with "false imprisonment" for getting people arrested and then refusing to give evidence. After *The War Cry* highlighted the attacks on Lomas, *The Skeleton* hit back:

> If this is a specimen of the "religion" and of the "Captains" who furnish reports for the *War Cry* save us from their intercession. What can respectable people think of a man of this type, who talks about "outflanking the devil," or "Hallelujah" with an expression on his face that would lead one to suppose that butter would not melt in his mouth? What can we designate such proceedings but a rotten stinking hypocrisy.[15]

Meanwhile, Booth asked the magistrates to forbid Skeletons from assembling and to swear in special constables. They refused but offered more police protection for his followers. After temporarily suspending parading, Lomas was ordered to march.

On Thursday, 21 December, reinforced by 'Captain' Foster and fourteen 'soldiers' from Exeter, they marched out singing hymns. They tried to parade outside the town hall but were attacked by the Skeleton Army, who had brought along their own band. It was Christmas Market Day with reputedly 2–3,000 people on the streets. During the collision between the two 'armies', market stalls were overturned. The police tried to intervene but were covered with flour and failed to make any arrests. One Salvationist sustained a large cut on the head after being hit by a brick. The Salvationists managed to scramble back to their hall. A reporter wrote:

> . . . the scene in the hall is difficult to describe. The Salvation officers were clad in red jerseys, which were partly covered with flour and mud, and they looked more like a number of football-players who had recently returned from a "good

15. 16 December 1882.

> scrimmage" than "preachers and teachers." These mixed with the general crowd, who were shouting against the Salvationists' attempts to say prayers, while a wounded soldier at the back of the Hall with a bandaged eye added to the characteristics of the scene.[16]

The *Pall Mall Gazette* criticized the magistrates and William Harcourt, the home secretary, for refusing to interfere:

> Mob law reigns in Honiton; the authorities have practically abdicated. It is no longer a question of processioning. It is the right of public meeting that is attacked, and the Bench and the roughs appear to have entered into a league to drive the Army out of town by brute force. This is scandalous enough, but it is perhaps even more scandalous that when the facts were laid before Sir W. Harcourt he replied that "he refuses to interfere with the discretion of the local authorities".
>
> . . . On Thursday night the streets of Honiton were some hours again in the possession of a brutal, disorderly mob. For a fortnight past the Salvation Army have been unable to hold services in their hall. The skylights have been repeatedly broken, the uproar of the roughs has been deafening and their general conduct very violent. The skylights were replaced and wire put over them, but the roughs threw shot, marbles, bullets etc. high into the air and let them drop on the windows. The Salvationists have had to hold services in private houses, and their windows have been smashed.[17]

In fact, however, Harcourt, who had sympathy for temperance reformers, did send a letter asking the magistrates to explain their decisions and statements. He urged them to take action against the Skeletons and provide Salvationists with more police protection. He also censured them for refusing to convict Samuel Stone, a labourer, for throwing a bag of flour over a Hallelujah lass even though two policemen were only three feet away and witnessed it. Henry Hook said the defendant – who had only been cautioned – was 'an inoffensive lad'.

* * *

16. *Exeter and Plymouth Gazette,* 22 December 1882.
17. 23 December 1882.

A reporter from the *Western Morning News* was sent to investigate. He discovered Honiton was attracting Skeleton "batteries" from all the neighbouring towns and that respectable tradesmen were supporting them. 'Boycotting and ostracism has been pursued which has resulted in much petty annoyance not only to the Salvation Army but to anyone who dared to offer them protection or associate with them in any way'.[18] Skeleton leaders went under assumed names and had a secret committee of fifteen which was commanded by a 'Lieutenant-General'. When one of the young female officers of the Exeter Army had written to the 'Lieutenant-General of the Skeleton Army', Honiton, complaining about being hit by a brick, she had received a reply from Edward Dent, a well-known tradesman of the town.

The reporter discovered that the editor of *The Skeleton* had announced Skeleton agencies were to be opened in every town invaded by the Army. As 'Major' Davey of Exeter was showing the reporter around Honiton, he witnessed local resentment when a publican refused to let them pass through his yard, which was a common thoroughfare. The reporter left town admitting it was not easy to understand why in such a usually quiet town there should be so much disturbance. He concluded that it had been 'infected' by Exeter, only 17 ½ miles away.

In January 1883, a large poster was put up in the Market Place, advertising three days of Salvation services from January 27–30. On Saturday 27 January, the Skeleton Army marched out to the railway station in full force with a big drum and other "musical" instruments: triangles, pieces of iron and a sheet of tin. They were expecting Salvationists to arrive from Exeter. The procession was headed, in a mock funeral, by a large coffin borne on the shoulders of four men. On the sides of the coffin were the words 'Purgered [*sic*] Salvationists' and, on the lid, a skull and cross-bones. Behind it was a big placard: 'Showing up General Booth and his Sham Army'. It was followed by a four wheeled carriage, 'Mr & Mrs Booth's War Chariot'. Two men sat in it, one dressed in military style wearing medals. Behind the 'chariot' there was a large flag, 'Booth at Home', representing a skeleton with a glass, bottle and pipe. On another large flag was written, 'His Satanic Majesty' and 'Salvation Army Confederate' with the words 'Fanaticism', 'Blasphemy' and 'Hypocrisy' written beneath.

---

18. *Western Morning* News, 23 December 1882.

The procession was followed by a vast crowd. To their surprise, no Salvationists arrived at the station. Instead, Skeletons turned on the local parade. They smashed the coffin across heads and threw pepper mixed with paint over them; the effects lasting a few days. Two men tried to get the coffin over Lomas's head and hit him with it repeatedly. He and his small band of sixteen went to the mayor's house to ask for protection but were turned down. There were only three policemen in town to quell the disturbance and they were helpless. They were also covered in paint, even in their eyes. Lomas's wife, Alice, was kicked by a publican.

The Honiton corps still didn't have a brass band,[19] so there was great excitement when the Exeter band, led by 'Captain' William Foster, arrived with supporters at the railway station the next day. The days' programme was as follows.

> 3PM: A GREAT HOSANNA MEETING WITH EXHIBITION OF TROPHIES RESCUED BY THE POWER OF GOD FROM DRUNKENNESS, SIN AND THE DEVIL AND ALL HIS WORKS. ADMISSION 3d. ALSO A GRAND MEETING AT 6PM; TICKETS 1/- INCLUDING ADMISSION TO HOSANNA MEETING.

The bottom of the programme read:

> AND ALL THE LIARS SHALL HAVE THEIR PART IN THE LAKE WHICH BURNETH WITH FIRE AND BRIMSTONE. PREPARE TO MEET THY GOD.[20]

At the station, Foster with fifteen 'soldiers' and seven bandsmen were met by 1,000 Skeletons carrying a banner, 'Reception to Exeter'. Charlotte Hartnoll had her face covered with mud and the small party were beaten up as they made their way to the hall. Stones, bricks, broken bottles, paint and other missiles were thrown. Teeth were knocked out, black eyes inflicted. They were covered with paint and so much flour they looked like millers. Foster was punched and kicked and had to run for his life after hearing shouts of 'Murder that Fellow!' Only 20 policemen were on duty. One of them was hit with a stone on the side of his face

19. It would not have one until the end of July 1883.

20. *Chard and Ilminster News,* 3 February 1883.

whilst others were covered in flour. Two Salvationists suffered serious head wounds. When Foster arrived at the hall, he said that, when Lomas tried to speak, he was greeted with pistol firing and wild yells. It was like the Wild West. Inside there were so many wounded it resembled a hospital. A local newspaper suggested Salvationists, covered in paint, 'looked like Red Indians rather than Englishmen'.[21]

Skeletons bombarded the building with large stones pulled out of a wall opposite and started to use a sledge hammer against the door. By this time, they numbered 2,000 and even the reporter could not leave the building for fear of attack. During the service, police from Exeter came to arrest 'Captain' Foster for the non-payment of a fine.[22] As he was escorted out by two policemen, he told the congregation that he was willing to go to prison for Jesus. They shouted out 'Hallelujah' and sang 'Anywhere with Jesus'. Outside he was pelted with paint and soot.

After the service, Foster's comrades were too scared to leave the hall and make their way through the mob to catch the last train to Exeter. Meanwhile, back at Exeter station, their supporters, numbering 200–300, were waiting for them to arrive. Instead, they were surprised when Foster alighted in custody. They sang, 'We'll Stand the Storm, it Won't Be long', as they accompanied him to the Devon county gaol. At the prison gates, holding up his hands, he asked for silence and said 'I'm going to prison now but I hope you will pray for me'. They responded with 'amens'.

Back in Honiton, the mob outside the hall gradually dispersed. On their way home they smashed the windows of those known to be Army sympathizers. After being besieged and kept prisoners for hours, the Exeter Salvationists fled across the fields. Late into the night Honiton was described as 'in tumult' as Skeletons paraded the town with a big drum. The following evening, on the third day of the advertised services, the Salvationists decided not to hold a meeting in their hall. Denied their usual target, the Skeletons went through the town centre smashing windows and street lamps instead.

The *Exeter and Plymouth Gazette Daily Telegrams* was still unsympathetic:

---

21. *Exeter Flying Post,* 31 January 1883.

22. Foster and Charles Middleton, a tailor, had both been fined five shillings and ten shillings, respectively, for assaulting each other. Middleton paid his fine but Foster claimed he was innocent and refused. He alleged that Middleton had repeatedly tried to trip him up by kicking him.

> What on earth can it be but pure ignorance on the part of men and women to go jumping and dancing backwards through mud and mire on the Sabbath day, to the amusement of a few country visitors and the riotous lads of the town . . . The Skeletons are formed by a few of the most respectable young tradesmen of the place. Even Lomas has called them "respectable sinners" . . . I can assure you that prior and up to the time of the arrival of the Salvation Army a more quiet and a better-behaved town it could have been impossible to find in the West of England.[23]

Foster was released from prison after a man on instructions from Salvation Army headquarters paid his fine. When he returned to his hall, the congregation stood on their seats waving their handkerchiefs and singing and shouting at the top of their voices. Foster had previously served seven days in Winchester gaol for assaulting a bystander during rioting in Salisbury. Afterwards, the Army had sold two pictures of him, one before the rioting and one afterwards showing his torn clothing and battered condition. In May 1883, he would be sentenced to three weeks' hard labour – after refusing to pay a fine – for allegedly assaulting a Skeleton in Watford after having a dead rabbit thrown at him during a service.

* * *

Despite being repeatedly attacked and fined for assault himself, Lomas had bravely carried on marching. However, he was becoming increasingly pessimistic. The newspapers reported that pubs and beer shops were doing a thriving trade as a rendezvous for Skeletons, while Lomas was forced to escape meetings in disguise and learnt that a coffin had been made for him. He described Honiton as 'Hell-on-earth' and spoke of a reign of terror in the town. Salvationists were losing their jobs and the windows of sympathisers' houses were being smashed, despite extra police being drafted in. They were collecting no money as people were too frightened to come to their hall. He had also heard a rumour that some Skeletons had procured a barrel of gunpowder to blow it up.

Lomas's situation was not improved by one particular incident. For some time, local children had paraded past the Salvation Hall singing rude songs and waving their hands and arms, parodying the Army in

23. 21 February 1883.

a ridiculous fashion. Lomas had been outside the hall when a group of passing schoolchildren had thrown stones at him. One thrown by Beatrice Skinner, aged twelve, a labourer's daughter, hit him on the chest. He grabbed hold of her and asked for her name. She refused to give it, so he locked her up in a room until she told him. Her cries attracted attention and after ten minutes he let her go. He was summonsed and charged with assaulting her. In turn, he summonsed her mother, Mary, for 'riotous and indecent conduct'.

In court he was accused of dragging Beatrice back to the hall by her hair and locking her in a dark room. Lomas denied pulling her hair and said it was a light room, a claim supported by witnesses. However, four other schoolgirls supported the charge against him. A local doctor, Dr Shortbridge, was called to give evidence and said that, when he saw Beatrice, she was 'suffering from a severe fright'. Even though the doctor had already publicly declared he would not treat Salvationists as long as they disturbed the town (and had also told Lomas he would not treat his wife if she was ill), his evidence was believed and Lomas was fined ten shillings. After Beatrice had gone home, her mother returned to the hall and called Lomas 'a rogue, liar and used violent language' in front of witnesses. She was fined five shillings. In future, whenever Lomas made a summons against an attacker, he would receive one in response.

Subsequently, John Fredricks, a professional entertainer who did impersonations and sang, shouted at Lomas that: 'the Exeter Workhouse was full of Salvation Army bastards and that you are a miserable coward to assault a defenceless little girl while you are afraid to stand up and fight like a man'.[24] He told a policeman who came to arrest him to 'go to hell'. In court, he was fined £2 for using profane and indecent language. (Fredericks would be back in court the following week after shouting at the top of his voice, 'Go to Hell, you bastards', at a parade. He refused to pay his fine. His wife paid it. In January, they both appeared in Exeter in a show making fun of the Army.)[25]

24. *Exeter Flying Post,* 29 January 1883.

25. It was advertised as "Comic Personation, Entertainment under the patronage of "Regular & Skeleton" Armies. Go and be "Saved" from the "indescribable" scenes of "Blood, Fire and Slaughter down below". Go and hear Mrs Fredericks' new song of "I am Captain of the Salvation Army." *Echo & Express,* 8 January 1883.

In the same month, Fanny Green was summonsed for disturbing a meeting and calling Lomas a 'wicked wretch' and for shouting out that he should be hung. She was fined five shillings and costs. When Lomas left court, he asked the magistrates for police protection on his way home, which they granted. His reputation was hardly enhanced when the local press accused him of asking for police protection for a procession only to cancel it after extra police arrived.[26]

Next, a Skeleton, John Hussey, the local postmaster and auctioneer, described as a 'strongly built man' and alleged to be the Skeletons' standard-bearer, was taken to court. He had gone to the Salvation Hall with 200 roughs and kept his hat on and smoked. He encouraged others to do the same and disrupted the meeting. According to the Army barrister, Sutherst, if he had done this in an ordinary church, he would have been turned out. He was acquitted because of conflicting evidence. Councillor John Spurway, the landlord of the Fountain Inn, was also acquitted of assaulting Lomas and his wife Alice.

Afterwards, Lomas was transferred to Crediton, where he was styled the 'Honiton Hero'. Perhaps, at times, he had been over-combative, telling the Skeleton Army there that he had permission to summons up to 140 of them to court. Moreover, he seemed to have a short fuse where children were concerned. At Crediton, in May 1883, he was fined five shillings and expenses after being found guilty of pulling the ears of a boy who had shouted 'Salvation Canary' and 'Honiton Canary' at him.[27] He was replaced in Honiton by 'Captain' James Fairless who, with his sixteen-strong band of Salvationists, was greeted with rotten eggs by 400 Skeletons.

At a council meeting, Councillor Matthews, though not agreeing with the Salvation Army, insisted it should be protected and that it had been a mistake not to have sworn in special constables. For speaking out, he had been hit by projectiles and his life and property threatened. He believed: 'there existed at Honiton an organisation that somewhat resembled the Fenian Brotherhood, as persons allowed to contribute two or three pence a week towards defraying the expense entailed by any

---

26. *Exeter & Plymouth Gazette,* 15 February 1883. An article alleged that he had requested 50–60 extra police but had cancelled the procession once they arrived.

27. Ibid., 4 May 1883.

fines that might be imposed'.[28] He suggested harsher punishments. A motion to require county police to provide protection was unanimously carried.

The home secretary's censure of the magistrates seemed to be working. Moreover, a new county JP, who was deemed to be more impartial, now sat on the bench and Skeletons were facing far stiffer penalties. As a result of previous assaults, mainly against Lomas, Henry Woodbury, a labourer, was fined £3 18s 6d for two counts of assault and William Chard, a labourer, the full penalty of £2 for throwing paint. James Harris and Hermon Clarke, publisher of *The Skeleton*, were each fined £5 for assaulting Lomas with a coffin. In court, to laughter, Harris was asked whether he thought it was a funeral. To renewed laughter, he replied "yes", although he did not know whether a Christian was inside the coffin. When Thomas Sutherst, the prosecuting barrister, suggested that if he behaved like that with a coffin again he would be imprisoned, Harris replied 'I hope I shall see you there if I do, Sir.' However, some attackers were let off because of 'insufficient evidence'.

The riots were costing Honiton £200–£300 in extra policing. The disturbances were also becoming expensive for the Skeletons; their fines thus far totalled over £200. They had organized a central fund for nearby villages and towns to make donations but it was drying up. In January 1883, George Corner, the landlord of the Three Tuns Inn, had driven his 'war chariot' into a procession and had refused to move. He was fined £2 and costs. However, despite the fines, the harassment continued. George Turner, a drainer, was given the choice of a fine or one month's imprisonment for assaulting a Salvation 'captain' and also punished for attacking a former Skeleton turned Salvationist with a knife.

For six months from September 1882 to February 1883, the Army had faced vicious assaults. From now on, due to better police protection, the Skeleton attacks were sporadic and Skeletons only occasionally appeared in court. One of them, Hermon Clarke, *The Skeleton* publisher, was fined five shillings in June 1883 for trying to forcibly make his wife and child leave the Salvation hall. However, Salvationists were still being arrested. In July, nine young ones were arrested for 'loitering' on a footpath after leaving a midnight service. They had left in orderly fashion but were all fined. They refused to pay and were in custody briefly before headquarters paid their fines. The same month, Walter

---

28. Ibid., 2 February 1883.

Harris – who had dressed up as William Booth in a red uniform, decorated with three tin medals and a tin cross in an earlier Skeleton parade – was charged with kicking 'Captain' Lister during a procession. Harris made a counter charge; both cases were dismissed and they were made to pay costs. In August a young man, Alfred Stockman, was fined for disturbing a meeting. Laughably, he tried to claim he had been given alcohol by a Salvationist, which had made him drunk. He refused to pay the fine and was imprisoned.

In October, the Army's standing was not helped when 'Captain' Fairless and Henry Denner, a drummer, were fined in court for mistreating a pony. They refused to pay at first but eventually did. Subsequently, a seventeen-year-old youth threw sulphuric acid at Denner, badly burning his face and his clothes. In court, as it was not proved that it had been intentional, the youth received a lesser sentence of one month's hard labour.

On Guy Fawkes Night 1883, in a torchlight procession, effigies of Salvationists were hung up in a mock execution on a scaffold before being thrown onto the bonfire. The windows of sympathisers' properties were smashed. One individual who had gone to Exeter was advised not to return home that night. A Skeleton mob in disguise waited at the railway station until convinced he could not possibly return and dispersed. One newspaper asked: 'Where were the police? They were present but might as well have been on the moon.'[29] A 'Lover of Order' believed Skeletons were getting their support and money from the sons of respectable tradesmen.[30]

In March and April 1884, as Salvationists paraded, hundreds of people gathered to jeer at them. Eggs, stones, paint and several buckets of stinking cesspit water were thrown over them. The crowds were no longer described as the Skeleton Army. Several 'soldiers', including women, were cut on the head. As a result, Salvationists and their attackers were summonsed for obstruction or assault. 'All cases were dealt with on the evidence provided and both Armies received similar fines on a par with those offences not involving the Salvation Army.'[31] In November that year, Salvationists were accused of only parading in the poor areas and that they were neglecting 'rich sinners'.[32]

29. *Western Times,* 10 November 1883.

30. Ibid.

31. Horridge, *The Salvation Army,* p.166.

32. *Exeter & Plymouth Gazette,* 15 November 1884.

By July 1885, *The War* Cry was appealing to its readers to pray for 'dark Honiton'. Over a year later in September 1886, a Baptist wrote to a local newspaper:

> It seemed to me that the police would rather see men rolling about the streets tipsy, and hear them cursing and quarrelling than marching on an orderly procession and singing hymns, which never really disturb or annoy anyone. Thirty Salvationists preached the gospel in a wide street at 10.30am on Sunday and the leader ["Captain" Hunt] was jailed for seven days for obstruction.[33]

Later that year Hunt was jailed again for obstruction, this time for fourteen days. Whatever the opinion of the Court of Judges in London in respect of the Army's freedom to march, William Booth was clearly still struggling to get the support of public opinion.

The Honiton Salvation Army corps closed in 1889, reportedly never to return. This was due to public apathy as much as anything. The Army had been invited and did have strong supporters in the town,[34] but they were worn down by relentless personal and official abuse, particularly by the mayor and ex-mayor, John Murch and Henry Hook. Ten years later, when William Booth made a triumphal tour of the west, he visited Exeter and Weston-super-Mare but not Honiton. Although there is no corps there now, the Army did in fact return in 1925 when a new hall was opened by Mr and Mrs Booth-Tucker.[35] She declared:

> Those days of persecution had been turned into days of victory. It was significant that every one of the ringleaders of the Skeleton Army came to a tragic end. The Salvation Army had

33. *Exeter Flying Post,* 3 September 1886.

34. In a ward election, March 1883, a leading tradesman, Edward Ashly, thought to be a Salvation sympathiser, had beaten Edward Burrough, the landlord of the Star Inn, who had the backing of the Tories and Skeletons.

35. He had been married to William Booth's daughter, Emma, who tragically died in a train accident in the United States in 1903. His present wife was former "Colonel" Minnie Reid, whom he married in 1906.

> returned to Honiton after many years, and in circumstances far removed from those of the early days . . . We have come here and we mean to stay.[36]

Nevertheless, the Skeleton Army had won their first victory and it had taken the Army over thirty years to return to the town. Would there be others?

* * *

It is no exaggeration to say that in the early 1880s the West Country was ablaze with Skeleton Army riots. There were serious disturbances in Barnstable, Bath, Bridport, Colyton, Crediton, Crewkerne, Falmouth, Frome, Launceston, Stroud, Tiverton, Torrington, Truro, Woodbury, Yeovil and in many small villages. According to reports, some of the disturbances descended into "fisticuffs" between the two sides (Salvationists giving a new meaning to the term 'Muscular Christianity'). So rife were the riots in the region, one entrepreneur on 26 October 1883, placed an advert in the *Exeter &Plymouth Gazette* selling:

> 5,000 Military Shakos [a tall, cylindrical or conical military hat], made for the Bulgarian Army, 12 for 4/6d – ideal for Schools, Guy Fawkes Processions, Football Clubs and the Skeleton Army.

It demonstrates that the Skeleton Army had become normal and almost 'respectable'. In Liskeard, the Skeletons had even mimicked the Salvationists with their own song:

> *"Hold the fort, the forks are coming,*
> *Plates will soon be here,*
> *Pork is in the oven roasting,*
> *And Charlie's fetched the beer."*[37]

Overall, there was less rioting in Cornwall. In the early 1860s William Booth had conducted a very successful evangelical tour there, reputedly saving 7,000 souls. It also had the most members of temperance societies in relation to its population and was a Methodist stronghold.

* * *

36. *Exeter and Plymouth Gazette*, 2 September 1925.

37. *Cornish Times*, 27 May 1937.

At the annual convocation of bishops at Canterbury in 1883, the Salvation Army was widely attacked for its immorality and gimmicks. The Bishop of Lichfield claimed it was a harmful organization that did no spiritual good. The Archdeacon of Bath exclaimed: 'morbid hysterical shoutings of "Blood and Fire", histrionic buffooneries and gestures, imitating the madness of heathen worshippers accompanied their ministrations'.[38] Another deplored the language they used in their handbills, which talked about devil-drivers and hunters.[39] Later on, the Bishop of Salisbury called it 'incomplete, unsatisfactory and dangerous.'[40]

Roman Catholics attacked the Army for being emotional Protestantism. *The Times* condemned it for its 'mode of securing recruits by a sort of spiritual conscriptions, which disregard family ties and parental authority, its vulgar buffooneries . . . religion degraded to the level of the music hall, the use of masquerade as a means of conversion'. It believed the bishops were right to be wary of the organization and concluded rather rashly that 'it is probable enough that it has already had its day'.[41]

Booth hit back at the annual May meeting of the Army. He claimed the Skeleton Army had justified its violent attacks upon inoffensive Salvationists, including young women, by reference to the language of religious dignitaries. He believed the bishops' condemnation was inciting the Skeletons to attack them. He dismissed the allegation that one of his 'captains' preached whilst standing on his head and doing cartwheels as a bit of publicity to attract converts, which did not actually take place. He also denied that *The War Cry* had printed an adapted tune: 'For he's a Jolly Good Saviour' with the refrain 'Which nobody can deny'![42] According to Bramwell Booth

> The most persistent and unrelenting opposition came less from the drinking saloons than from the parsonages . . . Always the chief opposition was from the churches. Every conceivable calumny was spread abroad against us by fellow Christians. When our poor people were bullied and injured, the parsons were 'shocked' but seldom said so publicly or gave us any support when we were down . . . Clergymen who had

38. *Leeds Times,* 5 May 1883.
39. *John Bull,* 14 April 1883.
40. *Lloyds Weekly,* 30 July 1882.
41. 11 April 1883.
42. *Northern Echo,* 6 November 1882.

> never been to a meeting of the Salvation Army in their lives, denounced us from their pulpits and wrote letters of ill will to the newspapers.[43]

It was more difficult for William Booth to deny the showmanship criticism. The more famous converts were encouraged to speak at meetings all over the country and given names, just like music-hall acts, to attract working-class attention: 'Big Ben, the Yorkshire prize-fighter', the 'Converted Wife Beater', 'Ching-Wing, the Chinaman' and 'The Converted Clown'. (The last named was sentenced to four months for bigamy in 1881.[44]) It was reported that a man imprisoned for body snatching wanted to be known as the 'Converted Body Snatcher' but was apparently dissuaded from joining! The Army saw a virtue in exaggerating the past sins of its members to highlight the miracle of their redemption. Booth never denied using the antics of the music hall to attract people. The singing of a hymn 'Bless His Name He Sets Me Free', to the tune of 'Champagne Charlie is My Name' was an example. However, his direct appeal to working-class culture was bearing fruit.

In the early 1880s there were negotiations between the Army and the Church of England. Booth had met Archbishop Benson when he was Bishop of Truro. Benson admitted the Army were reaching people that the Church of England was not. There was to be no formal arrangement but an idea of co-operation. However, no sacraments and women officers were stumbling blocks. Neither was Booth willing to relinquish full control. Additionally, the Church showed no contrition for its previous public criticism. Although it would have enhanced the position of the Army in the eyes of the public and improved their finances, nothing came of the talks.

If 1882 was the high-water mark of the attacks on the Army, with 669 Salvationists attacked (including 250 women and 23 children) and 56 buildings partially wrecked, it was also a time of great growth, with 164 new Salvation Army corps founded and sales of *The War Cry* at 280,000 copies weekly.[45] Moreover, the movement was spreading abroad. That year 100 Salvation officers were sent to India, the United States, Africa and Europe. They were frequently met with opposition.

---

43. Bramwell Booth (1925), *Echoes and Memories,* Ch.4, Kindle edition.

44. *Weston Mercury*, 7 May 1881.

45. According to *The Cornishman*, 15 June 1882, it had 'the largest circulation of any Christianity-teaching newspaper in the world'.

Their processions were initially banned in Australia, Sweden and Canada. In Japan, they were beaten up by brothel keepers. In Bombay, seven Salvationist were arrested for walking through a Muslim area. In Switzerland, their offices were attacked by a mob and one of Booth's daughters was expelled. When she returned, she was imprisoned. On one occasion, an innocent Swiss sailor was attacked because his uniform was mistaken for the Army's. Five Hallelujah lasses had such a hard time in Ireland, they were forced to move every night. There were riots in France and in Paris a French Salvationist was murdered. Back in the British capital there were riots that threatened to get out of hand.

Chapter Five

London and the East End, 1882–83

Once William Booth had moved his family to Hackney in 1865, the East End became the centre of the Christian Mission and then the Salvation Army. After the name change in 1878, which distinguished it from the numerous other missions in the capital, attacks increased as it rapidly expanded. Although they occasionally occurred in places like Chelsea and Oxford Street in the West End – where a former skating rink was converted into a hall[1] – the worst violence was in the East End. It is probable that the use of the 'Skeleton Army' name in the capital was fuelled by newspaper reports about the rioting that had broken out in the West Country.

In his autobiography, *My Life*, George Lansbury, a young Salvationist, who became the leader of the Labour Party in the 1930s, recalled:

> Whenever the Salvationists went for a march or held a meeting there was also the Skeleton Army, making night hideous with their blasphemous shouting, singing and cursing. Often there was a pitched battle between those who supported the Army and those who hated it. I remember on one occasion outside Whitechapel Church finding myself in the midst of the most unholy, scrapping, kicking, butting, and hitting it has ever been my lot to be in. The Salvationists never fought, they took

1. It could seat 3,000 with standing room for 100.

> their grueling as all in the day's work, though new converts occasionally broke loose and gave the 'Skeletons' a dose of their own medicine.[2]

'Colonel' George Holmes, a boy Salvationist in 1881, later remembered seeing the Skeletons led by a seventeen-year-old teenager, Charles Jeffries:

> It was very rough. I remember attending an Open-air meeting one Sunday night outside 'The Blind Beggar'. Afterwards we marched to our hall in Whitechapel Road. The 'skeletons', directed by Jeffries, headed our procession, proceeding at a snail's pace and compelling us to do so. Thus handicapped, we were jostled and pelted with decayed fruit and mud. I was only a boy, and for safety was placed in the middle of the ranks.
>
> An enthusiastic Salvationist in our front rank wore a high hat with a Salvation Army band round the crown. Slipping behind him, Jeffries leapt upon his shoulders and deftly pushed the high hat over his eyes, whilst wriggling into the desired position. Then, using the top hat as a drum and his legs as a goad,[3] he 'drove' his victim in the procession to the hall. The Salvationists could have dismounted Jeffries only by rolling their comrade in the mud.[4]

Born in the East End in 1864, Jeffries was brought up by his widowed mother and worked for a tobacconist. He was a well-known local tearaway.

In November 1881, the Army asked magistrates to send John Jacon, a clerk, to prison for shouting out 'Glory to the Devil' during a service at Bethnal Green. He was fined £1 or fourteen days in prison. Sometimes the Army requested police to come to their meetings in plain clothes for protection. This led to arrests. When their new headquarters was opened – a six-storey, brick-and-stone tower, former billiard club in Queen Victoria Street, a block away from St Paul's Cathedral – police

---

2. George Lansbury, *My Life* (London: Constable & Co. Ltd, 1928), p. 85.
3. A spiked stick used for urging cattle forward.
4. Holmes, cited in Lilian Claughton, *Charles H. Jeffries: From 'Skeleton' to Salvationist Leader* (London: Salvationist Publishing, 1946), p. 3.

were stationed there every day. Frank Smith, a leading Salvationist and instigator of so many of their social welfare initiatives, recalled one occasion when he had to climb out of a window at the back of premises that overlooked the Thames and escape in a barge, such was the fury of the chasing crowd.

* * *

After the Army had managed to lease the Eagle Tavern and the adjoining Grecian Theatre – in the centre of a working-class area – on City Road in June 1882, most rioting took place in Hackney, Bethnal Green and Whitechapel. Known as 'The Bird', it had dancing gardens and a music hall between the tavern and theatre and was hugely popular. To Booth, it was a den of iniquity that produced sin. If he could convert the house of Satan into a camp of salvation, it would be a great triumph:

> Standing amidst a dense working-class population, and with a character far and wide such as makes it unnecessary to describe the scenes nightly to be witnessed there, the building will give us an opportunity far superior to any we have hitherto had of gathering tens of thousands of the worst of people together, and we trust that a great many of those who have formerly been seen there seeking worldly pleasure will soon be found on the same spot, rejoicing in the Lord and leading others to Him.[5]

On its acquisition, or, as Booth saw it, its 'capture', he created medals with the words 'occupied' and 'captured' inscribed. A fund was established to raise the £16,750 necessary to secure the lease, with even the Archbishop of Canterbury contributing. Queen Victoria gave her public blessing but did not contribute. More money was raised when 6,000 people were charged one shilling to attend Bramwell Booth's wedding to Florence Soper.

Hackney had fewer public facilities than other parts of the city. There were no swimming pools, baths or concert halls, apart from one music hall. There were only pubs. When Booth acquired the buildings and publicly declared no alcohol would be served, it seemed to be adding insult to injury as far as the local community was concerned. (*The Times* wondered whether the Army was trying to stop all amusements apart

5. William Booth, letter, *Morning Post*, 26 June 1882.

from religious ones.)[6] When the Army had its dedicatory service in the dancing grounds in August with 6,000 Salvationists thronging the streets, it provoked instant outrage. Whilst London was under gas-light they had assembled at five a.m. at Finsbury Square, singing, playing concertinas and violins. Astonished householders had left their beds, peering out of windows to see what was going on.

> Headed by brass bands and banners, the Army proceeded, three and four abreast, along City-Road, their progress retarded by the unruly mob, who derided and jostled them as they passed along. On reaching the Eagle gates some difficulty was experienced in entering but with the aid of the police, and after some sharp skirmishing and much crushing, the Army entered and, with cheers, secured the possession of their new premises.[7]

Before the Eagle's official opening as the temperance "Salvation Army Hotel" in September – the Grecian Theatre was renamed "a Temple to God" – a meeting nearby of various Christian denominations passed a resolution protesting against the "aggressive and presumptuous attitude of the Salvation Army . . .. contrary to the true spirit of Christ's Gospel".[8] When it opened a mob of 30,000 surrounded the hall, throwing mud at Salvationists as they entered. When they came out, they were showered with bags of flour. The police were completely outnumbered and could do little to protect them. Booth had to send a telegram to Scotland Yard for help and four hundred officers were stationed there that evening. Afterwards, Henry Gandee,19, Henry Wheeler,19, and a boy named Lucas were fined for throwing mud in the City Road. Wheeler was also sent to prison for ten days for assaulting a Salvationist.

The opposition wasn't just due to the fact that Booth refused to honour the drinks license or that he was taking over a working-class place of entertainment. There were also rumours the Army's financial activities were undercutting local labour in the East End. At their brand-new Congress Hall in Clapton, Hackney, it was rumoured the Army

6. Bailey, Victor, '"In Darkest England and the Way Out" The Salvation Army, Social Reform and the Labour Movement, 1885–1910,' *International Review of Social History* 9, no 2 (1984) p.134.

7. *East London Observer*, 17 August 1881.

8. *Northern Echo*, 22 September 1882.

was taking in washing. It wasn't. Later, in 1888, the Vicar of Bow, the Reverend William Adamson, made the false accusation that the Army was selling cheap matches. It wasn't. But such rumours were widely held to be true and increased working-class opposition in London.

In the first few months of its opening 10,000 Skeletons regularly marched in quasi military style playing instruments to drown out Army services inside the "hotel". Booth believed local publicans were sponsoring the mob. In fact, some newspapers referred to the Skeleton Army as "The Publicans Procession". One reported that £7 had been subscribed from local householders who objected to the disruption caused by Army parades. Edmund Lyon,[9] in his article about the opposition to the Army in the East End, found little evidence to suggest Skeletons received financial support from publicans.

Initially, the *Shoreditch Observer* was impressed calling the Skeleton Army in October 1882 'a splendid band of young fellows they would make if rightly handled we admit, for their order and discipline are good, and rough and ready is their work of correcting an unruly member'.[10] That month Skeletons were parading nightly in 'ultra-military clothing and are fine birds in borrowed plumage'.[11] However, their clashes with the police were becoming increasingly violent. In December, a costermonger, John Andrews, was given six months hard labour for attacking a policeman outside the Grecian Theatre. The officer had not been able to work since. Not long after, the *Daily Telegraph* was complaining that:

> it is an unfortunate fact, however, that there is scarcely a thickly populated district in London that is not plagued more or less with such an organized assemblage of rowdies and blackguards. They go in extensively for display. They somehow procure cast-off military jackets and helmets, and their marching banner is a sheet of calico, on which is drawn at full length a skeleton, and the ragtag-and-bobtail behind carry small flags, ragged coloured pocket handkerchiefs, generally attached to stout sticks handy for head-breaking in the possible event of a row. Musical instruments other than

9. Edmund Lyon, '"An avalanche of wrathful violence": Physical Opposition to the Salvation Army, 1881–1883', *Hackney History* 18, pp. 27–36.
10. *Shoreditch Observer*, 14 October 1882.
11. *Hackney and Kingsland Gazette*, 13 October 82.

> an old drum and a few tin-whistles they have no means of providing. But battered pots and kettles cost nothing, and, filled with stones constitute a "rattle' sufficiently deafening and hideous to satisfy the most inveterate peace-hating rough that ever handled one. . . . They are led by two 'captains' on horseback.[12]

New Year 1883 brought increased Skeleton activity and violence in the East End and arrests. It peaked in January. A cab horse driver,, William Burrows, was given the choice of a fine or fourteen days' hard labour for throwing stones in Stoke Newington. A labourer, Charles Young, was given two months' hard labour for trying to stab a Salvation hallkeeper in Whitechapel; and John Old, a 26-year-old labourer, was sentenced to two months for stabbing Timothy McCartney in the back. Old had shouted, 'There's one of them', and had mistaken McCartney for a Salvationist. In reality, he was a Skeleton.

James Flynn, a labourer and Skeleton known as 'The Devil' and described as a 'low-looking ruffian', received six months' hard labour for assaulting George Heywood. Heywood, an ex-Skeleton and retired seaman, was leaving the Grecian Theatre with two girls when he was followed by a mob. Flynn, with 200 Skeletons shouted: 'Here is Sailor!' and stabbed him in the arm with a penknife, 'Take that you Salvation bastard!' Heywood replied, 'All right, Devil, I know you', and carried on walking. Flynn and the others followed him and threw a dead rat and onions at him.

On Sunday, 28 January, Alfred Little, 19, a porter, George Clarke, 50, a labourer and Francis Canham, sixteen, a newsboy, were brought before the magistrates charged with assaulting police outside the Eagle Tavern. With 200–300 police present, Little, holding the flag, had shouted, 'Come on', to his comrades and charged the building. When a policeman had tried to take the flag away, Little had hit him over the head with a stick and, after a scuffle, the three of them had been arrested. In court, Little claimed the police attacked them, capturing their helmets and flags. He and Canham had either to pay a fine or go to prison for fourteen days. Probably, because of his age, Clarke received a month's imprisonment.

According to the *Daily News*, the Skeleton Army had been growing for several weeks. In the last week of January, they had a muster with banners, sticks and pockets full of stones. They told police they had

12. *Daily Telegraph*, 3 February 1883.

A QUIET SUNDAY IN LONDON; OR, THE DAY OF REST.

Figure 8. A cartoon in *Punch*.

as much right to march as the Salvation Army and were threatening a great gathering of forces from all over London on Sunday, 4 February. That day they started to parade the streets with a brass band at seven a.m. and, according to the *Pall Mall Gazette*, 'the streets of London were given up to a rabble of half-grown ruffians'.[13] A *Daily News* reporter described one making his way to the Grecian Theatre:

> At length, about 11 o'clock in the forenoon, we met a Skeleton warrior sauntering leisurely up the City Road towards the Angel at Islington. He was a miserable looking waif, not more than ten years of age and preternaturally small at that, hungry looking and panicked with cold. What the original fabric of his jacket and trousers might have been was an unsolvable problem, and he had evidently run short of pocket handkerchiefs. On his head, however, and overlapping the upper part of his wan face, he wore a secondhand volunteer's

13. *Pall Mall Gazette*, 9 February 1883.

> helmet; that seemed to be as large as himself. The boy was at first proof against the modern art of interviewing, responding to a question as to how he obtained the helmet with nothing more than a knowing leer. The tender of a coin opened his mouth somewhat and hoarsely whispered that the muster of the Skeleton Army had been postponed till later in the day. It was with a sad glance under the peak of the helmet that he added, as he went his way, 'No larks today, Guv'nor'.[14]

When the reporter got to the theatre – the 'cockpit of ruffianism' – he found a disappointed-looking crowd of 1,000 men and boys faced by over 100 police with another 600 waiting nearby in reserve. Since Booth took it over, the police on duty had been doing thirteen-hour shifts and had not had a Sunday off for months. They had made quite a few arrests, which had deepened the animosity against them. The Salvationists, quite wisely, decided to stay in the theatre and hold services there.

As the afternoon progressed, the crowd outside grew to between 10,000 and 20,000. Some Skeletons, aged twelve to 20, decided to divide into three 'battalions' of 150 and started to march round eight abreast. They waved dirty handkerchiefs and sang rude songs. They were led by a man on a worn-out horse. After three p.m., when the pubs closed, there were free fights between them and the police. When three Salvationists came out of the building escorted by police, they were pelted with rotten oranges and old shoes. Two Hallelujah lasses were chased into a shop and threatened with murder if they came out. At six p.m. the ordinary congregation of the Salvation Army began to arrive without being molested.

On the same day, two eighteen-year-olds were fined for riotous behaviour in Peckham High Street. They were leading a mob of over 200 with sticks with pocket handkerchiefs as flags. When a thirteen-year-old boy, William Jones, was brought before the court for attacking Salvationists, a policeman claimed that the boys were paid one penny a week to break windows or to stone all the boys who were not members of the Skeleton Army. If they failed to do this, they would receive a 'good hiding'. Jones was fined five shillings or five days' imprisonment. He laughed and pulled faces during the entire hearing. Frederick Rogers, a warehouse boy living in the East End (who later became a famous trade

---

14. *Daily News*, 5 February 1883.

unionist, writer and journalist), who used to go to meetings to 'scoff' at preachers and have 'heaps of fun', would later claim that you needed a subscription to join the Skeleton Army, which he could not afford.[15]

The names of the Skeleton leaders were rarely mentioned in the press. The 'organisation' was wrapped in obscurity. Poplar's 'Captain' Saunders was alleged to be a dwarf dressed like a drummer from a line regiment. He and four others, all aged under 20, were cautioned to keep the peace after leading a thousand-strong mob pushing people off pavements. They caused havoc in their neighbourhood and affected local businesses. Police had difficulty making arrests as the mob tried to rescue those stopped by the police. In court, they produced seized helmets, some heavy metal ones with the plume of the dragoons sticking in them, flags and two tattered 'standards' with skull and crossbones and 'The Brave Warriors of the Skeleton Army' inscribed. Newspaper reports were unsure whether they were genuine Skeletons or imitators.

A day after the latest disturbances the *Daily News* published a letter from someone who claimed to be the founder and leader of that 'great organization' known as the Skeleton Army:

> Having read with great interest in your valuable paper of the day, respecting the Skeleton Armies, which were rumoured to have mustered at the Eagle yesterday, and your correspondents' various comments about us, kindly allow me, as the founder of the Skeleton Army in the East End, and the now General, to correct a few statements. Firstly, we are charged with being roughs, only organized to assault Salvationists and create disturbances. This I declare to be utterly untrue as our aim is not to assault or do any one harm, and as for being roughs, I ask the public to come and hear and see for themselves, at our next meeting, whether we are such. Secondly, you state that we were going to muster at the Eagle to create a disturbance, which is also untrue. We should have marched there; but hearing that there were several hundred policemen with staves drawn to attack us when passing we resolved not to march in that direction at all, as we thought prevention better than cure. Thirdly, you state that the Skeleton Army was first begun at Hackney. This is also not true, for I first founded an opposition Salvation Army at Whitechapel some four years

15. *Westminster Gazette*, 22 August 1912.

> ago which has grown to the great organisation of the present day, and our intentions are greater than ever to march the streets and oppose by speech the results of Salvation Army teachings, and to parade the streets with bands and banners until an Act is passed in Parliament suppressing both armies. I beg to state that next Sunday we shall call a meeting at Victoria Park at three in the afternoon, to express indignation at the manner in which the police behaved on Sunday last [4 February] in the City Road.
>
> General Alfred Charrington,
> The Founder of the Skeleton Army,
> 13 Newnham St, Whitechapel.[16]

His insistence that the Skeleton Army started in Whitechapel may have been a reference to the 'Unconverted Salvation Army'. It was alleged that his 'lieutenant' was the teenage Charles Jeffries, who apparently fell out with him and briefly took over the leadership. Jeffries, in fact, along with some of his fellow Skeletons, dramatically became a Salvationist in early 1882, converted during a meeting he had come to disrupt. This led in the future to him being jeered and kicked by his former mates. He had a quick temper and would hit them back. As 'Captain' Jeffries he would later serve seven days' hard labour for obstruction in Maidenhead in March 1883. His triumphal return was ruined when he was knocked off his horse by a mob. However, he became one of the Army's greatest converts and years later was appointed the Army's Chief of Staff. (Jeffries attained the third highest rank possible in the Salvation Army when he was appointed Commissioner in 1919.)

Newspapers claimed 'Charrington' was an apprentice engraver with no organisation at his back. The *Pall Mall Gazette* called him a 'prentice boy, just out of his teens, who but the other day left the ranks of the Salvation Army to head the rabble of its assailants'.[17]

* * *

The events of 4 February were the last straw for William Booth. He feared there was a real danger of fatalities. Already a little girl bystander had been seriously injured by a stone in Hackney and other youngsters had suffered fractured arms and legs. One ten-year-old boy

16. *Daily News*, 7 February 1883.

17. *Pall Mall Gazette*, 9 February 1883.

had been run over by a cab, whilst following a Skeleton parade, and a 60-year-old bricklayer, Isaac Buckingham, watching a fight between the two armies, died of his injuries after being knocked down. (Just as relevant, perhaps, was Booth's own experience in Northampton in January. He had announced a two-day campaign there. When he arrived at the station a 20,000 crowd was waiting. There was a riot. Two of his 'officers' were dragged from their horses and Booth was thrown from his closed carriage. Instruments and drums were smashed and he was escorted by police to the vicarage under a hail of muddy missiles. A planned meeting in the market square was abandoned. The same month he had also been pelted with mud in Exeter.) On 8 February he wrote to all the national newspapers:

> Finding to my regret that a number of the Metropolitan police have for some weeks past been deprived of Sunday rest owing to the movements of the Skeleton Army and being anxious to give every assistance to the authorities in the event of their desiring to deal effectively with rowdyism which is rapidly making some of the streets all but impassable for worshippers of any kind on Sundays, I am instructing our officers in various parts of the Metropolis where there have been disturbances to suspend until further orders all open-air meetings and processions whatsoever outside the lines of our own property. London is the only large city in the United Kingdom where bands of persons formally organized for the express purpose of creating disorder in the public streets have been allowed so fully to complete their organisation as to render the thoroughfares impassable for peaceable citizens lawfully assembled for a lawful purpose, and which I am certain that the country will not allow them for any length of time to be prevented from prosecuting.
>
> Meanwhile I enter my solemn protest against any interference with religious liberty brought about in the Metropolis of this country so effectually by systematic neglect to repress disorder which authorities in small towns having at their disposal only a few constables, have shown it easy to suppress when the will exists.[18]

18. *Pall Mall Gazette*, 8 February 1883.

It was true that other religious groups were being affected on Sundays. That month five Skeletons were arrested for disturbing Divine Service at Portcullis Hall in Westminster; and the Blue Ribbon Army was attacked in Brentford. Booth was also aware that tradesmen near the Grecian Theatre were claiming their businesses had been ruined since the closing of the theatre. Nightly and Sunday disturbances were making their lives extremely difficult. The tradesmen had asked the police to stop the processions and they were preparing a petition to protest about disturbances near the Eagle. In addition, members of the Vestry of St Luke's Church in the East End were demanding all pubs be closed on Sundays as the roads were becoming impossible for respectable citizens.

One the same day that Booth's letter was published, the vicar of St Philip's, Bethnal Green, the Reverend Robert Loveridge, worried about the rioting in his area, invited the leading local branches of the Skeleton Army to a meeting 'to reason with them before God'. Some had already 'surrendered' but a large number were still parading. He was particularly worried that children of the neighbourhood were absenting themselves from Sunday School[19] to join marches and sing Skeleton mockery hymns. It was reported in the *Woolwich Gazette* that 'householders were subscribing to the Skeleton Army in the City Road in the hope of stopping marching kids absenting from Sunday School'.[20]

Loveridge had two policemen in the background just in case there was trouble. For half an hour no one came. Then six hundred Skeletons came in full marching order with a band playing, flags and wearing military-style uniforms. Loveridge assured them that Salvationists through their workshops were not underselling them in the labour market. He told them that Booth had found work for hundreds of men and women who would have been a drag on the labour market. He noticed that, when Skeletons marched past his church, they would stop singing in reverence to it. He asked them to stop their hostility to the Army and to remember that 'Christ is Everywhere'. At the end of the meeting, one detachment of Skeletons disbanded and handed in their colours, helmets and arms to the vicar and others said they would follow suit. Many of them were unemployed and Loveridge started to raise money to help some to emigrate or become costermongers.

---

19. Booth attracted criticism by declaring that he did not want his followers' children to go to Sunday School. He was hoping to organise an alternative service for them.

20. 10 February 1883.

The following Sunday, all was quiet outside the Eagle Tavern as a large body of police lined up. In fact, they outnumbered the crowd and Salvationists entered peacefully. (In the afternoon, a small contingent of Salvationists disobeyed orders and marched in Bethnal Green and were attacked.) In nearby Victoria Park, Skeletons and onlookers numbering 4,000 listened to an 'officer' on a stool address his 'brother Skeletons'. He warned them that the police intended to interfere with their procession but that they would march just the same. Fifteen hundred Skeletons with helmets and banners, marched off towards the tavern. They were intercepted by police who, after being attacked, made several arrests. As the police tried to take the assailants back to their station, they were attacked again. They took cover with one of those arrested in a barber shop and had to listen to the windows being smashed as the mob tried to rescue him. In court, with a policeman with his head bandaged standing by, Edward Fox, 18, Henry Jennings, 21, and George Fordham 17, all labourers, were charged with disorderly conduct and assaulting the police. Plain-clothed police had arrested them. Fox and Jennings, the leaders, received two months' hard labour, although witnesses said the police had attacked them, and Fordham was fined.

After Booth's ban on parades, the *North London News* predicted: 'the Skeletons will now probably retire into private life, and help to illustrate in a liberal sense the adage: "There is a Skeleton in every house."'[21] The *South London Press* was less optimistic: 'As a rule in the better neighbourhoods the Salvation Army is very much left alone. People have got used to it. But the feeling against it is still very strong amongst the lower classes. In the East End, the feeling is intense.'[22] Meanwhile, Salvationists were proclaiming great success: 'The work at the Grecian Tavern makes wonderful progress. Night after night thousands of the worst and blackest stamp of London roughs can be seen gathered together. . . . Several members of the Skeleton Army have been saved.'[23]

In March, it was reported that a Skeleton rally to protest about police tyranny and the right of public meeting was to be held on a piece of waste land in Mile End Road. When the Skeletons started to form into marching columns, the police, armed with staves, charged them. The

21. *North London News*, 24 February 1883.

22. *South London Press*, 17 February 1883.

23. *The Auxiliary*, 21 February 1883. The official organ of The Salvation Army Auxiliaries.

Skeletons fled amidst derisive jeers from the large watching crowd. In reality, they had fewer grounds for parading now the Salvationists had stopped marching.

In late March, by order of 'General' Alfred Charrington, the Skeleton Army held a demonstration at Epping Forest near Chingford. On police advice, a march to the Mile End was abandoned. He denounced the Salvation Army but a snowstorm disrupted the meeting. Although Charles Jeffries claimed that Charrington had left the Skeletons, in November 1883 he wrote to the *Barnet Press*:

> I am rather reluctant to trespass on your valuable paper, but a report of the case heard at the Barnet Petty Sessions on Monday, and published in your most valuable paper of yesterday, which states that the person charged with disorderly conduct and interfering with the Salvation Army procession styled himself a captain in the Skeleton Army, compels me to reply. The person is not as he admitted, a captain in the Skeleton Army for we have not at present a corps or any person representing the Skeleton Army at Barnet. I am, Sir, your most obedient servant, Albert Charrington.[24]

The newspaper's editor responded that there had been no mention in court of the man in question – William Overy, who was fined – being a Skeleton army captain. So, who exactly was Alfred/Albert Charrington? Was he really an engraver's apprentice as newspapers had suggested?

Two years before his original letter to the newspapers, Alfred Charrington was taken to court for attacking a doorkeeper at the Salvation Army Hall in Whitechapel in April 1881. He was fined £2 or fourteen days in prison. Living at the address he gave at the bottom of his original letter was an immigrant German couple, by the name of Bachert, with three children. In the 1881 census, the father was employed as a tailor and his son, born in 1863, an engraver called 'Albert'. Putting two and two together, it is more than likely that he was 'Charrington'. Of course, the family could have had a lodger with that name but the future history of Albert may give us a clue.

Albert Bachert became a serial writer to newspapers, particularly about the Jack the Ripper murders. At various times he claimed to have either seen or received letters from the Ripper. He also said he

---

24. 17 November 1883.

was the chairman of the Whitechapel (Murder) Vigilance Committee. Sceptical newspapers affirmed it was a committee with one member! Nevertheless, over a period of three to four years he was constantly in the papers on the subject of the murders. On one occasion, after telling the press he thought he had met the Ripper in a pub, he had graffiti written on the wall of his parent's house: 'I'd like to punch yer bleeding nose. Yours, Jack the Ripper.' One of his alleged Ripper's letters had at the top a design of a skull and crossbones, a skeleton and a coffin; identical to many of the Skeleton Army flags. Certainly, many reporters thought that Charrington and Bachert were the same person but, when asked directly he denied it, and he also denied ever being a member of the Army.

In 1889, he was acquitted of passing counterfeit coins. Because of his notoriety, a coroner in a local murder case refused to let him sit on a jury. In 1891, under the name, Albert Bachert, he was actually a witness at a murder trial at the Old Bailey, which ended in a 'not guilty' verdict. As well as the Ripper case, he got involved in local politics and addressed anti-socialist meetings of the unemployed. He was a witness at the trial of the leaders of the 1887 Trafalgar Square Riots and for a brief period was secretary of the Tower Hamlets Unemployed and Relief Society. It was whilst he was in this last post that he committed a fraud in March 1893; he took provisions, which he claimed were for a needy widow. He fled to Bristol. The Metropolitan Police found him there organising meetings for the unemployed and arrested him, which newspapers across the land gleefully reported:

> *Derby Daily Telegraph*: 'A Notorious Busybody in Trouble'
> *Middlesbrough Daily Gazette*: 'A Seeker of Notoriety in Trouble'
> *Southern Daily Echo*: 'Too Fond of Letter Writing'

In court he was described as 'smartly dressed and well-educated'. He was sentenced to three months' hard labour. It was reported that his friends were trying to raise money to send him abroad on his release. It is unclear whether he went. In the 1901 census he was recorded as living with one of his sisters in the East End. On one of the Ripper websites – www.jtrcasebook.org – he is described as having 'an authority complex and a penchant for self-publicity through Ripper hysteria'. Perhaps the same could be said of his role as 'Charrington' in the Skeleton Army riots.

* * *

Although Skeleton activity decreased in the East End after Army parades stopped, there were still outbreaks and disturbances inside Army barracks. Walter Langham, a marble mason of Bethnal Green was accused of being drunk and riotous during a service and assaulting a policeman. He had shouted out, 'More Beer', and, when asked to leave, started to kiss young ladies outside who were waiting for their 'brothers' to stop speaking before they entered. They screamed. He then offered a policeman £10 to fight him. Langham was lucky. As it was an unlicensed religious building in Bethnal Green, the case was dismissed.

In June 1883, Thomas Edumunds, 23, a tanner's labourer was charged with assaulting four Salvationists including a female, Jane Clark, in Bermondsey. They were on their way to the barracks, when he knocked out the teeth of one Salvationist and threw Jane Clark down and kicked her. As he was known as a Skeleton leader, he received one month's hard labour.

That month there was an action against Booth to recover the Eagle Tavern (and the Grecian Theatre) for a breach of covenant. Booth had signed a lease in June 1882 for seventeen years. He was accused of breaking the covenant by not selling alcohol and that Salvation services were causing annoyance to the other tenants. He had promised to do the former but had only sold coffee. However, the claimants could no longer complain about the rioting outside as Booth's ban on parades and police action had put an end to them. The court case took place in the Queen's Bench Division in front of Justice James Stephen. William Booth, in a defiant mood, was cross-examined by Arthur Jelf QC:

> **Jelf:** Accepting your motives to be of the highest character, do you work upon the feelings of the people to stir them up to religion?
>
> **WB:** We teach them to know right from wrong. Show a man he is wrong, and he will 'feel bad'. (Laughter).
>
> **Jelf:** Is there anything like external emblems and do shouts form a part of your system?
>
> **WB:** We recognize a song as being useful to get sentiment and truth into the peoples' minds. We rely upon the truth.
>
> **Jelf:** You use loud cries of 'Hallelujah' and 'Amen' to awaken their feelings?

> **WB:** No, our feeling is to persuade bad people to be good. (A laugh)
>
> **Jelf:** Do you touch the hearts of the people through the feeling?
>
> **WB:** I should consider that we take exactly the same course as a barrister who wants to persuade a jury to give him a verdict. (Laughter)
>
> **Jelf:** That is not very flattering.
>
> **WB:** I mean a 'sensible barrister'.

At this point Justice Stephen intervened, telling Booth, 'that is not a proper expression. You must conduct yourself properly in the witness box'.

> **Jelf:** In a spiritual sense, do you consider yourself an aggressive body?
>
> **WB:** Yes, against the powers of evil, decidedly. We do not always meet with opposition of a violent physical character.
>
> **Jelf:** Do you meet with any at Henley?
>
> **WB:** None. . . . [but] The devil is against us everywhere.

The judge told Booth off for preaching. One of his witnesses, 'Captain' Stonehill caused laughter and incredulity by claiming that a Salvationist could play any musical instrument even if they had never seen it before! His claim did not exactly help William Booth's case and added to the public perception that Salvationists were, at the very least, eccentric.

In his summing up, Justice Stephen declared that: 'there was no doubt the defendant had broken both covenants. The defendant had from first to last been in the wrong. He took the lease intending from first to last to evade one of its terms.'[25] However, the verdict did not stop the Salvation Army from purchasing several public houses for use as 'temperance hotels' and from manufacturing alcohol-free 'Booth's Beer' in 1891.[26]

---

25. *The Daily News*, 7 June 1883.

26. Spencer, 'The Fatal Gaze of this Moral Basilisk', p. 230.

In August, Booth agreed to an interim transfer of the spirit licence of the Eagle Tavern to William Trafford, a wine merchant. The tavern started to sell alcohol again but was reported to be less popular than before. Booth also withdrew his application for a licence for music at the Eagle Tavern and the nearby buildings. Nevertheless, the Grecian Theatre and music hall were still used by Salvationists and the corps was said to be 500 strong.

In November in Stratford, James Downey, a boiler maker, went to the Salvation barracks and hit the doorkeeper and another Salvationist in the face as they tried to eject him for disturbing the service. He was fined £1 with costs or fourteen days' hard labour. By then the Skeleton Army seemed to have almost disappeared from the East End. A reporter from the *Shoreditch Observer* went to witness an enthusiastic meeting at the Clapton Congress Hall: 'After the "captain" had delivered prayers, others join in with violent expressions of feeling; they wave their hands; they sink down on all fours, undergo ludicrous contortions as though some emotion possessed them which they could not express or contain.'[27] He warned his audience that: 'God could summons us at any time.'

The following year, in 1884, there was only sporadic anti-Salvationist activity in the East End. In June, plain-clothed police attended services in Leyton to keep an eye on men dressed in Skeleton 'uniforms'. In September, Charles Pelford, a van boy with a gang of roughs, threw mud at a Salvationist, Charles Smith, hit him with a stick and rolled him in the mud in the Old Kent Road. Pelford received fourteen days' hard labour.[28]

* * *

Once disturbances died down in the East End there were more clashes in other parts of London. In March 1883, in Chelsea, the Salvation Temple was attacked by a group shouting out, 'We're for the Devil!' Their ringleader was eighteen-year-old George Reeves. They viciously attacked 'Captain' Dear. As a result, one Skeleton received two months' imprisonment and two, one month each.[29] In April, Charles Reeves, a youth, and a boy, Thomas Fossey, received 21 days in prison and fourteen days, respectively. They had assaulted Cornelius Harvey, the doorkeeper at Alexandra Mews, Hammersmith, by knocking him

27. 18 August 1883.

28. *Reynold's Newspaper*, 10 October 1883.

29. Ibid., 4 March 1883.

through a window, tearing his cap and hitting him in the eye with an orange.[30] At Wandsworth, James Bell, a car-man, went to Livingstone Hall, Battersea to try and get his daughter back. He did not want her 'mudlarking in the street'. He shouted at the 'captain', George Sulley, and disrupted the meeting. He was warned he would get two months' imprisonment if he returned to the hall.[31]

In Hounslow, there were riots when the Salvation Army threatened to 'Storm the gates of Hell and Snap the Devil's Chain'. Their barracks, with sixteen Salvationists, were attacked by a mob, led by a publican, Edward Hamlin. He blew a horn and 700 Skeletons charged. After smashing all the windows, they tore the Salvation Army's 'colours' to pieces and kicked one Salvationist unconscious. Others were imprisoned in the barracks for an hour.[32]

Afterwards, six Skeletons appeared before the bench. Four received one month's hard labour and two were fined for assault and disturbing a place of worship. The Army barrister, Thomas Sutherst, publicly stated that he thought the fines would be paid by the publicans. A petition signed by 127 local tradesmen asked the magistrates to ban the Army processions in Hounslow. Quite deliberately, it was not signed by any publicans. Five months later, 800 to 900 Skeletons marched with a banner, 'Skeleton Army; True Religion Not Humbug'. After disturbances, their leaders, Henry Webber, 30, and W.H. Clarke, 36, were sent to prison for fourteen days.[33] In January 1887, it was announced that the Hounslow barracks had been closed for a few weeks because of a shortage of money, few participants and dissension in the ranks. The *Middlesex Independent* commented, 'latterly the Army has shown every sign of collapse'.[34]

In the early 1880s the police had been reluctant to protect the Army parades in London and the East End but in the end had been compelled to arrest the lawbreakers. In celebration, in May 1884, 'troops' from Chalk Farm, Stratford, Hammersmith, Woolwich, Whitechapel and Clapton, with flags, banners, brass bands, pipes and big drums, marched from the Eagle to Whitechapel. The procession was led by an ex-prominent former leader of the Skeleton Army, called Bachelor. He bore the brunt of the horseplay by roughs and some of his comrades were rolled in the

30. Ibid., 18 February 1883.
31. Ibid., 10 October 1883.
32. *Middlesex County Times,* 5 May 1883.
33. Ibid., 29 September 1883.
34. 19 January 1887.

mud. At the Whitechapel station, the 'People's Hall' was half full. Later there was a mass 'Lufrednow' (wonderful, spelt backwards) meeting. Of the converts there, the majority said they had been saved at the Eagle. It was followed by a tea for 250.

It was unusual for the poor's opinion of the Army to be expressed in the newspapers, particularly conservative ones. However, in October 1884, *The Globe* did just that. Under the headline, 'THE SAINTS OF THE SLUMS', they published a passionate letter 'From a Sinner's Point of View':

> Serious losses, caused by the failure of a bogus company, compel me for the present to live up a back street and I have, therefore, some opportunity of judging of the effect of persistent doses of 'Salvationism' upon my neighbours. I think I might say that by a very large majority they do not believe in the Salvation Army and I should very much like to know why I, and those living in this poor street, are to be worried and irritated by noisy fanatics who profess to be specially called upon to convert the world.
>
> I have read the newspapers long enough to know that the members of the Salvation Army are continuously appearing in our criminal courts, and only a week or so back I noticed three cases in the paper – the first being embezzlement, the second fraudulent bankruptcy, and the third bigamy. Now I do not say but what the same sort of mishaps may occur among other sects; but I do object to anybody, whose members are constantly subject to similar weaknesses, setting itself up as the heaven-appointed saviour of the human race.
>
> *Truth* says 'Let the Army go where it is wanted'. Well, it is not wanted down our street – at least we poor sinners are bold enough to think so. Most of us work hard all the week, and when Sunday comes we like a quiet pipe and a bit of sleep; but when the 'Salvation' row begins it generally drives us into the public-house, and produces precisely the opposite effect to what is, no doubt, intended. Then, again, why should we be singled out for special attack? Are there no sinners amongst the rich? I think I remember reading (a long time ago, I am sorry to say) that the Apostles of old were not afraid to stand before Emperors and Kings and to rebuke 'wickedness in high places', but our modern martyrs (under police protection) seem afraid to do so for fear that subscriptions should run

short. If Salvationism is truth, then let the rich have a taste of it also. Let Regent Street be paraded at 12.30 a.m., give them plenty of 'Blood & Fire' songs down Pall Mall between six and eight p.m., and let the grand combined 'Hallelujah' attack be made on the Stock Exchange, Tattersalls, the theatres and all the places of amusement – of course, always excepting the Alhambra,[35] under the new moral regime. These proceedings, combined with occasional 'Hurricane' demonstrations in our most aristocratic squares, could not fail to produce a profound 'moral effect'.

It should not be forgotten that working people know far more about this question than those who sit at home at ease and read stirring accounts of the Salvation Army riots, in which the 'Skeleton Army' is depicted in the blackest colours, and the opponents of the Salvation Army are most indiscriminately called 'roughs'. Only those who live among the poor people can understand the irritation which is caused by the presumptuous parades of the Salvationists, whose 'converts' are in many instances the veriest [real] hypocrites, and who yet are allowed to come out to 'save' their neighbours, numbers of whom are much nearer heaven than they. The fact is there is no 'Skeleton Army' as an organized body. The opposition proceeds from the poorest classes of working men, who are most worried by the Salvationists, and have no power or influence to make their voices heard in any legitimate way.

By-and-by it will be admitted that the so-called 'rough' has been administering a wholesome check to the tyranny of religious fanaticism and has unconsciously been fighting in the cause of civil and religious liberty against an organisation which threatens both.

It has been said that the Salvationists are attacked because they endeavour to teach people to use self-denial and self-restraint. This is not the case, for priests, missionaries, district visitors and total abstainers can go without fear of insult or injury; nor are they obliged to call upon the police to protect

35. The Alhambra Theatre of Variety in Leicester Square: primarily a music hall, it had started to have 'patriotic demonstrations' celebrating the British Empire and British military success.

> them any more than Christ and his Apostles had to call the Centurions to protect them from the poor 'roughs' of the early Gospel days.
>
> What we poor sinners want is a little more effort to understand us on the part of those who are placed in better circumstances and for them to think that the despised 'rough' is, after all, a 'man and a brother', with like passions to his richer neighbour, and needing somewhat similar relaxations and amusements to prevent him from being utterly brutalized by his surroundings. These are the sentiments of 'our street', and the philanthropic individuals who are wise enough to recognize the truth of these words, and will help to put an end to the reign of cant, will be saving the people in real earnest.[36]

His contention that there was no 'Skeleton Army' as an organised body is interesting. A cynic would suggest that it was in many people's interest to say there was. The letter echoed a common criticism of the Army from social commentators: that it did not understand the causes and complexities of poverty and offered simplistic solutions. It also substantiates Edmund Lyon's findings in the East End, that working-class communities (as represented by the Skeletons) were acting on their own volition in their physical opposition to the Army and were motivated by a defence of their pastimes and amenities and a protest against the Salvation 'row'.[37] The support of the publicans and brewers and the issue of temperance was of secondary importance.

There were complaints in the local papers that the Army was marching in poor areas at seven a.m. in the morning.[38] However, according to 'A.M.' in the *Hackney & Kingsland Gazette*, the Army did not confine itself to the East End. He found Salvationists on Sunday and weekdays 'prowling through some of the principal streets of the West End'.[39] When he complained to Army headquarters, he was told to move away.

In October 1883, the Congregationalist, Andrew Mearns, published *The Bitter Cry of Outcast London: An Inquiry into the Condition of the Abject Poor*, which exposed the horrors of slum life: overcrowding,

36. *The Globe*, 18 October 1884.

37. Lyon, '"An avalanche of wrathful violence": Physical Opposition to the Salvation Army, 1881–1883, *Hackney History* 18, p.28.

38. *Islington Gazette*, 8 February 1882.

39. Letter, 18 October 1882.

unsanitary housing, low wages and high rents. In its wake, the Army began to develop its social work. 'Slum sisters' went to work in the poorest areas in the East End and, in January 1885, a home for 'fallen women' was opened in Whitechapel. A Drunks' Rescue Brigade and Prison Brigade were also formed. In May, there was a monster rally at the Congress Hall, Clapton with 2,000 'troops' and several bands: 'The females were in their distinctive blue dresses, coal-scuttle bonnets, playing their tambourines. The long string of Salvationists was brought up at the rear by several wagons full of "little soldiers" waving banners and singing revival hymns'.[40]

The following year, an Army poster gleefully announced: 'Thrilling Scenes Nightly at the Old Grecian!' with 'Salvation for Costers, Cabmen, Cats-meat-men, Loungers, Lords and Stealers, Policemen, Pirates and Political Agitators'. Two brass bands would be playing plus female singers and 'Thousands of Angels in Attendance'. It was religion with the attractions of a music hall for the curious. Moreover, in the East End, the Army was expanding with new 'slum corps' at Borough, Walworth and Rotherhithe.

By 1889 February, there were six homes for 'fallen women' in London and several in the provinces. In three years, Booth claimed the homes had received 2,099 girls and that 1,676 were now living 'honourable and hard-working lives'. During September 1889, the Army provided free meals for thousands of starving dockers and their wives and children in their hall in Poplar during the Great Dock Strike. Strike leaders said the distress would have been much greater without the Army's assistance. The previous year, the Army had contributed funds towards the Matchgirls' Strike at Bryant and May's factory, also in Poplar. Up until then, according to *The War Cry*, Salvationists had been driven away from the dock gates and forced 'to run like sheep' after being pelted with paint, filth and dead animals.[41]

Away from the East End there were still occasional persecutions of Army members. In 1889, several in Chelsea were imprisoned for obstruction after parading outside the Enterprise public house on a Sunday. According to witnesses, they had not been playing music or singing and were attacked by police with the encouragement of local roughs. In the Strand a procession of 100 former Salvationist prisoners – gaoled for preaching – in prison uniforms, were stopped by police and

40. *The Times*, 26 May 1885.

41. 25 December 1889.

had their banners seized for causing an obstruction to the traffic. In September 1890 Commissioner Frank Smith – who used to enter towns on horseback facing the animal's tale to attract attention – was jailed for three weeks for refusing to disperse his parade in an area that contravened the Trafalgar Square regulations brought in after the demonstrations of 1887.

On the spiritual side, the Army was heavily criticised for its lack of success in London. Llewelyn Davies, the vicar of Marylebone, declared the Army was 'a failure in a unique degree'.[42] He claimed it was refusing to give him the names of converts in his area and that it only converted people who would normally join other congregations. He reasoned that, if they could not reach those who did not usually go to church, then they had lost their *raison d'être*. Another vicar said he had not heard of one conversion. However, they could not deny the success of its social work and influence. The famous preacher, the Reverend Charles Spurgeon declared, 'if the Salvation Army were wiped out of London, five thousand extra policemen could not fill its place in the repression of crime and disorder'.[43]

After Booth's lease ran out on the Eagle Tavern and Grecian Theatre, the buildings were demolished and a new pub was built in 1901. Today, the Army has no corps in Hackney or Bethnal Green.

* * *

Over time Skeleton Army riots spread across southern England and the Home Counties in places like Dorking, Gravesend, Guildford, King's Lynn, Maidenhead, Newbury, Romsey and Tunbridge Wells. In Dorking, despite not singing or playing any instruments, Salvationists were brutally attacked by 'a band of savages on the warpath. . . . They offered no resistance, they returned no blows. Half of them appeared to be drunk and the other half mad.'[44] Some were seriously injured. To make sure there was a collision, Skeletons had a flag that extended the width of the street. When the Army took their assailants to court, the Skeletons were fined £8, which was paid by 'well-to-do people, who employ others to do their dirty work'.[45] Trouble only subsided once subscriptions dried up and Skeletons were imprisoned. In Gravesend,

42. *The Times*, 5 January 1889.

43. *Coventry Evening Telegraph*, 21 August 1912.

44. *Pall Mall Gazette*, 22 September 1887.

45. Ibid.

Army instruments and drums were thrown over a railway bridge onto the tracks below. However, some of the worst anti-Salvationist activity took place on the South Coast.

In January 1883, after three months in Folkestone, their evening parades were attacked by Skeletons who were described locally as a 'self-defence' organisation: saving the town from 'fanatics' who were demoralising the working class and disturbing peaceful Sundays. Their principal banner was 'We want peace in our town'. A policeman, Sergeant Butcher, was alleged to be their 'captain'. The magistrates asked the home secretary to ban the marches but he advised they use persuasion. During one parade, 50 Salvationists were attacked by 600 Skeletons wielding wooden swords and flagpoles. Eleven Skeletons were bound over, instead of receiving punishment, and one Salvationist was fined for assaulting a leader of the Skeleton Army. So many fireworks were thrown at them, *The War Cry* had its own version of 'The Charge of the Light Brigade':

Squibs to the right of them,
Crackers to the left of them,
Squibs before them,
Crackers behind them
Volley'd and thunder'd;
But out went the little band,
And all Folkestone wonder'd.[46]

Back at their hall, it was customary to prepare bandages and to be ready with basins of water and towels to wash the blood and dirt off the 'soldiers' when they returned from parading. Stones, rotten eggs and eggs filled with tar made them look like they had come from a real battlefield.

In July of that year there were reports that 2,000–3,000 Skeletons regularly congregated outside their hall on Sundays. Over 800 windows were smashed. One Salvationist told magistrates they had all been in fear of their lives for the last three months. There was even an altercation at the docks between a vessel flying the Army flag and one flying Skeleton Army 'colours'. At an election, it was alleged Liberals had lost a seat because they favoured Salvationists. When a Salvationist, William

46. *Folkestone, Hythe, Sandgate and Chariton Herald*, 7 September 1912.

Bugden, was charged with perjury – swearing he had not seen a 'soldier' assault a boy – it provoked a new song for local children to mimic the Army with:

Are you ready? Yes, I'm ready.
Only waiting for old Bugden's trial.
Keep believing and receiving
And he'll get six months in Maidstone Gaol![47]

Only after the original jury of twelve publicans was dismissed was Bugden acquitted. Once the magistrates started to sentence Skeletons to four to six months' imprisonment, the riots in Folkestone died down. The local newspaper, commenting on disturbances elsewhere, had a suggestion: 'The "Army" cannot exist long where there is no opposition. The lines from the old nursery rhyme "Little Bo-Peep" are singularly appropriate. "Let them alone, and they'll go home, and take their tails behind them."'[48]

The worst Skeleton Army riot up to that time was to take place in a seaside resort whose name today symbolises quiet retirement. A place to enjoy sea air, that sovereign Victorian treatment for delicate constitutions. A place where Oscar Wilde wrote *The Importance of Being Earnest.* Its relative proximity to London would give it a national media coverage far greater than the riots in the West Country. In the 1880s it had a large working class with a tradition of drunkenness, domestic violence and poor church attendance: a perfect challenge for the Salvation Army; one it could not and would not shirk.

47. *Folkestone Express,* 17 November 1883.

48. Ibid., 18 September 1886.

Chapter Six

Worthing, 1884

In 1883, Worthing, situated at the foot of the South Downs and 49 miles from London, had a population of 12,000. Most inhabitants were involved in the service industry and market gardening. There was a large influx of newcomers, especially expatriates from India who had come home to Britain to retire, and families from the rural hinterland. Nonetheless, the old landed families still held sway and the working-class families of Worthing were equally as conservative as their masters. There was still a strong tradition of 'rough-musicking'. On bonfire night in particular, it could be on a grand scale and was an opportunity for people to settle old scores. For the victims, it was often terrifying, with the clattering of metal objects, such as kettles and saucepans, and the blowing of horns outside their homes, the smashing of windows and the shouting of rude slogans.

Before disturbances began in Worthing, there was trouble in nearby Steyning and Shoreham. As early as Whit Monday 1883, Henry Upton, described as a Skeleton leader, had led a 150-strong mob through the streets of Shoreham mimicking Salvationists and was fined for obstruction. At Steyning in August, 200 Skeletons, with flags and banners flying and making a hideous noise with their musical instruments, followed an Army parade of fifes and tambourines. When a policeman told them to move on, one shouted back, 'Go to hell, we don't care for no bastard policeman. We shall move when we think we shall.'[1] Only two

1. *West Sussex County Times*, 20 August 1883.

policemen were on duty and several Skeletons put their instruments in the policemen's faces and blew hard. Afterwards, twelve were charged with obstruction and fined or faced seven days' hard labour.

In 1883, posters appeared to warn inhabitants that the Salvation Army was coming to 'attack Worthing' and save the population from their godless ways. Under 'Captain' Margretts, the Salvationists first met in a loft above a private house. Aged nineteen, Harry Standing, attended a meeting. Years later he recalled being fascinated by the sight of Margretts and his helpers, playing a banjo, violin and tambourines, as they marched round a platform singing all the time. It was so uplifting he joined up. Standing, who died in 1951, wrote:

> Worthing had one of the most successful openings of any corps. Hundreds of souls were converted, among them some of the worst characters. . . . I had one man in my Brigade. I never knew him out of prison for more than a few days. I have seen him take six policemen and then they had to strap him on a barrow to get him to the police station.[2]

Initially, the Army did not parade much nor enter the poorer areas. Margretts sent headquarters a telegram after their first public outing in September:

> Worthing attacked yesterday; whole town moved; powerful morning meeting; knee drill good; 50 present; crowds in the market at 10; short heavy firing – hit straight; glorious march to the hall, rather tough – hall filled, good order; much conviction. Great gathering, rough element in afternoon completely overwhelmed; closed meeting early. Hall packed at night, crowds outside, stormy meeting, many wounded. Glorious prospect; great victory near. Our King shall, and will reign! Police rendered assistance. Report coming.[3]

---

2. Standing, Harry, 'Reminiscences of Early-Day Fighting,' in *The Officer's Review*, May-June 1947. This was a monthly publication for serving Salvation Army Officers that periodically featured 'Reminiscences of Early-Day Fighting' by officers.
3. *The War Cry*, 22 September 1883.

Their arrival was not welcomed by either the local roughs or the elite. Hoteliers and boarding-house owners feared their noisy parades would drive visitors away from the town. The ultra-conservative *Worthing Gazette* reported:

> The long-threatened invasion of Worthing by the hyper-zealous fanatics of the Salvation Army has at last taken place. . . . As soon as the declaration of war was posted in town last week, bearing the signature of 'General' Booth . . . the 'enemy' was to be seen assembling in large knots about the streets planning all sorts of defence, and gleefully anticipating all kinds of rowdyism. . . . Salvationists are excitable young men and hysterical young women who mistake a quasi-religious revelry for Godliness.[4]

The 'enemy' (local roughs) formed a Skeleton Army and were supported by the *Gazette* partly because its editor and co-founder, George French, was an arch conservative against any kind of change or reform. According to Chris Hare, director of History People UK, author of the excellent *Historic Worthing: The Untold Story*, and an expert on the Worthing riots and the town's history: 'I have little doubt that it was his provocative and condemnatory comments regarding the Salvation Army that did more than anything else to fire up the Skeletons in Worthing.'[5] In fact, the *Gazette* had come out the same year as the Army's arrival – 1883 – and, with its lurid accounts, was soon outselling the other two local newspapers. Local religious leaders like the rector of Broadwater, also 'attacked what he called religious clamour, communism and "the morbid craving for change"'[6] encouraged by the Army.

Once parades started, the hostilities were immediate. Salvationists were hooted and hustled by Skeletons and one convert, Fuller, was set upon as he left the barracks. He retreated to the house of a relative and water was thrown on the heads of the mob below. Before services, Salvationists walked the streets for 30 minutes singing. People threw eggs, soot and even the contents of chamber-pots at them from their top windows. They were spat at, had pins stuck into them and their shins kicked. Opponents thought that after a few attacks they would go away.

---

4. 20 September 1883.
5. Hare, email 25 July 2020.
6. Ibid.

This was a serious underestimation. For Salvationists believed that the more they were attacked, the more their attackers needed salvation! Their own newspaper, *The War Cry*, asked rhetorically in April 1883: 'Are you being persecuted enough?'

The local newspapers portrayed the Salvation Army as a shambles and caricatured Salvationists as half-wits.[7] (Some of the toy shops and stationers sold caricatures on cards depicting cats and dogs dressed in Army uniforms). They even encouraged a subscription list to be set up to finance the Skeletons. Prominent on the list was Worthing Hospital Committee's Henry Tribe, who offered a £20 reward to any man throwing a Hallelujah lass into the sea.

After a few noisy parades in which they were manhandled, Margretts agreed to cease the Sunday processions and to hold prayer meetings only at their barracks. Disturbances decreased so much that by October his successor, 'Captain' Kirby, could declare that he felt really at home in Worthing.

In April 1884, the Salvation Army obtained their first proper premises, Prospect Place barracks in Montagu Street, from a sympathiser, 44-year-old George Head, who owned an ironmonger's shop. As a young man he had been imprisoned for larceny and this seems to have been the catalyst for his religious conversion. In 1863, he had brought a summons against his violent, alcoholic father for assaulting him and his mother (who was an invalid). He had had to restrain his father from attacking them with a poker. As a result, his father was fined. George, a quiet, bearded resolute man became a staunch supporter of the Temperance movement. He was now a fervent Salvationist and a Liberal.

The barracks shared an alley with a liquor store and soon the walls were covered by Skeletons in black sticky tar and linseed to stick to the uniforms of Salvationists as they passed. Head also leased the Army Montagu Hall (now Waterstones) for their services. It is alleged someone tried to bribe him with a large sum of money to break his agreement. Without his assistance, it would have been impossible for the Army to stay in Worthing. He was to become the Skeletons' number one target.

---

7. Booth didn't mind. He once said "We have no reputation to lose. . .Everybody has now settled it that we are fools if not a great deal worse, therefore we can go into a town and do exactly what we think best without taking the least notice of what anybody may say or wish". *Daily Telegraph* quoted in the *Leamington Spa Courier* (23 August 1912).

In the spring of 1884, the arrival of a new 'captain', Ada Smith, a 23-year-old from the East End, changed the mood. She arrived at Worthing station following a difficult placement in the North where she had found some of the people 'very very rough and wicked'. Pretty and deceptively demure, she always sang with her right hand raised. Her initial impression of the town was that it had an air of respectability. That soon changed.

After a few days, Ada avowed: 'If the Devil doesn't attack us, we ought to attack him.' Her words seemed to have antagonised the whole town. She planned to re-introduce marches and parades midweek and on Sundays. There were soon, according to the *Gazette*, 'disgraceful scenes' as Smith led parades through traditional working-class areas such as the fisherman's quarter, fewer through the town's graceful Regency streets. They were pelted with eggshells filled with blue paint. When Salvationists shouted, 'No Beer!', Skeletons shouted, 'Plenty of Beer!' As a result, two local men were sentenced to hard labour for two months and another fined £2 13s. for assaults.

The Skeletons were led by 'General' Arthur Reed, a 24-year-old groom and leader of the local bonfire society, and by 33-year-old 'General' James Tee, a pastry cook. Reed had been a private in the army and had served in the Zulu wars: 'Tee was probably the foremost Skeleton in Worthing. The chief constable, Captain Drummond, noted how the

Figure 9. Ada Smith as depicted in *The War Cry*, 17/9/1884.

mob followed his directions. He had been in trouble with the police since he was a child and was arrested for bonfire night disturbances in 1879 for directing rockets towards the Royal Hotel.'[8] According to Hare:

> The people who made up the Skeleton Army were, for the most part, related and lived in adjacent streets in the working-class districts of Worthing. For these young men beer and drinking and meeting mates at the local pub was the very hub of their social world. Life was hard and beer and the company of friends somehow made life more tolerable.[9]

The Worthing Bonfire Boys were also known as the 'Skull-and-Crossbones Brigade' and there was a very close correlation between them and the Skeleton Army. The Skeletons wore a yellow ribbon with the motto 'Excelsior' – the name of their bonfire society – or 'Skeleton Army' on their caps. Their supporters sported king-size sunflowers in their buttonholes. Their flag was a human skeleton topped by a grinning skull against a black background and they dressed as they usually dressed up on bonfire night. They carried sticks with skeleton figures. Most were males with an average age of 20. They sang, 'We'll Hang old Head from a Sour Apple Tree', to the tune of 'John Brown's Body'. Skeletons were often recruited at the George Tavern. Some were described as young men with respectable positions in the town.

With the arrival of Ada Smith, the young Salvationist Harry Standing immediately noticed a change of atmosphere. In his memoir article, 'Reminiscences of Early-Day Fighting', Standing recounts:

> We soon lost the help and sympathy we had been enjoying. We began to feel the bitterness brewing. The articles in the press got stronger and more bitter and called upon the Army to confine its meetings to its own hall. . . . Finally, they asked the Army to cease its work and leave the town. . . . The press further suggested that, seeing the Army went out and fetched sinners in, the opposition should annoy them in their inside meetings by organized disturbances.[10]

---

8. Hare, email 24 July 2020.
9. Hare, (April 2021) *Worthing Village Voices.*
10. *The Officers' Review*, May-June 1947. Quoted in Bovey (2015), p.262.

Tradesmen and residents were angry that the customary quiet of the town was being disrupted and many supported the activities of the Skeletons. As the attacks against Salvationists increased the *Gazette* laid the blame squarely at their door:

> The good people of Worthing have had just upon twelve months' experience of the Salvation Army, and taken altogether, the experience has not been a happy one. The hitherto quiet peaceful Sabbath characteristics of the town have at length degenerated into rowdy carnivals and Sunday is now looked forward by the inhabitants with dread on account of the disgraceful rowdyism which takes place. It may be urged by sympathisers with the Salvation Army that they are not the direct cause of such disgraceful scenes as those enacted on our streets on Sunday last; but the fact is undeniable that the processions of the Skeleton Army are traceable to those of the force under the command of General Booth. It may be necessary, in the interest of the Army, for the simple-looking youths and the girls in poke bonnets, of which the Worthing contingent of the Salvation Army is composed, to parade the streets on Sunday singing sacred words to the tune of music hall songs; but the ends achieved in Worthing certainly cannot justify the means employed.[11]

However, the Salvation Army marched on: on Sundays in the morning and afternoon, sometimes with texts on their back, 'Victory is the Lord' and 'Prepare to meet thy God'. One morning they were surrounded by Skeletons and found it impossible to continue. During the attack:

> a determined assault was made upon the bearer of their 'Blood and Fire' banner and some half-a-dozen of each force clung to the pole, eager to obtain possession of it. The Salvationists managed to retain it temporarily, but a wild hurrah denoted that the flagpole had been captured by the enemy.[12]

They retreated in disorder to their hall followed by Skeletons, singing and shouting at the top of their voices. In the afternoon, the Army did not parade and the Skeleton Army paraded the streets: 'One of

---

11. 10 July 1884.
12. Ibid., 13 July 1884.

the banners bore the words, "Worthing Excelsior Skeleton Club" (and looked extremely like that formerly used by the Excelsior Bonfire Club), and another bore the words "Long live the Queen".'[13] When Salvationists paraded singing one of their favourite hymns:

We'll fight beneath the banner till we die,
And go to our home on high.

The Skeletons sang:

We'll fight beneath our colours till we die,
And drop on old George Head by-and-by.[14]

The danger was not only when the Salvationists marched out. At their hall meetings the doorkeepers were often pelted with rotten eggs and mud. On leaving to make their way home, they were assaulted again. There was an incident when one Salvationist was surrounded and dropped on his knees in the streets and started praying. As his attackers started to rip away his uniform, he was rescued by sympathisers. Years later, the first Worthing convert, George Mariner, a waterman, who was made 'colour sergeant', remembered on one occasion leaping out of a first-floor window over the barracks into the mob below to drive them off. On another he thrust the 'colours' under his jersey to safeguard them. Harry Standing recalled that so much filth was thrown at them, they started to wear special suits for the marches.

The Army temporarily suspended marching. They applied for a summons against those who had assaulted them and torn down their banner. However, the magistrates refused to grant one, blaming *them* for not staying in their barracks. The magistrate, W.F. Tribe, commenting on one Salvationist's summons, declared: 'you know what you do provokes others to interfere with you, and then you come to us for protection. It is disgraceful for any body of Christians – and I suppose you call yourself a Christian – to provoke these disturbances.'[15] His fellow magistrate, E. Henty, declared, 'it is a desecration of the Sabbath and you provoke all this riotous behaviour'.[16]

---

13. Ibid.
14. *Sevenoaks Chronicle*, 18 July 1884.
15. *Sussex Express*, 19 July 1884.
16. Ibid.

Booth wrote to the home secretary, Sir William Harcourt, to protest but he refused to interfere. Booth replied, 'having now for two weeks suspended our open-air work in Worthing . . . we have now instructed our people to march on Sunday leaving the responsibility for the maintenance of order with those to whom it belongs'.[17] Harcourt also received a petition from local residents who claimed that the Army were deliberately 'bawling' songs outside churches just before divine service and ruining hitherto quiet Sundays. When the Skeletons passed by, they were quiet. In June 1882, Booth gave specific orders to corps not to pass churches on Sundays but, if they did, to do so in perfect silence.

Meanwhile, George French, editor of the *Worthing Gazette*, used his weekly column 'The Chiel'[18] to lambast and denigrate Salvationists at every opportunity. He described them as 'tramping down the gutter, gesticulating like maniacs' and said the only protection they deserved was the type of protection offered to inmates at the local lunatic asylum at Haywards Heath. Such inflammatory comments added to the fevered atmosphere developing in the town. The unusually hot summer did not help.

On Sunday, 17 August, the Army started parading again. As a reprisal, George Head's shop was violently attacked by Skeletons and there followed four days of rioting. The *Gazette* declared 'never in the history of our town have more serious scenes been enacted in our streets'.[19] As Salvationists marched out, Skeletons deliberately marched in front moving at a snail's pace through the streets. They drowned out their attempts to sing with their own rude songs. Several policemen (including reinforcements) accompanied the procession but made no attempt to disperse the vast crowd assembling. By the time the procession reached the town hall, there were 3,000–4,000 people. The Skeletons turned around and charged:

> The placid stretch of Bath Place was suddenly a sea of screaming men, battling amid brick-dust and broken glass. The crimson-and-blue 'Blood and Fire' banner swayed, then toppled like a sapling. Truncheons flailing, the police burst through; with bottles and boots, the Skeletons fought back,

17. Letter, HO 45/9960/x2676.

18. "Chiel", meaning Child was taken from a Burns poem, "There's a chiel among ye takin notes."

19. 21 August 1884.

Figure 10. George Head's shop during the Worthing riots.
Source: The War Cry 3/9/1884.

> intent on retaining their own banner. Nimbly, clutching their instruments, the Salvationists ducked from the melee, escaping [to] the barricaded sanctuary of Montagu Hall. Reluctantly Ada Smith cancelled that evening's procession.[20]

The police tried to arrest the Skeleton leaders but were kicked and had their helmets knocked off. Next day several Skeletons were summonsed to appear at the police court. In the evening they marched with the summonses pinned to their banner towards George Head's shop and smashed his windows. Then they smashed the windows of the Army barracks and the police station with rocks. They defied the police to come out but none did:

> As time wore on towards eleven o'clock, the rough element seemed to be in complete control of the neighbourhood. As stone after stone was flung in quick succession, the crash which followed every missile brought forth repeated cheers of the mob.[21]

20. Collier (1965), p.99.

21. Ibid.

Head's premises were the main target as he lived over the shop. Skeletons entered it and James Medhurst, a 22-year-old 'fly driver' (a two-wheeled horse-drawn cab) hit him with a loaded stick.

On the third day of the riots, Tuesday, 19 August, Skeletons from other towns came and congregated in front of Head's shop again. A large thousand-strong mob marched past singing, 'We'll jump on old Head by-and-by; If you are not quiet, we'll have another riot.' Head took his family, including two sons and a daughter, to the back of the shop and sent for the police. The police force in Worthing, small in number – only twelve – did not come and were holed up in the station guarding the prisoners arrested the day before.

The mob rammed Head's front door with a timber pole, threw down oil and wood in the shop and threatened to burn it down. His goods were thrown out and scattered on the pavement outside. Six men entered but retreated when they saw Head and his sons with shovels. There was a lull. The men re-entered only to be met with six shots fired by Head, one wounding Arthur Reed in the wrist. Head saw a teenager named Eldridge, a jeweller, just about to set fire to the oil and shot him in the face too. Eldridge was taken to a doctor who dressed his wound and sent him home. Head afterwards claimed he had shot over the heads of his attackers and that, if his son had not given him a small revolver, his shop would have been burnt down. He said his son had been wounded.

Head had appealed to the police for help in the afternoon and evening of 19 August but none was given although his shop was only five minutes' walk from the police station. His wife and the three youngest of his children escaped from the back of the premises at midnight and took refuge in the house of a relative. Because of the attacks, Head's shop was closed for four and a half weeks and he had to employ men to watch his premises at night.

After four days of disturbances, fifteen Skeletons appeared before the bench and were found guilty of causing an obstruction and fined ten shillings each with 3s. 6d. costs. Six were given one-month prison sentences with hard labour for assault. When one of the magistrates left the courtroom in the town hall, a crowd of 400 Skeletons outside tried to unseat him from his horse.

On the following Saturday, thousands filled the streets around the town hall protesting against the sentences and the Army. The magistrates feared for their lives as the mob stoned the police station and the police and threatened to rescue the prisoners due to be taken to the railway station the next day. The chief magistrate, Lieutenant Colonel Wisden, decided that he might have to read the Riot Act and called in the dragoons from Preston barracks in Brighton. When 40 arrived, clattering outside the town hall at ten p.m. in their scarlet tunics with blue facings, they were cheered by the mob who sang, 'We won't go home till morning'.

Wisden asked the rioters to go home. His speech was polite enough until he told them he would *bloody* make sure they did. The *Worthing Intelligencer* takes up the story:

> The concluding portion of the Colonel's speech was met with howls of derision which lasted a considerable time and terminated in the people singing 'Rule Britannia' with special emphasis on the chorus 'Britons never, never will be slaves'.
>
> 'I don't want you to be slaves', shouted the Colonel.
>
> 'Then speak as a gentleman ought to speak and apologise', roared a man in the crowd, and 'apologise' was angrily exclaimed in all directions.
>
> 'Now will you go home quietly?' asked the Colonel, and from a hundred throats came an emphatic 'No.'
>
> 'Don't you mean to go?' he again enquired, and again the mob replied 'No!'
>
> 'Very many times you have listened to me', he commenced to say.
>
> 'Not when you swear', interrupted a voice, amidst much laughter.
>
> '. . . I'm here to help Worthing tonight. I've tried to do a little bit for you, and now I want you to do a little bit for me. All that little bit is to disperse quietly and go home. You'll be doing me a favour and conferring a great boon on the town.' (Cheers and a voice, 'You've insulted us and we won't go until you apologise.' Another cried, 'What did you bring the soldiers here for?')
>
> 'For your own good and the good of your fellow townsmen do go home', the Colonel again said but all expostulation was in vain, his appeals only exciting jeers.
>
> 'Try to speak pretty and apologise like a gentleman', cried one.
>
> In reply to a further request to go home, a man near the officers said, 'We'll all go home if you will withdraw.'
>
> 'Withdraw what?' said Colonel Wisden.
>
> 'Why that word.'
>
> 'I withdraw nothing', said he, 'you must go home.'[22]

[22] 23 August 1884.

While this confrontation was going on, groups of boys were sent to collect stones from the beach for the rioters. Finally, Wisden read the Riot Act, the only time it had ever been read in Worthing. The soldiers drew their sabres and started to clear the streets followed by the police. By one a.m. order was restored but not before a certain amount of revenge brutality. All day the policemen had been taunted by Skeletons and their station pelted with stones. They drew their truncheons and laid into the crowd with a vengeance. A 25-year-old Italian pastry cook, Giacomo Semadini, standing outside his shop, was so badly beaten he died of his injuries two years later. Two tradesmen and a girl were also seriously hurt.

The next morning the Dragoons escorted the prisoners to the railway station followed by a large, threatening mob. At Brighton magistrates court, the Skeleton's leader, Arthur Reed, Edward Standing and Edwin Eldridge were charged with riotous assembly and for attempting to demolish Head's shop and house. They were remanded for trial at Maidstone assizes in October. The *Gazette* started a subscription for their defence.

With tension in the town rising, the first batch of special constables was sworn in. Three Skeletons volunteered their services but were politely declined. The fire bell of the town was to be the signal for the specials to assemble. In a three-week period, 230 were enrolled.

With many visitors leaving for Brighton, the *Gazette* started to change its tune: 'Although the unparalleled scenes which have been witnessed in our streets may be traced directly to the pig-headed obstinacy of General Booth and his crazy followers, we strongly advise the Skeleton Army to desist from further action.'[23] However, George French in his column, still supported them and laid the blame elsewhere:

> The accounts of the disturbances in Worthing have been so exaggerated, that I shall soon begin to think the Worthing people know very little of them. I had thought I had seen everything: even the charge of the dragoons, and the savage attack made by the police upon the orderly inhabitants. But I must confess that even these sank into utter insignificance, when I read some of the accounts in the London papers. But the most glaring departure from the truth is quoted by the 'War Cry' and depicted by the 'Illustrated Police News'. But, there, the object of both these publications is to excite the morbid passions of the people.[24]

23. *Worthing Gazette*, 28 August 1884.
24. Ibid., 28 August 1884 – Included in email from Hare, 4 August 2020.

The Skeletons still had support from the local elite. A clerical visitor to the town wrote: 'The opposition is not that of the publican. The universal opinion is that persons of influence above the class of tradesmen are finding money for the opposition, from the idea that the Salvation Army is injuring the town and keeping away visitors.'[25]

Ada Smith, instead of being frightened by this turn of events, saw it as a sign that the Salvation Army was winning:

> So with loaded guns, and with Holy Ghost ammunition, we are in the field, and with all our might are pouring red-hot bullets of calvary, death, judgement, heaven, and hell into the ears and hearts of the vast crowds of people, and by the power of God it is taking mighty effects. . . . The Lord has been wonderfully near, upholding us by His power, and our whole confidence is in Him. When in the barracks with stones and glass flying in all directions, His strength is enough casting out all fear. Hallelujah![26]

The police gave Salvationists six-chamber revolvers, shotguns and pitchforks with which to protect their hall. Young Harry Standing and five others were put on sentry duty from eleven p.m. to six a.m. in two-hour shifts. (Although Standing had been so badly injured in one riot that the doctor believed he might not walk again, he had recovered.) They were told to fire on anyone – after being challenged three times – who approached the building acting suspiciously. For several weeks Standing had to sleep on the floor when not on duty. He was thankful they never had to fire on anyone.

The Skeleton Army were still determined to get rid of the Army and, in particular, George Head. They even had their own song, 'The Skeleton Hymn', a parody of the Salvation song, 'This Is a Happy Land'. Below are selected verses:

The Salvation Army we must drive,
Far, far away,
For cannibals to eat alive,
Far, far away.
We will pepper and salt them too,

---

25. *Pall Mall Gazette*, 22 August 1884.

26. *The War Cry*, 27 August 1884.

And make them fit for a rare good stew,
And old Head shall sail with the crew,
Far, far away.

The nuisance we must try to send,
Far, far away,
Or none will come with money to spend,
Far, far away.
Our Local Board who these things view,
Knowing well the harm they do,
Must help us or go to Timbuctoo,
Far, far away.

We want disturbance and mob law
Far, far away,
Things have come to a dreadful pitch,
We'll drown the Army in a ditch,
Far, far away.[27]

On 4 September, an eyewitness wrote to *The Times* to say that there had been no justification for the attacks on the Army. He claimed that it had never paraded with a band but had received donations to buy instruments and was now practising. According to the letter, no more than 100 Salvationists were attending meetings and the 22 Hallelujah lasses were modestly dressed and quiet-mannered. Despite the presence of the chief constable, Captain Drummond, and 100 special policemen, the Skeletons continued to assault Salvationists. On one occasion they tried to throw Ada Smith and 'Lieutenant' Alice Griffin off the pier but they were protected by sympathisers. Others were pelted with bags of lime and flour, including Ada, who was hit by the former thrown from an unoccupied house.

On the afternoon of 7 September, after the brass band was due to play for the first time during the service at Montagu Hall, Skeletons invaded the balcony shouting and booing. Two or three climbed onto the penitent stage and started to sing, 'Wait Till the Clouds Roll by, Ginny', a popular 'hit' from America published the year before. Ada Smith asked a policeman to intervene but he told her he could only do so if they caused a disturbance *after* the meeting began. She asked

27. *Sussex Coast Mercury*, July 1884.

the band to play the loudest they could to drown out the Skeletons. It was not enough. Ada blew a small whistle and a posse of constables swept in:

> Now a jungle-screech of execration burst from the balcony: the narrow stairs to the main hall were choked with savage clawing men bent on destruction. A seething trampling mass of bonnets, helmets and cloth caps battled amid a blizzard of torn song books, toppling across overturned forms. . . . As the police hauled the ringleaders to the station, they were followed by a running fire of rocks and soot.[28]

Unfortunately, the policemen beat a thirteen-year-old boy, Frederick Thompson, over the head with a truncheon. It seems he was an innocent party. As they took him to the station with his head bleeding, they were followed by an angry mob. His wound was treated and he was released. The policemen locked their station doors and stayed inside. Meanwhile, George Head's daughter fetched him home after seeing a mob march past his bow-fronted Montagu Street shop. Head gave this account:

> Soon after my arrival home the mob returned to my shop and recommenced stoning the windows, one stone striking me on the forehead and cutting my temple. Seeing men climbing over the hoarding, and again no police in sight, I, being alone in the house with my daughter, fetched the small revolver I had used on 19th August and fired, slightly wounding one young man. The mob then drew back but made two or three faints as if to renew the attack so I deterred them from further mischief with a double-barrelled shotgun.[29]

Head had shot Edward Oliver, a fly driver, in the neck. He was taken to the local infirmary and had a bullet removed. That evening Drummond arrived with policemen and special constables. He advised Head to place himself under police protection at the station. He refused as 'I considered my post was at home to assist in protecting

28. Collier (1965), p.102.

29. TNA HO 45/9960/X2676.

my wife and family.' Drummond returned later with a warrant for his arrest and he was taken to the police station, hissed and booed all the way by a mob. Standing on a taxi-cab, the chief constable addressed the crowd waiting outside Head's home. He was cheered by men waving their hats in the air, the women their hankies. He told them to leave Head's house as inside were only a defenceless woman and her children.

The next day, Drummond asked for 50 additional special police and sent them to guard Head's house. Some were Salvationists. Head was remanded in custody and refused bail. He was charged with 'unlawfully, maliciously and feloniously wounding Edward Oliver'. The *Gazette* reported that Oliver had 'sustained a severe wound'. However, Head recorded:

> My solicitors then had the 'wounded' man examined by another doctor who pronounced his injury to be merely superficial and not in the slightest degree dangerous and my release was ordered. In the meantime, I had been conveyed to Portsmouth gaol and was liberated on bail on 16th September after having been in custody 8 days. At the request of the Chief Constable I left the town and was away for the month.[30]

At the magistrates' inquiry, he claimed that, during the attack on his house, he had received wounds to the head and had only fired to defend himself. He protested 'everybody was against me except the Lord'. Drummond had a difficult job trying to explain to the magistrates why there were no police officers present on the night of the attack. Head was sent for trial at Maidstone assizes in October and stayed with friends at Sydenham. With Head on bail, the Skeletons had a new song:

Old Head's got bail today!
Old Head's got bail today
If you don't be quiet, there'll be another riot
Old Head's got bail today![31]

---

30. Ibid.

31. *Horsham,Petworth,Midhurst & Steyning Express*, 23 September 1884.

Despite the serious nature of the disturbances, *Punch* took a light-hearted view:

> The Skeleton in the Cupboard
>
> Mistress: I thought I heard a man's voice down here, Jane, I do trust, after all I told you about the last cook and her Salvation Army friends, that you have not admitted any______.
>
> Cook: Oh lor, mum! That you should ever think that of me! ____which I can't abide the Salvationist, mum, _____and my young man a 'skeleton' and at this minute at Worthing a fightin' the 'orrid wretches![32]

* * *

For the local churchmen there was a dilemma. The Reverend Francis Cruse, vicar of Christ Church from 1864 to 1891, articulated it in September 1884's parish magazine:

> Are the 'Salvationists', so called, justified in the aggressive action they are engaged in? Are they doing unmixed good? Are they to be commended? We fear the answer to each of these enquiries must be in the negative. Not that we would dispute the sincerity, even the excellence, of their motives. Nor even the assertion that some amount of good has been done. But, on the other hand, the question forces itself upon us – is not the amount of evil resulting from their action so serious as even to counter-balance – if not to overbalance the good?[33]

He was particularly critical of the Army's irreverence for Church traditions and what he considered to be their blasphemy:

> Do the tactics of the Salvation Army combat evil or rather incline to creating it? Is it really doing God's service to raise opposition by the very unyieldingness of our aggression? Is it

32. *Hampshire Telegraph,* 27 September 1884.
33. Hare (2021), *Worthing in the Bad Old Days,* p.37.

> tolerable that the quiet – we may say the sacred quiet – of our Sabbaths should be invaded by unseemly and noisy and even irreverent public demonstrations?[34]

Nonetheless, he condemned the violence of the Skeletons as morally indefensible:

> The moment anyone, even in trying to put down a nuisance, passes the limits of the law, that moment he puts himself in the wrong, and his very lawlessness awakens sympathy with the party thus improperly opposed. And we add that the very title 'Skeleton Army', suggesting so terribly the opposite of 'Salvation', or, Eternal Death as opposed to Eternal Life, is in itself so shocking that it can only emanate from one secret and ultimate source. And if it be irreverent with right intention to thrust holy things wrongly on public notice, how much more irreverent must it be, with a wrong intention, to parody those holy things themselves, and deliberately and designedly to turn them into burlesque ridicule.[35]

Cruse concluded by advising the Skeletons to desist and that, if the Army continued their 'aggressive' tactics, a petition from residents should be sent to the 'proper' authorities requesting them to stop. His advice was ignored.

* * *

Even without Head's presence the disturbances continued. The day after his arrest, 100 Salvationists marched out at 7.30 p.m. They were surrounded by 4,000 Skeletons – many had poured in from other towns and villages – singing, 'Wait till the clouds roll by', and throwing fireworks. The Salvationists quickly returned to their hall. Skeletons tried to sabotage the meeting and then went to the absent Head's shop to shout abuse.

The following day when the Army paraded, blue paint was thrown from windows and their caps were thrown into the air despite police protection. One lad named Millard was given fourteen days for throwing bags of soot and lime from an empty house in Chapel Street, which landed in the midst of the parade and also showered the police.

---

34. Ibid., p.38.

35. Ibid., p.39.

Drummond placed several of his officers, disguised as labourers, within the Skeleton ranks and, as a result, more and more were arrested. Walls and hoardings were now covered with police notices threatening to arrest Skeleton Army members and their subscribers. After disturbances on Sunday, 5 October, six were fined ten shillings each and one £1 by the magistrates. Two could not pay and were sent to prison. There was growing resentment from Skeletons towards the magistrates who had previously supported them but now were sentencing them. As a consequence, their houses were attacked.

The rioting peaked on Sunday, 12 October. Over 500 Skeletons, including women, waited for the Army to exit their barracks. They wisely stayed in. Despite the presence of Drummond and 250 police and special constables, the Skeletons marched through the town shouting abuse outside the homes of magistrates. To reduce trouble the police walked in twos and threes amongst them. All along the route yellow ribbons and hankies were waved to show support. The Skeletons went to the seafront and a man in yellow on horseback – apparently trying to imitate the horse riding Drummond – was told to dismount. Then the mob walked the seven miles to Shoreham, trespassing on private land and demanding pubs open. Tipped off, the local police had already asked the pubs to close. (As it was Sunday the pubs and inns were supposed to be closed during 'divine service', although they could open for 'travellers').[36] The Skeletons forced their way across Norfolk toll bridge, which spanned the Adur River. Some refused to pay tolls and smashed the toll-house windows.

They attacked Shoreham police station and smashed all its windows and then forced the King's Head pub to open and serve them. Next, they bombarded the Army barracks in West Street with stones even though Salvationists no longer held outdoor parades in Shoreham. Their local leader, 'Captain' Sarah Broadhurst, was badly struck by a stone and had to escape by the back door. When she died in February 1892, it was alleged that it was a result of her injury.

Next day, 21 Skeletons were arrested, refused bail and committed for trial. As they were taken handcuffed in cabs to the railway station, crowds cheered and sang. In the days leading up to their trial 'a great many women accompanied [Skeleton] processions wearing yellow ribbons and flowers. They were chiefly the mothers, sisters, wives or sweethearts of the young fellows, either imprisoned or awaiting their trial.'[37] (In other

---

36. Chris Hare, email 24 July 2020.

37. *Horsham, Petworth, Midhurst and Steyning Express*, 21 October 1884.

towns it was reported that female Skeleton sympathisers often collected stones in their aprons and piled them up on the pavements along the parade routes of the Army.)

On 30 October, at Maidstone County Court, the 21 Skeletons were charged with rioting at Shoreham. Their ages ranged from thirteen to 43. Sixteen were bound over and released to keep the peace; thirteen-year-old James Hunt, who had spent five days in custody, was released without charge. However, one of their leaders, James Tee, was sentenced to three months' hard labour and three others were given two months'. Meanwhile, Reed, Eldridge and Standing, aged 24, eighteen and nineteen, respectively, received four months' hard labour for wrecking Head's house and shop in August and for 'unlawfully and tumultuously damaging a place of worship'.

At George Head's trial, also in Maidstone, without hearing any evidence for the defence, the jury acquitted him on the grounds that he had no malicious intent and was justified in his conduct. The judge, Mr Justice Manisty, agreed with them. However, he had some harsh words for the Army:

> He had witnessed in the processions of the Salvation Army; howlings, noise, music, dancing, and other things, which made him almost doubt whether he was in his own country. Proceedings of this kind must be put a stop to, and if they were persevered in, all those concerned in them would find that the law was too strong for them, and that they would render themselves liable to serious punishment.[38]

Back in Worthing, a popular, well-known shopkeeper, charity donor and self-publicist, James Baker, who had previously strongly supported the Skeletons, started to change his tune. He addressed a crowd and pleaded with them to fight the Army through parliamentary means – by procuring a bill to ban Army marches – and not on the streets. He could see the damage the protests were doing to the town. The wealthy visitors who usually came for the winter season were not coming.

One London visitor, Mr Cussans, after a visit to plan a month's break with his family, wrote to *The Globe* newspaper complaining about the Army parades and 'determined not to take apartments in

[38] *The Standard*, 1 November 1884.

Worthing at any price'. He asked four young 'warriors' outside their barracks why they did not go to the thirteen other places of worship in the town:

> 'Not likely', was the reply, 'our cap'n, Jesus Christ, came into the world to make a row, and he did make a row, and we're a goin' to keep it up.'
>
> 'Are you not ashamed', I said, 'to take that sacred name so lightly in your mouth? To me it sounds absolutely blasphemous.'
>
> 'Ah! I can see what you are. It is certain I shan't meet you in Heaven; for thanks to the Lord, I'm washed in the blood of the Lamb.'
>
> I told them I wouldn't come now and spend £60.
>
> 'Well, I s'pose nobody has harst you to come.'[39]

Cussans took his family to Herne Bay instead.

* * *

After the convictions at Maidstone, the Army temporarily discontinued their parades and Skeleton activity declined. However, there were reports of hundreds of women, wearing Skeleton Army colours, still hanging about the Army barracks. George Head returned home on 1 November but immediately faced hostility:

> On Sunday 2nd November the Skeleton Army mustered in great force and awaited the appearance of the customary Salvation Army processions, hooting and groaning at each of the latter body as were to be seen making their way to the meeting room. Directly I and my wife appeared in the streets on our way to the meeting we were saluted with even louder cries and yells than the others. For about an hour the mob lingered in Montagu Street but finding the usual procession did not take place, it gradually dispersed. . . . Most of the roughs as on previous occasions wearing a yellow flower or ribbon as a badge.[40]

As the fifth of November approached, there was fear disturbances could get out of hand. For Head, it was a particularly trying time:

---

39. 2 October 1884.

40. TNA HO 45/9960/X2676.

On the evening of 5th November, a mob of several hundred roughs dressed in various disguises was suffered to assemble on the Parade near the end of South Street, where a large bonfire was lit. They began to parade the streets, passing and repassing my shop four times at intervals, stoning the upper windows on each occasion, breaking several and singing:

'We'll down with the barracks bye and bye,
We'll jump on old Head bye and bye' etc.

These and similar cries being generally sung by the Worthing mobs during the last few months. Two policemen were present but were of course powerless to cope with a disturbance that had been allowed to assume such proportions as this. Twice the roughs marched to the Salvation Army Barracks, the windows of which were already riddled with stones and pelted it with such violence that the greater number of their missiles passed completely through the building (which is 40 to 50 feet distant from the road) and out at the other side. One policeman was stationed here to protect the building.

The house occupied by my eldest son, who lives close by was also attacked, six plate glass and one sheet glass window being broken. Over a dozen stones entered the sitting room, to the great alarm of his wife, who was in the room at the time. One stone weighing 8 or 9 lbs fell close to the cradle in which their baby was lying ill. Had this stone gone a slight distance further it must have killed or injured the child. The mob also attacked the police, who resisted their attempt to roll a lighted barrel into South Street, stoning them and injuring the Chief Constable and several others. I was informed from a reliable source that this barrel was intended to be rolled into my shop. One gentleman who assisted the police had his head badly cut by a stone. No arrests were made or summonses issued in consequence of these occurrences, although several police were sent from other towns amongst the mob in plain clothes to witness their actions.[41]

41. Ibid.

Figure 11. Salvation Army barracks in Worthing under attack. Stones were thrown with such force that some passed through the building and out the other side.

The Army marched out again on 10 November led by two young Hallelujah lasses. The mob hooted and yelled at them along the entire route. The implacable George French was unrelenting in his criticism of the Army:

> 'Skeletons' Drowned
>
> Those of our readers who were charitably inclined to credit the 'Salvation' Army with a desire to save souls, should read the following item of news from the 'War Cry' of Saturday last: 'The fishing boat Prudence has been run down by the steamer "Mentone" near London. They had made a good catch of mackerel. Five of the men were saved, the other two, who were prominent "Skeletons" at Worthing, were drowned.' A more heathenish exultation over the sudden ushering into eternity of two human beings I have never read.[42]

42. *Worthing Gazette*, 13 November 1884 (email, Chris Hare, 4 August 2020).

The persecution of George Head continued unabated. His garden shrubs would be damaged and broken at night. An occasional window would be smashed and men were often seen lurking around the door of the barracks in a suspicious manner in the early hours of the morning. They fled only when a guard approached. Men who had been sent to prison for breaking into Head's place in August hung about his shop, 'uttering threats, making insulting remarks and otherwise endeavouring to annoy and intimidate me and my family and deterring customers from coming in whilst the police seem to be utterly powerless to stop them'.[43]

However, by the end of the year the Army were marching out virtually unmolested. This was due to the stiff prison sentences passed on Skeletons and because the town authorities were no longer supporting them. They had become bad for business, with the tourist trade ruined by the riots. That summer the only people coming to visit had either joined the fighting or watched it, some from as far away as Eastbourne.

Disturbances started up again in the spring of 1885. By this time the young 'soldier' Harry Standing had lost his job and, with employers reluctant to employ Salvationists, had left the town. Head and his sons did not go to bed until the pubs had closed and after they had checked the streets near their properties. He was convinced that the local magistrates and police were giving him little protection because he had complained about his treatment to the home secretary.

On Easter Monday 1885, local Salvationists marched to the station *en route* to joining their comrades in Brighton. They were accompanied by a very large crowd singing threats and hustling them as they made their way. Near the station, a man deliberately rode his tricycle into the Army band. In the uproar that followed some were hit including George Head who received painful kicks. The sergeant and two policemen present drew their truncheons and did their best to restrain the mob and the Salvationists managed to get to the station. No arrests were made, despite the assailants being easily identifiable. Head complained again to the home secretary:

> is this the protection for which I have been paying rates and taxes in Worthing for the last 25 years? A great deal of this ill-feeling and spite against me has, I feel certain, been engendered by the local tory papers. They are evidently

43. TNA HO45/9960/X2676.

> taking this opportunity of rewarding me for the part I have taken in opposition to them in political matters. What am I to do? If I attempt to take my own part, I am arrested and sent to goal. Am I to stand by and see myself beggared? My little property I have toiled all my life to acquire is no sooner repaired than it is again attacked and destroyed and at the time of writing this I do not know from one hour to another how soon I may be attacked again. I appeal to you as an Englishman to know why I am left to the tender mercies of this vile and brutal mob and why the law is not employed to protect me as expeditiously as it is put in motion to arrest me if I make a false step.
>
> Finally, I ask you to do one of two things; either to afford me the adequate protection for which (as a subject of the Queen and a taxpayer) I have been subscribing for the last quarter of a century, or else give me permission to take such measures as I find necessary to protect my own person, that of my wife, those of my children and my property, from future attacks.[44]

In September 1885, Edward Standing, nicknamed 'Doggy', and two others were arrested for being drunk and disorderly and singing anti-Head songs. In court it took six policemen to restrain him in the dock. As he was taken down the town hall steps by a police sergeant after being sentenced to one month's hard labour, he slipped his grasp and headed for the beach. He plunged into the sea, swam a hundred yards and climbed up onto the ironworks of the pier and perched on a support. The chasing police were reluctant to enter the water and waited alongside a jeering crowd on the shoreline. After two hours, with the tide coming in and with his friends begging him to give himself up, Standing did. The police grabbed him and had to draw their staves to escort him, through a hooting and groaning mob, back to the police station. The police sergeant, despite seventeen years' service, was reduced to the rank of constable: 'Popular sympathy was thus still clearly on the side of the Skeletons. So, to some extent, were the magistrates and press. When the

44. Ibid.

police asked the magistrates to withdraw the licences of two cab drivers because they had been convicted as Skeleton leaders, the magistrate, Mr Wythe, refused.'[45]

In July 1886, one local paper was still complaining about the Army:[46]

> The Salvation Army at the present time have got the law on their side, and they can with impunity infect our streets, make night hideous with their so-called music and singing, frighten horses and disturb invalids and cause no end of mischief without their being any chance of stopping them.

It reported that the chief of police had actually gone to the magistrates for advice. Numerous accidents had occurred and two men had been injured after their horses took fright at the Salvation band. The magistrates said they were powerless to stop the processions. In September, Head wrote again to the home secretary. He complained that for three years he had had to endure attacks on him, his family and his property. His shop was:

> wrecked, stock destroyed and stolen, customers frightened. Anonymous and threatening letters. Despite appealing for help, the abuse is on the increase again. The police make so far promises only. We intend the next time we are attacked to do our best to protect ourselves without further reference to the police. If we are prosecuted in the future we want these letters to you as testimony.[47]

Eventually, Head received £147 in compensation from the courts for the damage to his property. He had applied for £200.

From April 1887, special constables, usually local tradesmen, protected the Army parades. Not that the local traders had any more sympathy for the Army but the town needed the holiday visitors to

---

45. *The Skeleton Army and the Bonfire Boys*, Chris Hare, *Folklore,* Vol.99, No. 2 (1988) p.223.

46. *Sussex Daily Telegraph.*, 31 July 1886.

47. TNA HO 45/9960/X2676.

return to the once genteel seaside resort. The last incidents occurred in the spring of 1887. Worthing Salvationist, Bill Lucas, wrote in his diary:

> [in the afternoon] no sooner had we got outside than we were surrounded by them – they got in front and we obliged to go ahead very slow. . . . The SKILTS [Skeletons] sang all sorts of songs – it wasn't much good us trying to sing. . . . We got in [the hall] alright. Had hardly done so when up came the SKILTS – we would not let them in – there was a row for about half an hour – regular fighting – Mariner got a black eye – stones of all sizes were thrown – it was ructions – our chaps partly cleared them when the police came and finished it.[48]

The following month, as the foundation stone of their new citadel was put in place, people threw clods of earth at them to try and stop the ceremony. Despite this, they continued to march out aided by the support of the local clergy who marched with them. Moreover, presumably much to the relief of George Head and the Army, George French finally died and his column with him. No one had been more against them than him, including the magistrates. He had depicted the Skeletons as heroes. Hare comments:

> The Worthing rioters would have benefitted from the greater literacy brought in by the 1870 Education Act. . . . Imagine the excitement of seeing your exploits described in print, and more than that, praised and encouraged. Is it too much to think that some young Skeletons might have thought of more outlandish acts they could commit just to see them recounted and sanctioned by 'The Chiel'? Without French the trouble in the town might have been contained earlier.[49]

The turning point for the Army in Worthing was the typhoid epidemic that broke out in 1893. Nearly 200 people died and 2,000 were taken seriously ill. A lot of people left the town but the Army stayed and did good work. This enhanced the Salvationists' reputation and they faced no more hostility.

48. *Diary of Bill Lucas*, 27 March 1887, quoted in Bovey (2015), p.287–8.
49. Email 4 August 2020.

George Head, who bore the brunt of the riots, continued to be a hate figure for some time. However, after surviving bankruptcy, he was gradually accepted as a respectable man of the town and held in high esteem. After several years of poor health, the old 'warrior' died aged 63, in November 1900. At his funeral, the Army band formed part of the procession, which included a hearse and six mourning coaches. It was led by two policemen who kept the roadway clear to the cemetery, which was full of spectators. Head's survival and continued residence in Worthing was testament to the courage of his strong Salvationist convictions in fighting for an unpopular and persecuted cause. Not many could have survived the abuse he and his family put up with for so many years.

In December 1902, Edward Standing, the Skeleton who had fled to the pier, was sentenced to eighteen months' hard labour for housebreaking. It was his 22nd conviction. The following year, Lieutenant Colonel Wisden, the magistrate who had read the Riot Act and had refused to withdraw a 'swear word', died at the age of 68. By then he had become rather a notorious figure having fathered fifteen children from two marriages and a large number of illegitimate ones around the town!

In 1906, Ada Smith, now 'Brigadier' Woods, returned to Worthing and addressed a large meeting. Recalling the riots, she remembered:

> when we had open-air meetings we had to wash our hands and faces under a pump before daring to go inside the hall. . . . Many of us felt inclined to run away and leave it all. We could have said it was dangerous, for certainly we were in danger of our lives. We always had to go out with an umbrella for the sight of a bonnet was the incentive to throw stones at us or filth. But always the presence of the Angel saved us.[50]

When William Booth came to open the new Army barracks in August 1907 all the past bitterness had gone. He was on a 33-day tour covering a thousand miles. At the Theatre Royal:

> the huge throng of people in the theatre, and it was packed closely to the very doors, rose to its feet and every eye was strained to catch a glimpse of the wonderful old man as he passed through the stage passage. As the venerable figure,

50. *Worthing Gazette*, 19 December 1906.

> white head bowed, came into sight a perfect thunderclap of acclamation rang again and again through that building, echoing and re-echoing as he sank wearily into an armchair.[51]

In his welcoming speech, the mayor, Frederick Linfield, recalled how he had sheltered two Salvationists for nearly a fortnight during the riots and that sympathisers had been dismissed from their jobs and refused work. The rioting had subsided once the council had put up notices threatening three months' hard labour without the option of a fine for anyone who subscribed to the Skeleton Army.

Worthing 1884 was probably the last time that the Riot Act was read in Southern England. Ironically, because of widespread press coverage, the riots had made the town famous. Much to the annoyance of local dignitaries, a London firm's small almanac of 1910 listed the Worthing riots of 1884 as an important historical event. The Salvation Army, too, had benefited from the publicity and been able to portray the heroic struggles of Ada Smith and George Head to good effect. It is true to say, however, that bad feeling amongst some Worthing families against the Salvation Army survived well into the twentieth century.

The last word goes to Mary Chandler, a schoolgirl at the time. Fifty-four years later she recalled: 'we children thought it was great fun as we were not old enough to realize the seriousness of it'.[52] Perhaps she had even visited toy shops with her friends to buy some cards with dogs and cats dressed up as Salvationists.

51. Ibid., 20 August 1907.

52. Ibid., 13 January 1940.

Chapter Seven

Brighton, 1884

In the second half of the nineteenth century, due to railway expansion, seaside resorts grew more quickly than any other type of English town. They offered rich opportunities for new organisations and societies. Brighton and Margate were among the first towns the Christian Mission established itself in outside London. As early as 1869, Catherine Booth had visited Brighton and given a series of talks at the Dome. She 'opened' many of the seaside towns up and because of her precarious health volunteered to do so. After a thirteen-week campaign, the result was the opening of a Mission station in December. In six months, it had a membership of 150. However, a year later, much to William's annoyance, the Brighton Mission seceded[1] from the main organisation and became independent of the Booths. Subsequently, Catherine visited Hastings along the coast and opened a station there on Christmas Day 1870.

In 1879, barely a year after the Salvation Army was officially formed, William Booth came down and spoke at three meetings at the Brighton Pavilion. He was described as a 'thin man with iron-grey hair and beard' who had started a movement 'avowedly stimulated by eccentricity'.[2] He told his audiences the Army was not trying to appeal to respectable people who went to church but to the great mass of the 'humbler classes' who went nowhere near one. He justified gimmicks to attract attention,

1. The decision was made by the evangelist in charge and the treasurer after receiving independent financial backing.
2. *Brighton Herald*, 25 October 1879.

as long as they were legal, endorsing the actions of one 'captain' who lay down in the snow until a crowd collected and another who led a new convert by a halter round the streets. At the meetings he introduced 'Yorky Liz' who recounted how she had been thrown out by her husband.

By the 1880s Brighton had a population of well over 100,000 and, although only twelve miles away, was a very different resort to Worthing. It was far more cosmopolitan with a community less inward looking and conservative. In the 1881 census, the majority of the Brighton workhouse inmates were not even from the town. It was a much more attractive place for the rich, the famous and the day trippers. It was also not so deferential. In fact, on her visit in 1845, Queen Victoria complained about locals making faces at her through the windows of the Royal Pavilion. She never returned and sold it to the corporation in 1850. By 1881, she had become a much more popular figure and, when the Prince of Wales came to open the Princess Alexandra Children's Hospital, he was greeted with a giant banner: 'Next Time Bring Your Mother'.

In October 1881, one of the first negative reports about the Army appeared in the *Brighton Herald*:

> Orderly street preaching is one thing; the howling of hymns by an excited procession of men, women and children is another. It is not decent or proper that the quietude of a Sunday should be broken as it has been broken more than once in Brighton within the past few weeks by the shrieks and shouts of a tumultuous mob. . . . They are the main cause of the uproar and disorder. It is intolerable that howling mobs should inflict their presence on usually quiet streets; and, if the Salvation Army cannot appreciate that fact, and be induced to treat their neighbours with a little more Christian charity, the sooner the authorities teach them a lesson the better. There is plenty of scope for appealing to the masses without indulging in the unseemly displays with which the Salvation Army is now, unfortunately associated.[3]

In 1882 there was a report of a dispute between the Army and Professor Shoggrass and his Punch and Judy show. The best pitch on the seafront was just in front of the Bedford Hotel and the Professor

3. 15 October 1881.

had been there for years. When Salvationists tried to take it over, his supporters physically moved them on. That year, two Hallelujah lasses started to conduct meetings in an old attic over a stable in West Street.

In January 1883, George Knowles, a sailor, was fined 50s. for disturbing a meeting. Afterwards, he knocked down a Salvationist and punched 'Captain' Sarah James who was leading a procession walking backwards. As he struck her, he shouted, 'fifty shillings or a month'. The magistrates gave him two months' hard labour.

In April 1884, Catherine Booth returned to open the Brighton Congress Hall in Park Crescent. With seating accommodation for 3,500 people, it was the largest private building in the town. It cost £7,000 and was financed by a local man, George Freeman. (He had previously also bought Conway Hall in Hove for members there). With many shut out, her speech in the morning could hardly be heard because of the abuse shouted by some of the audience. In the evening the Army decided to charge an entrance fee to reduce the attendance of the 'baser sort'. The first weekend campaign was led by William Booth and special trains were run to hear him speak. Three hundred 'soldiers' came down from London and on the way back they were met by an unruly mob at the station. It cannot be a coincidence that this was the same month that serious attacks on Salvationists in Worthing began.

By August, the Worthing riots had spread to Brighton. Three marches a day in the northern part of the town had antagonised locals. On 24 August, a crowd of 2,000 waited outside the Congress Hall by the Level – a green open space – expecting the Worthing Skeleton Army to arrive. Extra police were drafted in. As Salvationists left and re-entered after their parades, they were stoned and their hall invaded. Skeletons tried to hurl them down the stairs to the balcony. The police ejected the troublemakers and were themselves attacked, one given a prominent black eye. Several were arrested and carted off to the police station on the Level. Salvationists left the hall through the back way.

The following day, seven Skeletons were brought before the magistrates at the town hall. A crowd waited outside, some wearing red, white and blue ribbons. William Collins, 31, a labourer, who in July had been cautioned for parading in the town with a Skeleton Army flag, was alleged to be the leader. Apparently drunk, he had shouted, 'Let us drive the ****** coppers down to the station and make them shut themselves into it, the same as in Worthing.'[4] There was laughter in court when he

---

4. *Brighton Argus*, 25 August 1884.

Figure 12. Congress Hall, Brighton, 1884. Illustration from *The War Cry*, 2/4/1884.

Figure 13. Brighton Congress Hall after being attacked.

complained the police were picking on him for carrying the flag. He was given fourteen days' hard labour: 'The prisoner, by way of expressing his thanks, threw his hat in the air and caught it as he left the dock.'[5]

George Savage, 25, was sentenced to one month for inciting mobs to break windows and for being drunk and disorderly. It was his sixth appearance before the bench. The others, all under 20, received fines or seven days' hard labour, mainly for attacking the police rather than for harassing Salvationists. The youngest was Albert Knight, fifteen, who had been eight years in Sunday school and attended Bible classes. The magistrates were clear in their summing up: 'The Salvation Army must and should be protected . . . it is wrong to interfere with perfectly lawful proceedings.'[6]

It was hoped the severe sentences would be a deterrent but they were not. Local papers reported crowds of between 6,000 and 9,000 waiting outside the Congress Hall. On 7 September, when 60–80 Salvationists marched out in the morning without police protection, they were attacked by 500 to 600 Skeletons. (A similar attack was taking place in Worthing.) On their return, the Skeletons tried to get their flag. Several Salvationists were knocked down, including two 'soldiers', Muggeridge and Hoadley, who sustained severe injuries trying to defend their standard bearer. Others were bruised, received black eyes and had their teeth knocked out. They were followed into the hall by a large body of lads whom 'Captain' Stonehill managed to persuade to leave. The Salvationists still left for their evening march at six p.m., this time with protection. A bigger crowd followed, continuing the harassment. Returning to their hall, the police had to force a way through for them and throw the Skeletons out. Windows were broken but there were no arrests.

On 8 September, reinforced by members from London, 100 Salvationists with their band marched out. A crowd of 2,000 followed, drowning out their singing with 'Wait Till the Clouds Roll By' and 'Rule Britannia'. Fifty policemen were on duty. Matches and fireworks were thrown and one Salvationist had his cap set on fire. Police tried to arrest one offender but he was rescued by friends. As Skeletons rushed to grab the flag, a dozen 'outsiders' intervened and helped Salvationists to rescue it. 'Captain' Stonehill was struck on the back of the head and, as they re-entered the building under a hail of stones, windows were smashed

---

5. Ibid.

6. Ibid.

and cymbals stolen. The next day the *Brighton Argus* complained about 'the grossest brutality and outrage against society' and recommended that those responsible should be 'punished without mercy'.[7]

A week later, *The Times* reported, on 15 September, that, due to effective police arrangements, the disturbances had been quelled. Sixty police were escorting the processions at the front and back. The Skeletons were reduced to just hooting and groaning. However, the optimism was misplaced. The next day the afternoon service was interrupted by disorderly behaviour inside the hall caused by a group of lads. 'Captain' Stonehill again persuaded them to leave. On leaving the hall, James Barker, a strong supporter and chemist,[8] was followed by Skeletons and had to be escorted to his home in Trafalgar Street by police. Barker had made himself conspicuous by distributing tracts amongst the crowd. His windows were later smashed and, for this, a seventeen-year-old, Herbert Peckham, was given a fine or fourteen days' prison.

A reporter for the *Brighton Argus*, calling himself 'One in a Crowd', gave his account of being in a mob of 2,000 following a parade: 'Many Skeletons were aged 20–25 and bore the mark of the rough both in their countenance and in the nature of their attire.'[9] There were boys and girls but he did not see any 'respectable females'. The Salvationists were apprehensive of being attacked and the order went out to 'Close up, never mind the heels' but there were no assaults because of the police presence. When they tried to sing, they were drowned out. Inside the hall, the reporter noticed how the service was continually interrupted; one man repeatedly shouting, 'Sing you beauties, sing'.[10]

It was clear Skeletons were arriving from Worthing, especially at the weekend. On a typical Sunday, Salvationists would meet at their hall for knee drill at seven a.m. At ten a.m. they would begin their march out and make their way through the guarded masses outside towards the 'lowest' parts of the town. There would also be processions in the afternoon and evening. On one occasion, 'Captain' Stonehill told *The War Cry*:

7. *Brighton Argus*, 9 September 1884.
8. Also described as a phrenologist and dentist.
9. *Brighton Argus*, 15 September 1884.
10. Ibid.

> In the afternoon having received information of the intention of the Skeletons to prevent our marching and to capture our colours, before leaving the hall we re-consecrated ourselves to God for his service in the Salvation Army, to do or die. When we formed in the courtyard, we saw thousands of people whose front seemed to present an impassable barrier. The band struck up. 'Forward I' is the word of command. Crowds separated like the Red Sea. 800 yards from the barracks the disturbances began. Between 300 and 400 charged us to get the flag. They deliberately struck our bandsmen in the face.... Night was the crowning time. As we marched out it reminded us very forcibly of the first march at the Grecian, masses of men as far as the eye could reach. . . . They rushed us. For a spell of ten minutes blows fell thick and fast. Police had to force a way into their hall to let them pass. They stopped too many from entering the hall. On Monday, there was a crowd of 10,000 people, 100 salvationists and a strong police presence. Near the Level, all hell broke loose. A dozen big men in the crowd rallied round us, helped the police just at the critical moment and saved the colours. At last we reached the hall and had to wait 45 minutes for the police to clear the entrance. Stones came crashing through but thirty came to be saved.[11]

On 21 September, there was only one procession but the service inside the Congress Hall was disrupted by lads. Again, Barker was hooted at and groaned at as he left the hall with his wife and friends. A mob followed him home to his shop. Stones were thrown at his house and the police were also stoned. Five Skeletons were arrested and charged with assaulting a policeman, who had been hit in the eye with a stick and kicked in the ribs when he tried to disperse the mob. A 24-year-old man, W.H. Hill was arrested hiding in a cart. He received one month's hard labour and four others between seven and fourteen days' hard labour. They were aged sixteen, seventeen, seventeen and 25. The Army in Brighton reported 100 'casualties'. The *Brighton Gazette* was cynical:

11. 17 September 1884.

> Oh, how General Booth must rejoice over the recent riot reports in connection with the South Coast action of his army which have appeared from day to day in the Metropolitan and local journals. He must shake hands with himself heartily every morning and evening, and chuckle vigorously every noontide when he contemplates the *golden* result of his labour. . . . He is followed by loafers who love laziness, nursemaids with nocturnal predilections, holiday loving housemaids, spinsters of uncertain age, and those who traffic in musical instruments, emblazoned guernsies [*sic*] and salvation bonnets.
>
> Aye it is a good game; and it is surprising to find how readily the sensation scribblers are playing into the hand of the Blood and Fire General all through the country. One would have thought that, as experienced men in all worldly matters, they would have known better than to have given undeserved importance as they have to the recent broils between these nonentities and a parcel of juvenile blackguards whose earnest love for a lark or a row far outreaches any feelings of sanctity for the Sabbath.[12]

Indeed, William Booth well understood how articles were copied by newspapers all over the country and saw the reports of physical and verbal attacks as a help rather than a hindrance. In the Salvation Army's 'Orders and Regulations', he wrote: 'It is in the interest of the service to be in the [newspaper] columns as often as possible, no matter in what way.'[13] In fact, he wrote rules advising commanding officers how to attract the press, particularly the 'local gossip' journalists. Booth surmised that, even if the press was critical, it would result in increased attendances. He once said he would rather be kicked than not advertised.

Brighton town council met with nearby councils to decide whether collectively to apply to Parliament to get the processions banned. In the end, they decided not to and left it up to individual local authorities to apply. In the last week of September, a petition to the local council

12. 25 September 1884.
13. William Booth, *Orders and Regulations for the Salvation Army* (London: Headquarters of The Salvation Army, 1878) p. 70. Found in the Salvation Army International Heritage Centre and quoted from *Brighton Gazette*, 25 September 1884.

from 2,737 ratepayers living near the Congress Hall in Park Crescent, complained about the 'injury and annoyance' they were subjected to by the processions, especially on Sundays. Police protection had emboldened 'the processionists and inducing them with the aid of confederates from other towns, to persist in their irritating proceedings, have increased the evil, and, there is reason to fear, are creating a strong feeling against the police and the authorities who employ them in this work'. The petition claimed house prices in the vicinity of the hall had depreciated in value and predicted: 'should the present state of things continue that every part of Brighton will suffer from the reports which now almost daily appear in the London and local papers of riots and conflicts in our streets'.[14] It asked the council to seek powers to stop the parades. The council's Watch Committee replied that it had no power to prevent or regulate the processions of the Army. The committee insisted that it was Parliament's responsibility.

Referring to a cholera outbreak in Europe, a resident from Park Crescent wrote to *The Globe*:

> If the cholera has not yet reached our shores, the plague of Salvation Army processions has. . . . There is disgust and indignation at the helplessness at what is felt to be a coarse, blasphemous burlesque of Christianity . . . and astonishment and annoyance at the helplessness of the local authorities. . . . The persecution is by Salvationists against their unoffending neighbours, in persistently and consciously injuring peace, health and property wherever they go.[15]

The paper's editorial asked Parliament to strengthen the hand of the local authorities.

In October 1884, there was a truce of peace as Stonehill agreed not to parade with music on Sundays. He also agreed to concentrate their marches in the poorer areas – a large proportion of the complainants came from the business area – and to reduce the noise of the drum beating and trumpet zeal. The new relative quietude of the town was put down to the actions of the police and the Watch Committee in discussion with Army leaders – but also because of the stiff sentences passes on the Worthing Skeletons at Maidstone. In addition, the local

14. *The Times,* 24 September 1884.

15. 1 October 1884.

churches were more supportive.[16] From then on the attacks were sporadic. In November, a fifteen-year-old boy was fined 2s. 6d. or three days' hard labour for throwing a squib at Salvation leaders while they were marching in Lewes Road. His mother blamed the Salvationists.

The following year, 'Captain' Glover told *The War Cry* that:

> on May 30th, several attacks were made on our soldiers in the open air. . . . A scouting party usually goes out all the morning, who, whilst assaulting a notorious garrison of vice and misery, were severely repulsed by the enemy in force. Shot, shell and refuse were flying all round. Our soldiers escaped unhurt despite being hit by mud. . . . The darkness, bigotry, and misery of this beautiful town is simply incredible; a strange blending of aristocracy with the most abject poverty and vice render the situation one of unusual difficulty. Churches, chapels, Gospel agencies abound. Many, indeed, claim that Brighton is evangelized beyond the most favoured of large towns, yet it is cursed. . . . The more we dig under the walls the more its vice and sin is discovered. We are making some strides and some blessed captures. Yet, oh, my God, send a heavenquake, our hearts are full of joy, but it seems as a drop to the rivers of abounding misery and sin.[17]

Brighton had hidden its poverty well under the image of a lively affluent seaside town, largely a legacy from when the Prince Regent set up court in the Royal Pavilion in the early part of the nineteenth century. However, behind the façade there was a squalor equalled only by working-class areas in industrial cities. In 1881, *The Brightonian* had declared: 'Brightonians themselves never, or rarely penetrate its [the town's] shabby recesses; and officialdom, like a well-to-do relative, tries hard to banish from its mind the disagreeable fact that so poor a dependent exists. . . . Tabooed, neglected and isolated, like a dark, noisome corner in a beautiful garden.'[18]

---

16. In October 1884, the Rev J.G.Gregory invited Army contingents from Brighton and Hove to Emmanuel Church in Hove. There were no disturbances.

17. 10 June 1885.

18. 18 May 1881.

One Sunday in November, during the interment of a member of the Army, a mob of 3,000 to 4,000 arrived. Graves were trampled down and several Salvationists were beaten up. On this occasion, police were utterly unable to maintain order. The following month a fifteen-year-old boy was charged with twice hitting Thomas Wilson, who was leading a parade, over the head with a whip, whilst other boys threw stones. The boy's father pleaded with the magistrates to let him join a naval training ship. He was taken to the local coastguard's station but was found to be two inches below the standard height. The magistrates fined him five shillings with costs or seven days' hard labour.

* * *

In 1886, *The War Cry* – selling over 1,000 copies a week in the town[19] – publicised successes like the one below:

> I was a deep-dyed sinner when I entered this hall. I don't think anyone in the town was worse than me. I tried the pleasure of the world as deep as possible and with my old companions went into sin as far as man could go, but praise the God, 15 months have passed away since I came to Jesus.[20]

However, the harassment continued. On one occasion, youths hissed and stamped their feet during the service and sang during bible readings. Their seventeen-year-old ringleader was given fourteen days' imprisonment. Another attack included youths throwing peas and jumping on the backs of seats. The service had to be stopped. The youths were given fourteen days' hard labour. A certain George Juden, a bricklayer, was fined 15s. 6d. and a one shilling penalty for damaging a drum. That same year, 1886, *The War Cry* optimistically reported:

> In the afternoon we had a march and took our stand in Robert Street and as one of our comrades was giving his experience a window was opened and a shoveful of coal was thrown on us, which only tended to give the fire an extra stir. At our next stand the Captain was pelted with mashed potatoes. At

19. At one time more copies were sold in Brighton than in any other town.
20. 27 March 1886.

> night there were three thousand people present. The power of God was present and took hold of the vast congregation – we wound up with nine souls giving God the glory.[21]

Three years later, in February 1889, William Booth came to the Dome accompanied by 400 of his staff to conduct half a dozen services:

> When Booth and his chiefs were about to enter the room, the command went up 'Fix Bayonets!' Up went the right arm of everyone on the platform in the form of a salute. When Booth walked to the front of the platform, the command 'fire a volley' and all shouted 'Amen', a blast from the brass instruments, a flourish on the violin and the organ, a clash from the cymbals and a roll from the big drums. The General was sometimes serious, flippant and satirical. As an organizer, the General is a genius; as a preacher he has less claim to admiration.[22]

By then, physical attacks on the Army had almost completely subsided. The *Pall Mall Gazette* put this down to the town's 'vigorous local government' and the fact that the Skeletons could only have some success in 'dead alive country towns' like Worthing.[23] However, the conservative *Brighton Gazette* was still critical:

> The Salvation Army is changing its skin and we are sorry for it. When it was started it was everywhere declared that it was not intended to interfere with other religious bodies . . . now rapidly deteriorating into a mere sect. . . . Salvationism is a system of violence and aggression, and the self-dubbed General Booth is its Pope.[24]

This was after it had reported that a cab driver who had driven his horse-drawn cab through the ranks of a Salvationist procession in Baker Street had struck a Salvationist across the face with his whip for trying to seize

---

21. 6 March 1886.
22. *Brighton Herald*, 2 February 1889.
23. 25 August 1884.
24. *Brighton Gazette*, 20 April 1889.

his horse by the head. The Army asked a magistrate to grant a summons against him but he refused, saying, 'it was the duty of the Army to get out the way'.

A *Gazette* reporter described the Army as a 'religion for young people of weak intellect and excitable temperament and a great curse to religion as it sets aside bible study and give themselves up to a mere reiteration of their individual "experiences". . . . It is indeed the bathos of ignorance, with noise and excitement superadded.'[25] Booth once exclaimed that 'reporters were past praying for', although he told stewards at one meeting he was addressing not to overlook them for monetary purposes when they came to meetings as the 'Lord loveth a cheerful giver'![26]

Part of the above 'interference', alluded to by the *Gazette*, might have been the success of the Army in raising donations, which impacted on other religious bodies' finances. In addition to being successful at fund-raising, the Army also had its Self-Denial Week, when its officers and soldiers would give up 'luxuries' and donate the money saved. Launched in 1886, the money was used to finance foreign missions. Even Booth's eldest son, Bramwell, would get his family to live on bread and water for a week. In October 1889, two 'slum sisters' wearing brown shawls and large white aprons came down to Brighton for Self-Denial Week. They and a speaker from India spoke at the Congress Hall. 'Captain' Annie Bell declared that they hoped to raise £500 and that wealthy benefactors would match whatever they raised. Some of the local officers decided to give up a week's salary.

By December 1889, it was reported that there were long, successful meetings. At Christmas, the Army provided 500 teas for poor people on Boxing Day. The next day there was a tea for 3,000 poor children. These became annual events and added to their popularity.

* * *

In March 1890, Commissioner Booth-Clibborn, the husband of William Booth's eldest daughter, Kate, gave a speech at the Congress Hall calling the year 1888–89: 'a year of triumph, progress and extension, mingled with imprisonments; a year of insult, assault, and illegality, but crowned with the Lord's blessing'. Not long after, a householder living near Brighton complained bitterly about Salvationists playing music and singing outside his house. When they

25. Ibid., 9 May 1889.

26. *Exeter and Plymouth Gazette*, 22 August 1912.

refused to desist, he set up 20 hidden water hoses in front of his garden and when the band came back the next day they were showered. They never came near his house again. (During riots in Bethnal Green, an Army critic had sarcastically suggested forming a 'water brigade' and that attacking them with hydrants might be legally defended as playing brass instruments!)

In May 1890, a journalist from *The Referee*, quoted in the *Gazette*, described the Army band as:

> the strangest I ever came across. As it banged and blared and crashed through the main thoroughfare and the side streets, horses stood on their heads, dogs crept into secluded corners and howled, and cats with their fur on end and their tails swollen by gigantic portions fled howling and spitting over the garden walls. Even the goats in the goat-chaise and the old gentleman harnessed to the Bath-chairs reared and curvetted as that awful band breathed furious defiance to tune and time and the holy Sabbath calm. . . . If the music was awful, the men who made it were worse. They wore on their heads old battered pantomime white helmets, tied round with bright blue gauze veils and the white and blue of their hats and the scarlet of their guernseys so horrified the sun that he blinked and precipitately retired behind a cloud.
>
> I marched through the back slums of Brighton, until we arrived at the Congress Hall, and this I entered to hear the service. The captain got a flying start, and made straight for the collection. The Collection Stakes is generally the principal item at a Salvation race meeting, and I will give this captain credit for being a surefoot at the game. . . . We were hardly settled in our seats before he started the collection[27] and while we were feeling for our shilling and sixpences he put up a young gentleman to say that the captain begged us not to laugh, because it wasn't a comic song. I took down the words of the new departure in Salvation blasphemy. This was the chorus in which the audience heartily joined.

---

27. In the Army's regulations, Booth had written: "It is a mistake to make any other announcements or sing anything requiring a book during the collection as it divides attention too much."

It's no good a-standin' and a-lookin',
If you stick to old Satan you'll be took in,
If you stand on the edge you'll be sugared,
It's no good a-standing and a-lookin!

> After the audience had roared at the song and encored it, I retired . . . a blasphemous song on a Sunday too much.[28]

In March 1891, 'Captain' Simpson, was accused of being a street-singer and was fined £1 or fourteen days in prison. A wine-seller had complained about him singing and playing music outside his house. Against his wishes, Mr W. Willet, a well-known Liberal supporter of the Army, paid the fine. That month, Simpson was again summonsed for being a 'nuisance' after refusing to desist from singing and playing music in front of the Rising Sun public house in Tidy Street. The pub owner, Mr Flowers, complained that his son was dangerously ill and this was confirmed when he actually died. Flowers decided to drop the charge after receiving a letter from Simpson:

> I am extremely sorry to hear of the death of your dear child. Respecting your wish for a public apology, I regret my inability to accede to the same, but repeat the promise made viz. that no more music should be played by my people in the street as long as any of your family are unwell. We are most anxious to prevent anything that shall cause annoyance in any way and am sorry that you should consider we have in any way injured you. God bless you. Please accept our deepest sympathy in your loss.[29]

There were still isolated disturbances outside the Congress Hall; one such instance resulted in a rough being sentenced to 21 days' hard labour for attacking a policeman. A publican complained about Salvationists shouting, 'Lord save the landlord and the poor creatures who go to him for drink', for two hours! When he had customers, they were greeted with 'There's another poor sinner going to hell and taking his poison cup.'[30] However, on the whole, things had quietened down considerably. Now

---

28. 8 May 1890.
29. *Brighton Gazette,* 14 March 1891.
30. Ibid.,19 March 1891.

the Salvationists needed only two policemen to guard their meetings. Once they had required 69. Moreover, on the Level in front of their hall, where they had been harassed so much before, they managed to stage a 'great saved drunkards' demonstration'. Their parades were 300 strong, not a mere handful with a band consisting of a big drum.

In 1894, the *Gazette*, whilst admitting the Army had 'done much to Christianize our poorer brethren', complained about the band of the Edward Street contingent playing music so badly that it 'set all the dogs in the town howling!'[31] A few years later, George Bernard Shaw, who was an experienced music critic, would vehemently defend Salvation bands and describe them as very good.

The Skeleton Army's impact on Brighton had been minimal. Decisive magistrate and police action had helped, as did Stonehill's leadership and the town's importance as a tourist destination – not forgetting the deterrent effect of the stiff sentences passed on Skeletons in Worthing. Another reason was that, in contrast to that town, Exeter, Weston-super-Mare and Honiton, the Salvation Army in one form or another had had a presence in Brighton since the late 1860s.

31. Ibid., 13 September 1894.

Chapter Eight

Torquay, 1886–88

Torquay was one of the fastest growing seaside resorts in the nineteenth century. It was run like other resorts by a small number of rich, conservative families. Because of its mild climate it attracted wealthy visitors in the winter as well as the summer. Unlike Worthing and other Sussex coastal resorts, the cost and length of the journey to Devon from most centres of population restricted the holiday market to the middle classes and above. After the French Revolution in 1789 and the closure of the Continent because of the revolutionary wars, many wealthy English tourists sought a destination with a similar climate to that of southern France in their own country. South Devon was ideal and became known as the 'English Riviera'. With its bathing beaches and medical baths, Torquay was reputed to be one of the best places in England to live if you had a lung disease (consumption). One observer described it as 'the south western asylum of diseased lungs'.[1]

Torquay had red sand to stroll on, grey cliffs to scramble over and rocky coves to bathe in. Its culture was polite, peaceful and quiet; ideal for retirement and also for writing: Sir Arthur Conan Doyle wrote the *The Hound of the Baskervilles* whilst staying there; Oscar Wilde visited several times; and Agatha Christie was born there. A large part of the population worked in hotels or the service industry. They catered to the needs of those whose successful enjoyment of Torquay depended on them doing no work at all!

1. Kneale, (2018), p.85.

Since 1843, Torquay had had a Temperance Society, which had, by the 1880s, a large membership. It even had three alcohol-free workmen's pubs. One of its strongest supporters was Edward Vivian, a banker, JP and a Liberal. He would become a prominent supporter and defender of the Salvation Army in the town.

The ruling by the judges, which overruled the ban on marching in Weston-super-Mare in 1882, could only be circumvented if a town introduced a byelaw. Along with Hastings and Eastbourne, Torquay introduced one. In 1886, the Torquay Harbour and District Act went onto the statute book. Section 38 of the Act prohibited non-military musical processions on Sundays and was directed against the Army. The argument was expressed in a petition signed by certain ratepayers:

> It is our wish that the town of Torquay, which is much resorted to by invalids and visitors, should be protected from the continuance of these processions on Sundays.[2]

It was soon nicknamed the 'smuggled clause' for it appears that neither most of the town's ratepayers nor many MPs knew about it. Six hundred ratepayers signed a petition against Section 38. On the other hand, the Local Board received a memorial from town worthies supporting it. At the local elections five men who were strong supporters of the Act were elected. Although as Salvationists pointed out, ownership of property had a great deal to do with the result, as those without property could not vote.

Respectable society in the town had little sympathy for these religious newcomers. As in other resorts, most of the town councillors were connected with the hotel trade. One letter in the local paper claimed that 'their [the Salvationists'] only object is to make a large collection at every meeting and under any pretence'.[3] However, it was reported that Salvationists were supported by members of all the other denominations.

Before the Act the Army had been marching on Sundays for six years without a problem although one 'captain' had had a glass of spirits thrown in his face and been told 'we don't want any preaching here'.

---

2. Wilson, P.W. (1948) p.88.
3. TNA HO 45/9965/X18313.

Four weeks after 'opening fire' in February 1882, under the leadership of nineteen-year-old 'Captain' Florence Richardson and 'Lieutenant' Emily Bright, their meetings were attracting 1,000 every evening and they claimed 600 converts. On their Sunday morning meetings, which started at seven a.m., they had similar attendances. *The Torquay Times* declared 'the Torquay people appeared to take kindly to the Army, and had rallied in the most kindly way around them'.[4] Despite the success, there was criticism. In September they appealed for 20 people to donate £50 towards the formation of a band. A letter declared:

> Soft-headed people abound, and possibly twenty may be found to add another drawback to Torquay as a place of residence. The poor invalids who come here with shattered health in search of quiet and repose are of small moment; they must be pushed aside to make way for commercial cant.[5]

In 1884 it was reported that an over-zealous female 'captain' had put up posters declaring: 'Cholera Raging in Torquay'.[6] The magistrates let her off after she promised to withdraw them. Although Booth positively encouraged dramatic and flamboyant tactics to attract attention, some of his early followers went a bit too far.

By 1886, the Army was well established in the town. They had two corps consisting of fifteen sergeants, fifteen bandsmen and 224 soldiers, a 'Home of Rest' for worn-out or ill officers and many local sympathisers. The Torquay Harbour and District Act came into force that year and coincided with William Booth laying down strict regulations for a timetable to be followed by every corps on Sundays:

> seven a.m. Knee-drill
> ten a.m. Procession and open-air meeting [Evangelical outreach]
> eleven a.m. Holiness meeting
> two p.m. Procession and open-air
> three p.m. Free-and-Easy
> six p.m. Procession and open-air

4. 3 March 1882.
5. *Torquay Times and South Devon Advertiser*, 8 September 1882. Letter by A.N.H.
6. *Sevenoaks Chronicle*, 29 August 1884.

seven p.m. Indoor Salvation meeting
eight or eight-fifteen p.m. Prayer-meeting begins[7]

The afternoon 'Free-and-Easy', like the music-hall singalongs, was a praise meeting with an emphasis on music and song, designed initially to attract those who had been drinking in the pubs, which were required by law to close at three p.m. Looking at the timetable it is easy to imagine why communities might be upset by the all-day activity of the Army on hitherto peaceful Sundays.

In August 1886, three Salvationists were arrested and charged with contravening the Act. After failing to pay their fines, they were sentenced to one month's imprisonment without hard labour. Edward Vivian, one of the most senior magistrates on the bench, tried to suggest to his colleagues that a less severe sentence was more suitable, especially as this was the first time the Act had been contravened. He was cheered in court but was outvoted. As the defendants, the 'captain', 'lieutenant' and 'bandmaster', all single men, were conducted to their cells below singing 'Glory to God', they waved their caps to their comrades in court. Outside it, Vivian was cheered. The prisoners were taken to the police cells where they had little food, no bedding and no light before being transferred to Exeter prison. At the station they were given a 'Hallelujah send-off' by their supporters: women waving handkerchiefs and the band playing. As the train steamed out, people lined the banks for several hundred yards to wave goodbye.

The *Pall Mall Gazette* believed: 'the Salvation Army is fighting the battle of the masses. . . . On the other side are ranged local "society," black-hatted respectability, the Church, practical Toryism, the Army's "betters" generally.'[8] The local Army commander, 'Major' Roberts agreed. He thought they were being persecuted more by the local elites than by the ordinary Skeleton roughs, although the latter needed little encouragement to join in the harassment.

In an attempt to compromise, the Army agreed not to hold any musical processions on Sunday. However, after the conviction of one of their 'captains' – Tom Kyle, convicted in 1887 of playing a

7. 'Order of Service,' in William Booth, *Orders and Regulations for Field Officers of The Salvation Army* (London: International Headquarters of The Salvation Army, 1886), pp 305–306.

8. Kneale, (2018), P.85.

concertina – was overturned by the high court in January 1888, the Army restarted its processions. On 25 February, the *Western Times* reported news of new arrests:

> The Torquay police yesterday arrested and brought to Exeter gaol four of the Salvationists in that town, who were recently fined by the Torquay Bench for taking part in Sunday musical processions. Each man has to serve seven days in lieu of payment of a 20s. fine.

After serving his sentence, 'Brother' Kingston said prison was one of the 'happiest times of my life. . . . I only got two or three hours' sleep because I was singing all the time.' A 'Captain' Hopkins ended up in the prison hospital after having his wooden arm taken away. On his release he was summonsed again and this time received a month's imprisonment. Meanwhile, William Booth had initiated a 'Torquay Defence Fund' and donations poured in from all parts of the country. This was partly to cover legal costs but also to support the families of those imprisoned.

The Torquay Times condemned the Local Board and claimed it was 'out of harmony with a large number of the ratepayers' and that the Army had been successful in 'reclaiming the drunkard, the depraved and the irreligious'. It did admit though that 'the methods of the Salvation Army may be peculiar and as such not to command universal approval'.[9]

By March 1888, fifteen Salvationists had been imprisoned and they started to appear in court in batches; some more than once. At their hearings the absurdity was pointed out that in the local parish of St Marychurch, a fifteen-minute walk from the court, they were allowed to play music and march on a Sunday. In fact, the nearby resort of Dawlish had the same powers as Torquay but, because of the Army's good work, there they were allowed to continue their marches.

By April the summonses ran to well over a hundred, with 30 already in prison and it was reported that young Skeletons were flocking from the countryside to indulge in rowdyism and riot during the parades.

9. 17 February 1888.

Outsider Salvationists and their supporters were coming too. The town's police superintendent decided to write to the chief constable of Devon for advice:

> Since the members of the local Salvation Army have been sent to gaol they do not come out on a Sunday and march in processions accompanied with instrumental music, but they have strangers at Torquay who when the police ask their names, they refuse to give.
>
> I should wish to know if when any of them refuse to give their names, when asked, could they legally be arrested? There is nothing in the Torquay Harbour Act in regards to it, and I have searched several law books in regards to it, and cannot find any authority for arresting on the grounds stated above. Mr Bridges [solicitor] is of the opinion the police can arrest when the name is refused or else the law becomes a dead letter.[10]

The chief constable's reply is not recorded but we know Salvation bands from Newton Abbott, Exeter and other places 'slipped into Torquay, marched and played, then vanished beyond the range of local authority'.[11] A youthful looking policeman was put in plain clothes and told to march with Salvationists to try and identify them. He was soon recognised and told to 'run along to his mother'.

As the arrests and disturbances continued William Booth decided to send his 23-year-old banjo-playing daughter, Eva, to Torquay. She had been active in the East End since the age of fifteen. As a teenager she had started a free 'broken toy' repair service for children in London and had sold flowers with other flower sellers to raise money. She was already a national symbol in her bonnet and cape and Booth always sent her to trouble spots. She was philosophical about her mission: 'The majority in the world are sinners, and are quite against goodness, and I'm afraid it is the same in Torquay.'[12] One local hotel owner offered £10 pounds to anyone who could shut her up.

A reporter from the *Western Times* described one of her first meetings:

---

10. PA/1/15/58 (Devon Heritage Centre). Letter dated 10 April 1888 from Superintendent Barbour.
11. Wilson, PW (1948) p.90.
12. *The War Cry*, 19 May 1888.

> Imagine a huge bare room like a varnished barn – the 'Public Hall' – capable of holding 2,000, and packed from floor to gallery; a stage; on it a hundred men and women, wearing badges, red jerseys etc. In the centre, a girl, tall, slender, with large, well-marked, regular features, framed in dark hair and a prodigious coal-scuttle bonnet. They lend a strange old-world look to a face, those queer bonnets. She is in black; slung across from the left shoulder is a white sash. A clear voice, better for speaking than singing; not a word is lost. By her a concertina and banjo. That is Miss Eva Booth come to fire the Torquay soldiers.[13]

Figure 14. A young Eva Booth.

Eva spoke:

> We don't know classical music, but our noise gets at some peoples' hearts if not at others' ears. Why not blow our message through trumpets and drums . . . Have you ever seen a crowd in London surging past backwards and forwards in a busy street [and she described their blank looks] and yearned to touch them, speak to them, help them – and can't; and then put a cornet to your lips, or take a banjo in your hand and play, 'You've got a mother praying for you in Heaven'. I have done though and know how they come and stand open-mouthed.[14]

The reporter was sympathetic, believing Salvation bands were a big improvement on 'the usual man with the grind-organ, who said on a placard that he was blind, and made you wish you were deaf; there was the brazen bronchitis of the inevitable German band'.[15]

13. 10 April 1888.

14. Ibid.

15. Ibid.

Torquay's MP, Richard Mallock, wrote to the home secretary to protest about Section 38. He replied merely that there were similar acts in other towns. William Booth tried to negotiate with the Torquay authorities without success, so the arrests continued. Over the months, the Army was reinforced by bandsmen from Exeter, Newton Abbot, Crediton, Barnstable and Ilfracombe. During their processions, local sympathisers formed a bodyguard to protect them from the police and from hostile residents.

On one occasion when Salvationists were arrested:

> a great crowd gathered at Market Street, waiting for the prisoners to be taken to the railway station. The Royal Hotel bus was hired, and the prisoners were placed in it in charge of four constables. The progress of the vehicle was greatly obstructed while proceeding down Market Street, and on turning the corner it was nearly overturned. The confusion was so great that many people, including two constables were thrown to the ground, and the bus passed over the leg of PC Cole. He could not walk and, seriously injured, had to be removed to his home. The other officer had his arm hurt, his clothes were torn from him and his helmet was crushed to pieces.[16]

In May, six Salvationists, including 'Major' John Roberts, were imprisoned after failing to pay their fines. Roberts received one month's hard labour because he was the commanding officer. His wife took over whilst he was away. He later wrote a pamphlet about his prison experience.[17] After declining to pay his fine, whenever he left his house he was uncertain whether he would return. Ten days of suspense passed between his sentence and arrest. On his arrival at Exeter prison, he changed into the prison uniform and had a bath. He was taken to a cell with a brick wall, stone floor and plank bed:

---

16. *The War Cry*, 17 March 1888.
17. *The Battle of Torquay and One month's Experience in the Devon County Prison.*

Figure 15. Bodmin Gaol, 1880s.
Source: The War Cry 2/6/1888.

> Presently my cell door opened, my dinner handed in, and the door immediately shut and locked. I sat down – not to eat – but to realize I was a 'Convicted Criminal Prisoner'. My mental agony then became so intense that I was quite unnerved and unmanned, and sobbed like a child.

For supper he was given eight ounces of bread and water. His spirits lifted when he started to read the Bible and hymn book provided. At midnight, he heard other Salvationists praying and singing praises unto God: 'One comrade paced up and down whistling which was against the rules so he hummed instead.' Roberts was allowed one hour's exercise every morning and then had to remain in his cell for the rest of the day picking oakum. In the Bible someone had written, 'Put him in the prison and the stocks.' Although prison was harsh, Roberts wrote:

> the universal testimony of all the [Salvationist] prisoners was that God's presence in prison had been more real to them than it had ever been before. . . . While my month's imprisonment was in one sense a time of real punishment, it was on the other hand a time of real blessing to my soul, and of communion with God.

On his release, five brass bands struck up and several thousand people proceeded through the main streets of Exeter, with banners flying, to give him a breakfast reception. One depicted a Salvationist in prison garb slaying a vulture, another Liberty holding a Bible and wearing a cap of liberty: 'Their caps of liberty and colourful banners celebrating justice and liberty would have been instantly recognizable to a whole range of nineteenth-century radicals.'[18] Roberts sang several hymns of his own composition with words describing his imprisonment.

In the evening there was a mass rally after a procession of thousands of Salvationists and supporters. A hymn opened the proceedings with the refrain, 'We will never give in'. Twelve former prisoners were in prison dress, including Roberts, who spoke about his prison experience.

In Torquay, Eva Booth's work continued. In May the *Pall Mall Gazette* reported:

> Before the service had proceeded far some four or five hundred people had collected, and a couple of police had sauntered up. After twenty minutes' prayer and singing a start was made: the Army corps, headed by Captain Hopkins and a girl lieutenant, with a banner, filed off in procession along the main road to the town, while the band, with Miss Booth and a banjo 'en tête', whirled up a side street. The crowd with much good-humoured laughter, for the most part followed the band and the police. Thus no organized procession followed the band, but whether these tactics will save either band or procession from being summoned remains to be proved.[19]

The police took no action. Later that day Salvationists again tried dividing into two processions. They started singing in the harbour surrounded by a mainly friendly crowd of 2,000. As Eva Booth led the band procession down the main street the two watching policemen withdrew and a gang of Skeletons immediately tried to attack her. Fortunately, local sympathisers protected her. However, some of the Hallelujah lasses lost their tambourines as roughs tried to snatch musical instruments. Others held them high above their heads. At the same time the other procession was driven into by a cab driver who

---

18. *Pulling the Kingdom Down*, Pamela J Walker, p.233.

19. 7 May 1888.

lashed his horse into them. A boy suffered an eye injury. Eventually, the Salvationists managed to return to their hall. The *Pall Mall Gazette* reported:

> Inside, the scene was indescribable; a struggling, panting, exhausted concourse of Salvationists filled the hall; the drum beat its loudest, the air was suffocating, and everyone felt that the battle had been successfully fought. Beyond a few black eyes there seem to have been no serious casualties. . . . The general opinion seems to be that the local board will take very little notice of today's proceedings. The fact is, the mass of the working people of the town are in favour of the Army, both because of the persecution it has undergone, but also because of the excellent practical work it has done during the last six years.[20]

The Army always had strong support from the *Gazette*'s editor, W.T. Stead, who had huge admiration for William Booth. Also, nationally the reputation of the Salvation Army for 'doing good' was growing. That year, at one of its hostels in London, it fed 4,000 people in one day. Apart from running soup kitchens, giving free breakfasts and clothing, its 'Cellar, Gutter and Garrett Brigade' of 'slum sisters' was visiting, cleaning, nursing and even living in London's squalid tenements.

It was quite clear the Torquay attackers were members or supporters of the Skeleton Army. Some had arrived from nearby Paignton where there had been disturbances since 1883. However, they seemed to be outnumbered by Army sympathisers and generally restrained by them. *The War Cry* reporter was informed that:

> at least the majority of the men who attempted to break up the band in the afternoon belong to a political organisation which prides itself on being the party of law and order and that several of them are in the employment of a gentleman who some time ago got up a petition against the Salvation Army.[21]

---

20. Ibid., 7 May 1888.

21. *The War Cry,* 19 May 1888.

After the latest clash on Sunday, nineteen Salvationists, including Eva Booth (who played a concertina) were summonsed to appear in court for breaking the Act. Despite the rain, many sympathisers stood outside. As she entered the witness box, the other Salvationists gave her a military salute. Their defence counsel, Thomas Sutherst, argued that the Army used its band to summon worshippers just as church bells did. He added that many would prefer a good band to the clanging of church bells on a Sunday 'but no one would think for one moment on interfering with the bells. What was the difference between the bells and the band except usage and custom?'[22] Although Eva was convicted the magistrates decided not to punish her or a female comrade. The male Salvationists were not so lucky. They had to choose between a fine or imprisonment. As few had much money, they all went to prison for two to three weeks.

Eva vowed she would continue to lead the procession and said she would rather die in prison than that the band should be stopped in Torquay or anywhere else. She thought there would be plenty of music in Heaven and, if not, she would take her banjo there and introduce it! So, the bandsmen continued to play every Sunday, and were then summonsed and jailed. A regular Torquay event became the musical procession that accompanied prisoners being taken to Exeter prison, and their welcome on return. Most of those charged and imprisoned were locals.

With every arrest, national and local sympathy increased. In May 1888, the *Pall Mall Gazette* claimed: 'The Salvationists at Torquay are unquestionably doing a political service to their country . . . it is affording an object-lesson of the danger of tyranny and violation of our common liberties, to which local legislation is always exposed.'[23] Edward Vivian, the Liberal and senior magistrate in the town, started to refuse to sit on the bench while Section 38 was in force.

After reporting back to her father, Eva returned once again to Torquay. Fifteen hundred people paid for admission to a public meeting at the Royal Public Hall to listen to this young woman in her simple uniform and white sash over her shoulder. She joined in the Army song, 'Bound to Win':

The Dawlish Board speak well of us,

22. *The War Cry*, 26 May 1888.

23. 18 May 1888.

But Torquay runs us in,
The L.B. [Local Board] says, on Sabbath Day
To play it is a sin.
And to bring about our fall,
With law do us assail,
But like Silas and St. Paul
We sing and pray in jail.
They grumble at the music,
They grumble at the drum,
They grumble at our marching
To make the people come.
They grumble at our uniform,
And say it's all display,
But still we are the people
That are bound to win that day.[24]

When Eva was asked, 'Why don't you stop?', she replied, 'Why should Torquay be deprived of the same privilege as that enjoyed by Plymouth and nearly every other town in the country?'[25]

When they next marched out, she again divided the procession into two: the Hallelujah lasses and their tambourines leading the crowd; and Eva and the band in another direction: 'Two legal points thus arose. Was a band permitted to march if there was no procession behind it? And was the sound of a tambourine at the head of a procession to be certified as music within the meaning of the law?'[26] The magistrates decided that Eva's concertina was a musical instrument and that a band was a procession. So, she was summonsed again. On receiving this second summons, Eva laughed and said she would have it framed along with the other one. It was reported that there was a crowd of between 20,000–25,000 outside the police court to witness her next appearance. This was probably either a misprint or an exaggeration as Torquay's population was only 20,000. Nonetheless, Eva was becoming something of a Victorian celebrity and many wanted to see her. When she faced the magistrates, they let her off again. She told them:

24. *The War Cry*, 12 May 1888.

25. Ibid.

26. Wilson (1948), p.100.

> I suppose that if a woman picked a magistrate's pocket, she would be let off! . . . Gentlemen, you have seen some of these men. They have been brought before you in this Court. You have imposed penalties on them for far other offences than playing a trumpet or beating a drum. You have fined and imprisoned them for being drunk and disorderly, for thieving, for other wrongdoings. What is to be said to you as magistrates when these men who are known to you as offenders against the law come back changed, sober, orderly, honest and guilty of nothing but praising God with the instruments of music authorized by the Psalmist and blessed by the Saviour of mankind? . . . We have two bands at Brighton parading on Sunday and surely Torquay could put up with one.[27]

Her speech did not stop the other Salvationists from being convicted and imprisoned in what *The War Cry* nicknamed Exeter's 'Home of Rest'. In May, after the Local Board suspended prosecutions, Henry Fowler, Liberal MP for Wolverhampton and a staunch Methodist, introduced a bill to repeal Section 38, with the support of the Torquay MP, Richard Mallock, and petitions, including one signed by 7,000 inhabitants.[28] It passed through both Houses of Parliament and received Royal Assent in August 1888. The Torquay Harbour and District Act was amended to allow Salvationists or anyone else to march and play music on any day of the week. Altogether, there had been 148 prosecutions and 56 Salvationists had spent from one week to a month in the county prison during the last six months. Some had been imprisoned two or three times. There were still residents, though, who saw the Army as anything but religious:

> I have never understood why, if they are right, we should not have some Sunday an Indian Fakir with a tom-tom or some dancing dervishes performing on the Strand, they would doubtless do good by alluring idlers from the public houses and as to the religion, the Fakir would most probably consider himself far in advance of the Salvationist.
>
> 'Common Sense'[29]

27. *Torquay Times*, 25 May 1888.
28. The population was 25,000 but there were a large number of children.
29. *Torquay Directory and South Devon Journal*, 4 July 1888.

Figure 16. The Torquay 'martyrs', prosecuted and imprisoned. Eva Booth is in the centre although she was not imprisoned.

In August, William Booth came down to celebrate the 'victory'. Not wishing to miss a commercial opportunity, *The War Cry* started to sell prints of Eva and 21 of the prisoners – 'Magnificent Portrait Group' for one shilling and 2s. 6d. – as mementoes.

A year later 600 Salvationists, some in convict dress, with bands and banners proceeded through the centre of Torquay, led by Herbert Booth (Booth's third son) on horseback. When they eventually reached their hall, some windows had been 'accidentally' broken by opponents. However, although some national newspapers applauded the town's spirited resistance to it, the Salvation Army had won.

James Kneale concludes,

> The trouble in Torquay was characterized by opposition from the 'classes', an 'official' persecution rather than violent disorder from the 'masses'. . . . Torquay's ban on musical processions was partly an attempt to preserve the

> peace and quiet that gave the town its character, and which allowed it to prosper as a successful resort for the better class of visitor.[30]

The main opposition had been the Local Board and the elite. The Skeleton Army had played a minor role, perhaps because its strength as a movement was dying out in the West Country.

In 1927, Eva Booth, now a Commissioner in the Salvation Army returned to Torquay. She was entertained by the mayor and most of the town council and was taken to the courtroom where she had stood in the dock and where so many Salvationists had been sentenced to prison. She recalled that on one occasion she had been knocked unconscious during one of the parades.

30. Kneale (2018), p.92.

Chapter Nine

Chipping Norton, 1887–88

The Skeleton attacks on the Salvation Army in London died down after the early 1880s, particularly since Booth had banned processions in certain areas. After the Black Monday[1] and Bloody Sunday[2] riots of 1886 and 1887, there was also a ban on public meetings in central London until 1892 and demonstrations were quickly stamped out by police. However, in towns to the north of London like Watford, St Albans, Stamford, Reading, Oxford, Buckingham, Newbury and Northampton, to name a few, there were still 'riotous' clashes during the rest of the 1880s with frequent arrests on both sides. More and more public figures, though, were speaking out against the attacks on the Army. Annie Besant, the feminist socialist and atheist, despite detesting its doctrines, told an audience in Northampton in 1887 that 'education and argument are the rightful weapons with which to attack them; brickbats and mud are the weapons of savages'.[3] She herself had been pelted with stones for her atheist views. Besant was speaking in Northampton in the wake of the vicious attack in January on William Booth and his 'soldiers' with sticks and stones. Allegedly, a mob of 10,000 had been on the streets. Threats had been made to kill him and Skeletons tried to drag him from his carriage. A stone knocked

1. The riot caused £50,000 of damage to the West End.
2. The unemployed had an encampment for the homeless poor in Trafalgar Square. It was attacked by police, which led to protest meetings.
3. *Northampton Mercury*, 12 February 1887.

a hole in his hat and he had to be rescued by police and supporters. Afterwards, he complained the police had not done enough to preserve order.[4]

Whenever possible, the Army used arrests to its advantage. At Stamford in September 1887 – where a Skeleton leader wore a white hat and marched with the effigy of a Salvationist on a pole and a banner, 'In Memory of the Whisky Drinker' – clashes led to twelve Skeletons and two Salvationists, 'Captain' Laurence and 'Lieutenant' Thompson, being imprisoned. At the end of their sentence, the Salvationists dressed in replica prison uniforms, rode back into Stamford on white horses and were greeted by a huge crowd. Their welcome home had been well advertised:

> Look out, Release of Captain Laurence and Lieutenant Thompson from Leicester Gaol, where they have passed fourteen days for preaching the Gospel. Tremendous demonstration. Massing of troops from the surrounding districts. Gigantic march, headed by ex-prisoners on horseback. Great welcome home meeting. Tickets 6d each.[5]

Shortly after, twelve other Salvationists in Stamford were sent to prison – although three were prematurely released on the order of the home secretary when it was proved they really did not have the money to pay a fine. They were found picking oakum in Leicester gaol and were given railway passes to Stamford. In Buckingham, too, when 'Captain' Deans and 'Lieutenant' Morris were released from prison – for playing a drum near a house where a man's wife was ill – the whole town came out to greet them. They also wore replica prison uniforms as 1,000 Salvationists, including four brass bands, serenaded them with 'Home Sweet Home'.

In Oxford, the Skeletons rioted in November 1882 but it was the Salvation Army's 'Captain' Paynter who was imprisoned for seven days for obstruction. On his release, he was hoisted onto the shoulders of his comrades and paraded around the town. The Skeletons also paraded singing, 'Rule Britannia' and 'Skeletons to the rescue'. Three cabmen sympathetic to or members of the Skeleton Army, drove into the Salvation parade. The Army summonsed the cabmen who in turn summonsed

---

4. When Booth returned in August 1888, a heavy police presence ensured protection.
5. *Warwick & Warwickshire Advertiser*, 3 September 1887.

Figure 17. 'Captain' Deans and 'Lieutenant' Morris welcomed home in Buckingham upon their release.

the Salvationists for obstruction. The magistrates dismissed both cases. This became the familiar pattern of summons and counter-summons. By the end of the decade, the Skeleton Army had virtually disappeared from Oxford. Complaints that its behaviour had caused undergraduates to move away from the city centre and tradesmen to lose business had forced the police and magistrates to take firmer action against Skeletons. However, the riots then spread to smaller market towns nearby. A case in point is Chipping Norton, a town of 4,000 people.

Chipping Norton, is eighteen miles northwest of Oxford. Today it is better known as the home of a group of media, political and showbusiness acquaintances (including former prime minister David Cameron) whom the media have dubbed the 'Chipping Norton set'. In hindsight, it is not surprising that trouble broke out there in the late 1880s as one of the main employers in the town was Hitchman's Brewery. A *War Cry* reporter described Chipping Norton as having a 'decidedly antiquated appearance, with hilly, irregular, straggling streets and a superfluity of pubs'.[6]

---

6. 14 April 1888.

There is no official record of the Army's beginnings in the town, but some years ago several elderly residents gave the local museum vivid accounts of the opposition its members encountered: 'An old lady, a member of the organisation since the age of eleven, told us that leaflets were delivered at every house in one day, saying that "The Salvation Army would open fire in Chipping Norton on March 11th 1887".'[7] By the end of the month, 'Captain' McFetrick reported: 'We have opened fire on this town in right good earnest. Our barracks, which is a club room connected to a public house, is filled every night. On Sunday afternoon, we were packed out and had an overflow meeting in the market-square attended by over four hundred people.'[8] However, resentment was soon apparent. Apart from publicans' opposition, a local curate preached a sermon against them. In July, the Army declined the mayor's invitation to participate in a public dinner for the Queen's Jubilee Day – it had its own meetings to conduct. In a letter to the corps commander – which was publicised – the mayor warned that the Salvationists' refusal could lead to unrest in the town.

When Eva Booth visited the following week, the mayor refused to let her use the town hall. According to *The War Cry*, he declared:

> that we had set everybody against us; that the leading men of the town had withdrawn their support – but, as the narrator naively remarked, that could not be, seeing they had never given it to us – that we had marred four thousand people's enjoyment, and that we were most disloyal![9]

Trouble first arose on Saturday, 8 October 1887. Prior to that, Salvationists had paraded without a problem although people objected to the 'unearthly row emanating from the drum'.[10] What sparked it off was a 'misunderstanding' with a theatrical company over where Salvationists could pitch their large Army van in the market square. As a result, when they arrived there, they were met by a man, James Burden, with a Skeleton flag with the inscription 'Death or Glory' and a skull

7. Letter of memoirs, email (8 June 2021) from Pauline Watkins of Chipping Norton Museum.
8. An account held at the Museum, dated "1970s".
9. *The War Cry*, 14 April 1887.
10. *Oxfordshire Weekly News*, 12 October 1887.

and crossbones, followed by a large crowd. (Burden had briefly attended Army meetings and had taken the penitent form before becoming a 'backslider'.) Salvationists tried to form their usual ring near the town hall but were jostled and prevented by the Skeletons. Their drum was burst and two female soldiers were hurt. Despite this, they kept on singing hymns till they got back to the room in the Fox Hotel where they held services.

It was thought that, without the Army's noisy drum, opposition to it would decrease but the opposite happened. Over the next two evenings the clashes worsened as Skeletons played 'clappers' (two sticks banged together) in their faces and threw rotten eggs. A few days later a letter in the local newspaper from a ratepayer asked:

> cannot something be done by the town authorities to stop the disgraceful rows which have taken place the past few nights by the Skeleton Army. So long as they are backed up, as undoubtedly are, by the licensed victuallers of the town, a set of lazy fellows will, for a few pints of beer, be ready to carry out their commands. A prominent publican, in an inn not a hundred miles from the market place, is where leaders of the Skeletons received their first tuition and that horrible rag 'The flag' first saw the light of day. . . . The original captain [Burden] has resigned. The new leader of the Skeleton Army is just out of prison for wife beating.[11]

Another letter demanded magistrates bring in a byelaw to ban all marching, especially 'as it was not right that our usually quiet town should be upset by a party of total strangers who pay no rates, and do not contribute one iota to the well-being or commercial success of the community'.[12] *Jackson's Oxford Journal* on 29 October reported that the landlord of the Unicorn Hotel, George Simmons, and a local foreman, Rueben Giles, would be contesting a vacant council seat. Allegedly, Simmons, a Tory, was the nominee of the Skeletons and Giles, of the Army. The candidates were put forward to test the feeling of the town with respect to its views on the 'rival' armies. Simmons received 259 votes; Giles 160. The Skeletons were jubilant.

---

11. *Oxford Times,* 13 October 1887.
12. *Oxfordshire Weekly News,* 10 October 1887.

The *Journal*'s headline summed up the situation:

> 'The Town Given Up to The Mob'
>
> There seems no disposition on the part of either of the rival forces to give way. Each evening after seven o'clock, the town is practically in the hands of these parties, who, after parading the principal thoroughfares, manage somehow or other to meet at different stations in the Market-square, where a continuous howling and hooting takes place, each party trying to drown the voices of its antagonists. Last Monday night in an affray that occurred the flag of the Skeleton Army was seized and torn to pieces.[13]

By the beginning of November, another letter claimed, 'the Army are doing no good. They are causing nightly disturbances. Their religion is simple mockery and nothing more . . . the Salvation Army asked for it . . . nine tenths of the ratepayers were against them'.[14] There was concern that extra policemen drawn from the local villages was leaving houses unprotected and vulnerable to burglars: 'The Skeletons carried an effigy and a coffin, which they declared, was for the leader, Captain McFetrick. They broke up meetings, tore up the flag. . . . Crowds would gather in the Market square to see the almost nightly tussle with the little band of 20 to 30 Army supporters.'[15] As a consequence sometimes they found themselves holding services in a field.

After clashes at the Fox Hotel, a Skeleton, John Allcock, was charged with assaulting Eliza Coleman, a Salvationist. He had punched her in the chin and chest. He said he was pushed into her. He was plainly drunk. Then he made a counter charge against a Salvationist, John Holloway, who took him to a room for Eliza to identify. Allcock was fined ten shillings and Holloway five shillings. In fact, it started a series of summons and counter-summons. In another case, the new 'captain', James Vincent, accused Edward Harris, a baker, of repeatedly bumping into him during marches. At the same magistrates' sitting, a Skeleton,

13. 29 October 1887.
14. Ibid., 2 November 1887.
15. Memories held at the Museum.

James Carter, who was employed at Hinchman's Brewery, claimed Vincent had kicked him. Both charges were dismissed with costs being divided up between accuser and accused.

Vincent was having a particularly hard time. Once he was chased by a mob for half an hour from the town hall to the railway station where they spat in his face and threatened to kill him. On another occasion, on returning from London, he had to disguise himself and arrange to be met five miles outside town and go home a back way to avoid the waiting mob. Skeletons regularly broke up meetings but, although some were arrested and charged, they were usually let off with a caution by the mayor.

As disturbances continued up to Christmas 1887, it was rumoured that, when a tramp arrived, he was bribed by publicans with drink to make anti-Salvationist speeches in the town centre. After two weeks he was thrown out of the town by police for drunkenness! It was well-known that one of the Skeleton 'captains' was the son of a popular publican and that his three brothers were also in the front rank.

By March 1888, Skeletons were forming processions of 300–400 behind an illuminated coffin (similar to the Honiton procession), a lantern ornamented with the figures of a swan, baker and bull (the surnames of Salvation soldiers) and a flag with skull and crossbones and the words 'Death or Glory' written on it. It was rumoured that a £5 reward was on offer to anyone who could put Vincent or his 'lieutenant' into the coffin. A Salvationist named Betteridge and several women were knocked down and indecently assaulted in the open streets. *The War Cry* reported 'night after night, these lasses, in passing up the narrow lane [to the new barracks] have to run the gauntlet of blows, kicks, obscene language and even indecent assaults'.[16] One 'sister' claimed:

> I was knocked down by a man, although he was asked not to push me down, and several fell on top of me. Falling on my shoulder on the kerbstone I was so injured that for over a week I was unable to work. I was going to summons him but the man got so many witnesses who were prepared to swear that he was not there that I thought it would be useless my taking proceedings.[17]

16. *The War Cry*, 31 March 1888.

17. Ibid., 14 April 1888.

The Army requested police protection in a special appeal to Captain Owen, the superintendent of the County Police, but he refused to interfere. They then asked William Sproston Caine, MP for Barrow-in-Furness, a Liberal and temperance advocate, to raise the matter in Parliament with the home secretary. He asked him: 'Did he know that the Army had repeatedly appealed to the local police for protection and had been refused?' This was his reply:

> the Chief Constable of Oxfordshire . . . informs me that the facts . . . are greatly exaggerated. The Superintendent of Police at Norton states that if the assaults referred to have taken place it has not been in view of the police. Neither himself or nor any of the police under him have been asked to take anyone into custody. I do not gather [that] the Chief Constable has refused to interfere; but he said it was not possible for him to provide a police guard for the processionists. . . . He has only four men at Norton; and he cannot, without great inconvenience to the rest of the county, provide more. If there is any ground for saying that the Chief Constable has been remiss in his duty, complaint should be made to the Justices in Quarter Sessions, under whose authority he acts.[18]

The War Cry sent its own 'special correspondent' to gather evidence. He set out to prove the facts had been understated and that the chief constable had misinformed the home secretary. He found that, during the year the Salvation Army had been in Chipping Norton:

> 'dancing-rooms' have been compelled to shut up shop, public-houses have been emptied, desperate characters reclaimed and a corps of one hundred brave Salvationists has been formed. One publican states that his takings are one pound per week less than formerly; and an Army convert who had probably contributed his quota to the one pound has failed to see the force of continuing to do so, and has become the fortunate possessor of two substantial pigs![19]

18. *Hansard*, 26 March 1888.
19. *The War Cry*, 14 April 1888.

The correspondent wrote: 'the horrible treatment the officers and soldiers have met with during the last six months cannot be adequately described'. They included black eyes, bitten fingers, bruised faces and ribs, indecent assaults and torn clothes. He admitted the real feeling of the town was difficult to get at:

> As far as I could glean, the general opinion is that the publicans and certain political influences are at present the backbone of the Skeletons. The wretched combination calling itself by this appropriate sobriquet appears to have got the upper hand over the authorities themselves, the consequence of the want of firm dealing in the beginning.[20]

A week later there was again a Skeleton procession with a coffin. The police did not interfere. However, the raising of the lack of police protection in the Commons did have an effect. Not long afterwards, a sixteen-year-old Skeleton called Robinson was arrested and sentenced to three weeks' hard labour for assaulting a Salvationist. As it was his first offence, a petition, signed by 1,300 residents, claiming that the sentence was 'severe, excessive and unjust' and asking for it to be rescinded, was sent to the home secretary. Leading Skeletons had visited every tap room to collect signatures. However, the petition was unsuccessful and, after this, street disturbances started to diminish. According to one petitioner:

> active opposition to the Salvation Army was already dying out before the sentence. It ceased because the Salvation Army was encouraging and inciting the disturbances in order that they might pose as persecuted people and make capital in the way of collections and donations. Now they also play instruments better, before it was torture.[21]

In the memoir held at Chipping Norton Museum: 'It is said that Colonel Dawkins [distant relative of Richard Dawkins, the biologist and author of *The God Delusion*], an influential Church member, was mainly responsible for persuading the troublemakers to leave the Army to hold its services without disturbance, and active opposition gradually ceased, especially as several genuine cases of reformation had taken place.'

---

20. Idem.

21. *Oxford Weekly News*, 28 November 1888.

In August 1888, the first stones of a building, to be known as the Salvation Army Citadel, were laid.[22] Herbert Booth arrived and led a procession to a packed town hall to hold a 'thanksgiving' service. On a side wall, a memorial read: 'These stones were laid by one hundred of those who through great persecution boldly and conscientiously served their God.' Four months later, Eva Booth held an open-air meeting and another one in the new hall. As she stood on its platform, an enthusiastic, noisy crowd waved handkerchiefs, hats and sticks. 'If I can't see the General, I'll have a jolly good try to see his daughter', someone yelled.[23]

However, the feeling of resentment against the Army did not disappear. In May 1889, there was an anti-Salvation rally at the town hall with a guest speaker, the Rev. George Brick, a former building surveyor and a former Salvation Army officer. Chairing the meeting was none other than George Simmons, who had previously denied being a Skeleton. Brick told the audience that he had been in William Booth's 'cabinet' and knew exactly what went on. He had joined in June 1882 and resigned six years later, allegedly fed up with the Army's antics. On signing up, he discovered that the other officers, rather than arriving from the 'gutter', had usually come from other churches and had a good knowledge of Methodist hymns. Most of them had now left because of the tight control of the leadership. Some also because of the financial hardship they had faced when setting up a new corps. Brick said there was a saying, 'as poor as church mice – or as Salvation Army mice, which would be poorer still'.

Booth had invited Brick to help with the opening of the Eagle Tavern and Grecian Theatre in August 1882. By 1884, Brick said, 'we became tradesmen to our sorrow'. He was not preaching but selling teaspoons, tambourines, knives and forks, alarm clocks and even tea in the Eagle. He told his audience that: 'General Booth is a man of business and if I was a betting man I should back him against any man in England for making money.' Then he gave a list of his grievances. One included Booth bringing over men from the United States, buying a load of feathers for them to stick on their head – to palm them off as Native Americans – and asking them to go around the provinces. The men refused and went home 'but a good trade was done in their photos'. He went on to castigate the Army's 'All Nights' where 'glory fits' (men and women foaming at the mouth) were ordered and encouraged. He also attacked Booth for his lack of transparency:

22. Today, there is no barracks at Chipping Norton.

23. 1970s account.

> You are told of the hundreds of officers who yearly pass through their training home, but you are not told of the hundreds a year who have left during the past three to four years. You are not told the figures. Officers sent abroad often have to beg to survive. . . . You put your money into the collection but you do not know how it is spent. . . . The management is getting into the hands of juveniles, it is not in the hands of good, godly men, such have gone before.[24]

Brick was interrupted several times by Salvation lasses who sang: 'The Old Time Religion'. Unperturbed, he listed various failed schemes for which Booth had raised money but never fulfilled. Firstly, 'Cavalry Forts' (furniture vans) were bought for £300 each but seven were now lying idle behind Congress Hall. The 'Italy in London' scheme, which was meant to help the 30,000 Italians living there, came to nothing. Then, there was the 'Iron Horse Artillery', when twin tricycles were to be bought for men to travel around the country. Nothing further was heard of this.[25] Brick claimed Booth had asked for £600 for the building of the Citadel in Chipping Norton, although he knew it could be built for £400. Booth had sent a 'Hallelujah' architect 'who couldn't tell glass from a slate' with the result that less than a year later part of the Citadel's wall had fallen down and dry rot had set in.

Brick ended his speech by asking: 'Where is the Salvation Navy? Where is the German Work in London? Where is the "nursery"? What happened to the "Cellar, Gutter and Garrett Brigade"? What is being done in the East End? It is a cruel shame to start these schemes to raise money, then abandon them, giving the public no intimation of their collapse, but he has not done so.' Brick spoke for two hours and was interrupted several times by a Salvationist 'soldier' called Hare who had come from Colchester. At the end, Hare went to the platform to try and make a speech denouncing Brick. He was dragged off the stage by several roughs who planted a Skeleton Army flag. In the melee, several benches in the front row were overturned and several ladies jostled. A few days later, the *Oxford Times* reported *The War Cry's* response:

> A publican took the chair, frankly explaining, amid derisive cheers, that he did so because there was no one else. Friends of the Army were there but there were no soldiers. Though

24. *Oxford Times*, 1 June 1889.
25. In 1892, bicycle "brigades" toured the Midlands and Cornwall.

> a Skeleton flag waved from the platform, no resolution was put to the meeting, which, like most of the chairs, broke up in disorder. The speaker and the publican escaped by a back door into outer obscurity.
>
> As bricks are not made without straw, there is a strong suspicion in the town that the 'trade' interest was behind this singular bit of business, especially as there was a deal of drinking during that and the next evening at somebody's expense.[26]

William Booth had a policy of not answering criticism, preferring the Army's work to speak for itself. It was well-known that the 'Cellar, Gutter and Garrett Brigade' was a branch of work performed exclusively by women. It was based in several East End communities. The 'slum sisters' would visit poor families (and even live with them), nurse the sick, assist new mothers, clean houses and evangelise at the same time. They demonstrated their sensitivity to those they were trying to help by wearing old clothes. The brigade also worked with 'fallen women' or women who looked like 'falling'. In fact, it was the great success of this work that had made the Army more acceptable in the East End.

The Army was reluctant to reveal the number of 'soldiers' it actually had and was cagey about how many officers had left. Moreover, although it produced balance sheets every year, the independent auditing was questioned. It was also true that the Grecian Theatre and Eagle Tavern had been selling Salvation goods. (The Army had set up its own trading department and sold clothes, musical instruments and a special blend of 'Salvation' tea). For this reason, in the early days, they were not exempt from paying local rates, as places of worship were, and Booth was taken to court over non-payment. He stopped selling products at the Grecian in 1886 but still had to pay rates on the Eagle and the other premises in the grounds. That year, 'Commissioner' William Corbridge was dismissed after complaining about the Army selling products on a Sunday and the poor salaries of its officers. He had suggested a fund for 'worn-out' officers. The whole of the southern division staff resigned out of sympathy.

Two months later, Brick returned to Chipping Norton town hall to give a talk on 'The Salvation Army Crisis'. Placards in the streets had proclaimed: 'The Beginning of the End of the Salvation Army'. At the same time a circular from Army headquarters was circulated

---

26. *Oxford Times,* 15 June 1889.

in the neighbourhood announcing, 'Brick Recants'. Brick made the extraordinary claim that rather than being financed by the drinks trade, the Army had given him an initial payment of £50 'hush money' to stop his criticism. It had also produced a signed letter in which he completely withdrew his allegations and threatened to publish it if he continued them. It turned out that the man, George Lampard, who had given him the money was an Army sympathiser but not a member. He insisted the money had been a loan to Brick because he was destitute. During the talk, Brick objected to publicans being accepted into the Army and emphasised that he was critical of the headquarters staff, not the ordinary Salvationist. Afterwards, he gave the profit he had made on the meeting to the local almhouses. The Army published his letter of recantation.[27] Whether Brick's allegations were true or not, they were damaging.

Brick's criticisms were echoed by other ex-Salvation officers, notably in two books: J.J. Redstone, *An Ex-Captain's Experience of the Salvation Army* (1888); and Samuel Horatio Hodges, *General Booth, the Family and the Salvation Army: Showing Its Rise, Progress and Decline* (1890). Redstone had been asked to leave by Bramwell Booth and so was obviously disaffected. Later, Frederick Rogers (mentioned in Chapter Five) agreed with Brick's proposition that those attracted to the Army were not necessarily from the gutter: 'That the Booth religious movement had its message for a certain class of people there is no doubt, though I have always thought that the same people would, without it, in all probability have found their way into the various religious sects.'[28]

* * *

Brick's allegations, whilst feeding general anti-Army sentiments, failed to revive the Skeletons in Chipping Norton. By the end of the century, William Booth made a triumphal visit and the local children were given a day off school. Criticism alone, without the support of the local elite, was not enough to sustain popular street protest. In the long term, Redstone's and Hodges' books made little impact on the Army's popularity. Yet Brick was not the only person to make anti-Salvationist speeches in 1889. That year a 'Father Devlin', in clerical garb and 'respectably dressed', claiming to be the chaplain of the Skeleton Army, toured Essex to publicly expose the 'villainy and humbug' of the Salvation Army. Using pubs as his base, he went to market-places to stir

27. *Oxfordshire Weekly News*, 31 July 1889.

28. *Westminster Gazette*, 22 August 1912.

up opposition and harangue it. He was greeted with cheers and hisses and reputedly drew bigger crowds than Salvationists. His meetings over, he sold leaflets in colour attacking them. He also told crowds he was an expert in the art of phrenology and that for 6d. he would feel their 'bumps' (on their heads) back at his lodgings. This was less remunerative than the leaflets.

When Devlin spoke in Braintree, Essex, in August, he advertised himself as an 'itinerant phrenologist' and 'profound scholar' who spoke six languages. For the previous eighteen months the Skeleton Army had been very active there, sabotaging the Army's meetings in halls by turning live sparrows loose and pelting Salvationists with stones from catapults. Skeletons also turned the gas lights off and threw rotten apples. Devlin's visit, according to the *Chelmsford Chronicle*:

> has provoked a good deal of opposition to the Army in the town. All last week the open-air meetings at the Fountain were attended by the 'Skeleton Army' in strong force, and a good deal of horse play was indulged in. Rotten eggs, water, and stones were thrown, and, after the meetings, a noisy mob followed the two female leaders . . . home to their lodgings, hustling them most unchivalrously.[29]

After heavy sentencing by the magistrates, Skeleton activity declined in Essex. However, two years later in July 1891, Devlin was still on tour, making anti-Salvation Army speeches, and he appeared in an unusual court case. The *Chelmsford Chronicle* headlines were:

STRANGE CASE AT MALDON

-

THE CHAPLAIN OF THE SKELETON ARMY IN COURT

-

EXTRAORDINARY EFFRONTERY IN THE WITNESS BOX[30]

Devlin accused a 60-year-old hairdresser, John Miles, of indecent assault. Miles, married with a family, pleaded 'not guilty'. Devlin's behaviour in the witness box was described as 'most extraordinary,

29. 6 September 1889.

30. *Chelmsford Chronicle*, 17 July 1891.

especially when under cross-examination. He interspersed his evidence with Latin phrases. His gestures and grimaces were no less strange than his language.' He described himself as a travelling lecturer, phrenologist and hat manufacturer in the United States and Germany, from Coleraine in Northern Ireland and 'a cosmopolitan of no fixed abode'. When asked if he was the chaplain of the Skeleton Army, he replied: 'Yes, every good man ought to be against that system, unless he is an idiot or a mug that gets his money from simple people.'[31]

Whilst he was watching a parade of Hallelujah lasses on the other side of the road in Maldon, he had publicly declared, 'if women conducted themselves in the States in speech and action as they do here, people would throw oil over them and burn them'. Miles, who was standing outside his shop, told him, 'there was much worse than that', and invited Devlin in. According to Devlin, he stayed 20 minutes in which time Miles kissed him, said he loved him and asked him to stay the night. Devlin agreed to return later. He went to the police, who advised him to go back to the shop:

> Again, he acted indecently with 'audacious brazen-faced impudence' and I felt like breaking my umbrella over his head. I told him he ought to do away with himself. I later returned with Inspector Halsey. When Halsey told Miles of the accusation, he replied, 'I don't know that I have.'[32]

Miles was a well-respected figure in the town and his lawyer, Salter, fiercely cross-examined Devlin. Salter told the court that Devlin used various aliases and in the United States called himself the 'Honorary Tom Collins' and had studied to be a Catholic priest. He asked him whether it was true that he had been turned out of his studies due to an entanglement with a woman. Devlin refused to answer and said he had been a Protestant and Spiritualist for the last fifteen years. Salter suggested Devlin had been thrown out of one hotel in Norfolk for non-payment and that he was constantly changing his appearance. At another hotel in Sudbury, he was asked to leave after discussing with the people in the bar the 'French methods of self-indulgence'. He said it was a lie.

31. *Essex Newsman*, 18 July 1891.

32. Ibid.

When Devlin was asked whether he was a consenting party to the assault, he replied, 'I am poor as a church mouse, but I am a gentleman', and fainted. He was carried out into the street. The fresh air revived him. On his return he said he had been very ill for a week and had not eaten that day. Salter argued that Devlin's evidence was unreliable and that the police were at fault for sending him back to the premises to obtain corroborative evidence.

The jury quickly brought in a verdict of 'not guilty'. Outside the court, Miles was cheered by a large crowd. Devlin, due to their hostility, remained in court for some time before being taken to the police station. Later, he was escorted out of town in a trap. The raucous crowd ran after him, booed and threw eggs from all quarters that missed their target and hit the police instead: 'Devlin, in a great state of excitement, vehemently gesticulating and vowing that were he armed he would teach them a lesson, left town.'[33] The *Chelmsford Chronicle* had little sympathy for either man and believed 'both equally guilty and would both get their desserts by being tied up in a sack and dropped into the sea'.[34] The 'chaplain' of the Skeleton Army was never heard of again.

* * *

The year 1890 was a turning point for the Army. Catherine Booth died from cancer on 4 October and the Army launched a social reform wing, which divided the organisation in two. Whereas sometimes William's passion had lacked direction, Catherine had provided the iron hand to guide it. Her insistence that women had a right to an equal role alongside men in the church was groundbreaking. (Initially, she and William did have doubts about putting men under the command of women but the Hallelujah lasses' great success as leaders of local corps laid these to rest.) She was a great speaker and, in many ways, a more successful one than her husband. In one year alone, 1881, she addressed meetings in 62 towns in eleven months and attracted huge crowds in Newcastle and Coventry.[35] In 1881–82 she conducted a series of talks in the West End before wealthy audiences, which had increased donations significantly. W.T. Stead described her as having 'intense humanity' and as 'the heart of

33. Ibid.

34. 17 July 1891.

35. Crowds of 7,000 to 11,000 in Newcastle and 5,000 to 7,000 in Coventry (*Surrey Advertiser* 15 October 1881). The *Manchester Times*, 2 September 1882 stated that in 23 years she had delivered on average four addresses a week.

the movement'.[36] One of Booth's closest supporters for 30 years, 'Colonel' Alex Nicol – who eventually fell out with him – wrote that 'but for Mrs Booth, there would have been no General Booth and no Salvation Army'.[37] In an interview in *The Herald*, Roy Hattersley, historian and one-time deputy leader of the Labour Party, said 'I started off thinking she was one of the most extraordinary women of the nineteenth century and ended up thinking she was 'the' most extraordinary woman of the nineteenth century'.[38] Losing his evangelical partner, William withdrew from the daily work of overseeing it. By the 1890s, Bramwell Booth, as chief of staff, was really in charge. As autocratic as his father, newspapers nicknamed him 'Baron' Bramwell.

Figure 18. Catherine Booth.

In 1890, the publication of William Booth's *In Darkest England and the Way Out*[39] offered a plan to eradicate urban poverty and vice for all time. It was largely written by his great supporter, W.T. Stead. It estimated that a tenth of the population, the 'submerged tenth' – three million – were languishing in a state of abject destitution and misery. It delineated a scheme of social salvation. Booth realised poverty was a serious impediment to being saved. He did not look at its cause but how to relieve it. He understood it was no good preaching to a man who wanted to know where his next meal was coming from. The book advocated a threefold scheme of self-help and self-sustaining communities. The scheme extended and formalised elements already present in the Army's work. The idea was that the homeless poor would initially be given food, shelter and work in the cities. When ready, they would be sent to agricultural 'colonies' in England where they would learn about farming. Finally, they would be sent to distant overseas colonies with plenty of land, particularly South Africa and Canada, where they could start a new life with the skills learnt.

36. *Elgin Courant*, 7 October 1890.

37. *General Booth and The Salvation Army*, A.M. Nicol p.48.

38. 6 November 1999.

39. A paraphrase of the explorer Henry Stanley's *In Darkest Africa*.

It was not long before the Social Wing dominated the public perception of the Army. From 1884, in tandem with evangelising, it had developed a miniature welfare state: shelter homes for prisoners and fallen women, orphanages, workshops, cheap food depots and even a bureau for missing persons. The first men's shelter in London opened in 1888. It also opened a massive shelter and food depot on Whitechapel Road. There were box beds for 160 and 4,000 meals were to be cooked every day for a half-penny or a penny.

Queen Victoria publicly backed the scheme but made no donation. It was immediately welcomed by the Dock Labourer's Union, still grateful for the support of the Army's cheap food depots during the London Dock Strike of 1889, which had helped to feed an estimated quarter of a million mouths[40] – even Salvationists from Australia had sent donations:

> This union records its heartfelt thankfulness to General Booth for his initiation of such a practical scheme of social amelioration, and knowing only too well the extent of the misery, starvation and helplessness of the many thousands who will be reached by this plan, we wish him every success in his undertaking.[41]

By January 1891, Booth had raised £115,000 – his target was a million – which in essence was applying Christian ethics to industrial civilisation. Although it was welcomed by politicians, church leaders and most newspapers, there were critics. That year, the atheist and republican writer, George W. Foote,[42] published *Salvation Syrup: Or, Light on Darkest England: A Reply to General Booth.* He accused Booth of being a 'clever showman who deals in religion' and that 'singularly and collectively these projects will no more affect "the unemployed" than scratching will cure leprosy . . . unemployment causes are political and economical'.[43] He concluded: 'the whole project, at bottom, is a new gigantic device for furthering the interests of the Salvation Army'. Thomas Huxley, the famous biologist and anthropologist, known as

---

40. *The Times,* 14 October 1889.

41. Ibid., 12 November 1890.

42. Foote had already served a one-year prison sentence for blasphemy.

43. Pp.5–18.

Figure 19. A cartoon in the *Bristol Magpie* mocking Booth's 'In Darkest England' scheme, December 1890.

'Darwin's Bulldog', and one of the Army's fiercest critics, denounced it as 'autocratic socialism, masked by its theological exterior'.[44] In a letter to *The Times,* he claimed that 'ex-members say it [the Army] has become a mere engine of fanatical intolerance and personal ambition '.[45]

Despite the scheme increasing the Army's popularity, there was often criticism that it was entering towns that already had a surfeit of religious groups. In April 1891, it announced it was going to 'attack' Lewes in East Sussex. Lewes already had sixteen places of worship, the Church Army, a YMCA, temperance groups, including the Band of Hope and so on, for a population of 12,000. The *Sussex Agricultural Express* declared:

---

44. *Social Diseases and Worse Remedies,* T.H. Huxley (1891) quoted in "Introduction" of *The Social Work of the Salvation Army* (New York 1909) Edwin Lamb.p.14.

45. 11 December 1890.

'the Salvation Army we fear, prefers to aggrandize itself at the expense of other religious bodies instead of seeking the lost in the great slum districts. . . . They have only 46 soldiers in Bethnal Green.'[46]

It was to be a Sussex town that would produce the worst Skeleton Army rioting of all, ironically, the place to which Huxley, their chief intellectual critic, chose to move to in 1890.

46. 3 April 1891.

Chapter Ten

Eastbourne, 1891–92

Most noble Eastbourne magistrates of judgement sublime
To beat a policeman a joke but to beat a drum a crime.[1]

The coastal town of Eastbourne is famous for its lush rolling landscapes, beautiful beaches and iconic sea cliffs. With its tree-lined boulevards and air of tranquility, it is surprising to learn that the worst Skeleton Army riots occurred there. In 1891, with a population of 35,000, Eastbourne was reputedly one of the healthiest, most genteel resorts in the whole of England. Almost halfway between Brighton and Hastings, nestling at the foot of the South Downs, it was a town built by gentlemen for gentlemen with no common shopkeepers allowed along the seafront. Full of hotels and public houses, two thirds of it was owned by one man, the Duke of Devonshire. It was a place where everyone knew their place.

George Meek, a bath-chair man, in his memoirs about the town, described it as 'the paradise of the idle and sometimes vicious rich, the rest-place of the jaded well-paid workers; but it is hell to the poor who try to live in it by casual labour'.[2] Recent newcomers to the town were either the well-off coming for a gentle retirement or the poor Sussex agricultural worker seeking employment after being thrown off the land

---

1. Walter Guy, *Marching with Music*, (Eastbourne Citadel Corps, 1964), p.12.
2. Huggins, Stephen 2019), *The Mob and The Mayor* p.19. Quoted from Nevill (1982), *Religion and Society in Eastbourne 1735–1920*, Eastbourne Local History Society (1982), p.12.

by increasing industrialisation. Tourism in Eastbourne was thriving; especially after the Cheap Trains Act of 1883,[3] which enabled working-class people to visit as much the wealthier clientele.

As mentioned earlier, in the wake of the disturbances in Worthing in 1884, Brighton town council had invited nearby councils to a conference, which agreed that councils should individually pass byelaws about Sunday processions. Only Eastbourne and Hastings eventually did. Crucially, Hastings soon compromised with the Army. Although there were Skeleton riots for a couple of months, the council agreed that, as long as Salvationists only sang during the procession, their band could play on the beach supported and protected by the police if necessary. However, this compromise came too late for 'Captain' Susannah Beatty[4] – the wife of 'Captain' William Beatty, gaoled in Weston-super-Mare – who, after being badly beaten up in a Hastings backstreet in 1884, allegedly died of that (and other injuries) in 1889. She was considered to be one of the first Salvation Army martyrs.

* * *

Resentment against new religious groups in Eastbourne was already apparent before the official arrival of the Salvation Army. In 1884, there were reports of attacks by a Skeleton Army on Miss Bell's Longstone Hall Mission – which Salvationists attended – for holding open-air services. The missionaries were set upon and beaten by the mob and pelted with rotten eggs. Hats and instruments were stolen and clothing torn. All the windows of the hall were smashed. As a joke one of the Mission members had a noose put round his neck and was taken to a lamppost before being rescued. Police were called out to protect the hall against crowds of 1,000–2,000. When police dispersed them, they sang 'Rule Britannia' and 'God Save the Queen'.

By December 1884, Salvationists were using the Welcome Coffee Tavern for their services. During one prayer meeting Skeletons collected stones from the beach. They tied up the doors from the outside, smashed windows and hurled logs of wood against the building. In court, large boulders and heavy trunks of wood were produced as evidence against three ringleaders who were each sentenced to one month's hard labour.

---

3. It obliged all railway companies to offer affordable "workmen's fares".

4. Sometimes spelt "Beaty".

In 1885 the Longstone Hall was attacked again. One attacker received one month's hard labour and another, ten days'. That year Parliament passed the Eastbourne Improvement Act, very similar to the Torquay Harbour and District Act, which forbade bands marching and playing music on Sundays. On 5 November, effigies of William Booth were burnt by the Eastbourne Bonfire Boys, no doubt influenced by the Worthing ones. A foretaste of the sort of welcome the Army could expect.

* * *

In late 1889, the Army officially arrived in spectacular fashion. Led by Eva Booth, with a band playing, it landed by steamboat from Hastings. Crowds flooded the streets to watch its procession to Langney road where the Army was planning to build its 'Citadel':

> Indeed, so great was the crush of people that many viewed the scene from the windows of neighbouring houses, and men and boys climbed up into the fine old mulberry trees which overshadow the gardens. . . . A platform and tall masts had been erected and were gaily decorated with the Salvation colours.[5]

Eva led the ceremony, which ran up the Army 'colours'.

In the evening, crowds assembled in front of the town hall awaiting the arrival of Eva and the Army's Household Troops Band for a meeting. The packed audience was described as well-dressed, including a large number of ladies. Eva told them she believed that there was scarcely anyone in Eastbourne who did not welcome the Salvationists to their town. *The War Cry* declared: 'Hallelujah! The prospects are most excellent. God save Eastbourne.'

In January 1890, the Army 'opened fire' at a crowded town hall. 'Colonel' Higgins, a Salvation Army commissioner, told his audience that Eastbourne 'had not denied them lodgings and the necessities of life' and he was grateful for letting them use the town hall. One young man named Harris recalled that he had been a Skeleton who had attacked the Longstone Mission Hall in 1884: 'I came here nine weeks

5. *The War Cry*, 21 December 1889.

ago to scoff and laugh at God's people' but now he was saved.[6] A local newspaper said the town had 'submitted to the Salvation Army without even a semblance of struggle', unlike other South coast towns.

By August, led by 'Captain' Emily Goss, Salvationists were parading, with music provided by an imported band, including on Sundays. The following month, the town council passed a resolution by nineteen votes to nine in favour of prosecuting them for contravening the 1885 Act. Amongst those against, the deputy mayor defended the Army on the grounds of religious freedom. He warned that its persecution in other towns had led to widespread sympathy from all classes.

The most prominent critics were Councillor George Chambers, a barrister, and William Epps Morrison, three-time mayor of Eastbourne and resident of fourteen years. Chambers called the Army 'a body built up with hypocrisy, on a foundation of humbug, cemented by false pretences'.[7] Morrison declared it 'was an outrageous, infamous and degrading movement. . . . All should be done to put down this business which is altogether opposed to true religion.'[8] He had already made a speech in 1884 condemning the Army and suggesting that the Skeleton Army could be used to put the Salvationists down and that he would consider joining the Skeletons. He later said it was a joke. The local churches, too, were mostly unsympathetic. There were three other Christian bands in the town but they did not play on a Sunday.

The Act was first used when Goss and a colleague were summonsed to appear before the magistrates in September 1890 for singing in the street. The case was dismissed. However, the following month, 'Staff Captain' Appleby of the Household Troops Band, was fined £1 and fifteen shillings costs or seven days' prison for being associated with a band of music. The fine was paid.

In January 1891, the Army appealed in the local newspapers for money to buy musical instruments. A total of £75 was subscribed by town residents. The donors were fully aware the Army intended to play music on Sundays. By the end of the month an 800-seat barracks, the 'Citadel' in Langney Road, opened. From the outside it was a plain-looking

6. *Eastbourne Gazette*, 19 March 1890.

7. *The Times*, 1 August 1891.

8. This description of Morrison's views is taken from 'Dare to be a Daniel', a radio programme about the riots broadcast on BBC Radio Sussex in the 1980s (archive audio kept at the Salvation Army International Heritage Centre). In the *Eastbourne Gazette*, 4 May 1891, he didn't deny making the statements.

castellated building but inside it was decorated like a theatre with a balcony, boxes and a raised platform. The seats were made in London by the unemployed and homeless at the Army hostels of its Social Wing. At its grand opening, the Brighton branch's brass band performed because the local one was still short of instruments and practice. There followed two days of celebrations.

Meanwhile, opposition to the Army was growing. The Bishop of Bedford visited the town to raise money for the East London Church Fund and made a speech to established religious groups in which he stated that the Salvation Army was the only group that had failed completely to convert anyone in the East End. As a local paper noted, 'His [Booth's] tapping of the successful Springs of charity had an effect upon the revenue of charitable institutions, especially in London.'[9]

In early May 1891, Booth's son Herbert, head of Army operations in the United Kingdom, wrote to the town council asking whether it could play in certain streets on Sundays as long as it avoided the wealthier areas and those frequented by visitors. In an animated debate, the proposal was rejected by seventeen to five with one abstention. Councillor Chambers dared William Booth to go to Parliament to get the Eastbourne Act repealed and 'let them put before the country as to whether our Sundays are to be spoiled all over the country by these tumultuous processions of which we have heard so much'.[10]

A few minutes after ten a.m. on Whitsunday, 17 May, headed by their 'Blood and Fire' banner, Salvationists left the Citadel and marched along Bourne Street, singing, 'The Light of the World is Jesus'. After their open-air meeting had finished, 'Captain' Robert Bell, a 35-year-old mild-looking man, a convert of eleven years who could reputedly play 40 instruments, ordered the band to play. It was immediately surrounded by a large crowd of Skeletons who started to pelt the Salvationists with rotten eggs and throw them to the ground. A big drum was damaged and chucked over a hedge. The chief constable, Fraser, pushed himself through the crowd to Bell and summonsed him and four members of the band to appear in court. They included a laundress, Louisa Clark, who had been playing a tambourine.

On 1 June, the five accused appeared before the magistrates. They were prosecuted by a formidable barrister, Edward Marshall Hall, who pressed for the maximum penalty of £5. The defence barrister, Symmons, pleaded with the magistrates to charge only a nominal fee and warned

9. *Sussex Agricultural Express,* 24 April 1891.

10. *Eastbourne Gazette,* 13 May 1891.

that, if the Salvationists were sent to prison, it would create widespread national sympathy for them – as had happened in other towns – and provoke criticism of the magistrates for punishing religious zeal. In addition, no tourist would come to the town because of the riots. At the moment, the Army was only parading in the poor part of the town where visitors never came. Symmons added: 'Salvationists reached hundreds and thousands of people that the ordinary established methods of other religious bodies did not reach. Processioning on Sunday was one of their methods of extending their religion.'[11]

His appeal fell on deaf ears. On behalf of the council, Marshall Hall declared that a 'strong hand' would be used against Salvationists who broke the law. The five were fined £5 or a month's imprisonment. They chose prison. One had his goods seized instead and the other four were taken to Lewes prison by train. As Morrison left the court, he was cheered by a vast crowd. The town council had won round one.

The result was a green light to Skeletons who believed they could now attack Salvationists with impunity. Local church leaders, including the vicar of Eastbourne, Reverend Ottley, wrote to William Booth requesting a temporary suspension of parades and the bands. Booth replied: 'These disturbances have been brought about by a mob and the blame lies with the magistrates of Eastbourne and can in no sense be attributed to the conduct of our people. . . . They should be allowed the rights that are allowed in every town in the Kingdom.'[12]

Another local vicar, the Rev. W.A. Bathurst, bitterly criticised the Sunday parades in a sermon:

> A body of religionists who have taken their place in our midst with professions of Salvation, and who act as though they felt themselves superior to all other agencies for good, openly defy law and trample on the powers that be, which are ordained of God for executing justice, and blatantly persist in rebellion and stubbornness in the face of all that is true and right and orderly. . . . They are willing to go to prison on this false unworthy issue. A local leader affirmed that 'she felt that the question of playing bands on Sundays was a part of her religion!' What are we to say of such blind fanatical utterances? What of the wild and mad disobedience which

11. *Eastbourne Gazette*, 3 June 1891.
12. *The War Cry*, 4 July 1891.

> they manifest under the shelter of the profession and name of Christ? And they call this lawless contention for the selfish pleasure and excitement of following noisy bands on the day of peace, rest, and quiet being 'prepared to suffer for Jesus Christ's sake.' . . . My friends, when such terrible language, bordering on blasphemy is publicly spoken, I cannot hold my tongue. These people are no martyrs. . . . They are spreading far and wide the spirit of lawlessness, confusion and rebellion, and doing this in the name of the religion of Christ.[13]

The War Cry declared there was a new blood sport: hunting Salvationists. It was rumoured Skeletons brought 'trophies': bits of petticoats, pages torn from bibles, parts of instruments, tambourines and drums and so on and laid them down across pub bars to get free beer. The paper started a defence fund to cover legal costs and before long £250 was raised.

Booth sent Eva and Herbert Booth to try and change the council's mind. When Herbert arrived, he was booed all the way from the railway station to the town hall. Eva, described as 'tall, slim and eloquent', conducted three meetings and spoke to a crowd largely consisting of sympathizers. She denied that breaking the law was an act of bravado:

> What could poor people gain by breaking the law and going time after time to prison for a month? . . . Many a time at Torquay it had meant the poor fellows losing their work while little children depended on them for bread. I have seen tears streaming from the mothers' eyes as they took their farewell. Surely the magistrates when they began to see these things would get their hearts broken.

She continued:

> What right had they to say there was sin in noise any more than there was in quietness? No one ever thought of condemning quietness, but when I was in church the other day I thought what a lot more good might be done if there was a little more noise. Why had we adopted music in the streets? Because we had seen how successful the devil had been in

13. *Eastbourne Gazette,* 1 July 1891.

> attracting thousands by all kinds of noise, not only in halls, but up and down the streets. . . . The devil had no right to all the music. God had a right to it, and we claim that by street music we attract the lower classes whom we can't reach by other means.[14]

She insisted people always came out of their houses to see a band out of curiosity, 'it was human nature; they could not help it'. Eva had a meeting with Mayor Morrison at the end of which she asked to kneel and be allowed to pray. Morrison, a devout Christian, followed suit, although Eva questioned the sincerity of his prayer as he had no intention of stopping the prosecutions. The magazine, *Truth*, parodied it:

Said Miss Booth to the Mayor of Eastbourne
'Ah! Your heart is hard, I see;
You are stubborn and stiff necked
And refuse to grant my plea,
So I'll pray to heaven the softer
Your decisions may be made,'
And with that the 'General's' daughter
Knelt down and loudly prayed,
'For,' said she, 'strong faith must triumph; and so great's the power of prayer,
It must even turn the purpose of a persecuting Mayor!'

Said the Mayor to the General's daughter
'P'rhaps the charge you make is true,
But at least you can't deny that
You are very stubborn too;
And till you are less stiff necked
Things in Eastbourne won't go smooth,
So I'll follow your example
And will pray for you Miss Booth!"
So, they both knelt down devoutly and then and there engaged in prayer,
Did that obstinate young woman and that most hard-hearted Mayor!

---

14. *The War Cry*, 4 July 1891.

And they prayed till they both were weary
With much fervency and glow
And of course when they had finished
Things remained in status quo;
The General's stubborn followers
Broke the bye laws as of yore,
While the Mayor sent them to prison
Just precisely as before
Which, once again, shows clearly it is foolish and unfair
To expect that mundane matters can be set to right by
prayer.[15]

Shortly, 30 Salvationists were summonsed to court for parading with music on a Sunday. They sat in two long rows in full uniforms. Those under the age of 21 were discharged but the remaining 15 were asked to stand up. If they promised not to repeat the offence, the sentence would not be passed. The magistrates asked them to put up their hands. Nobody stirred. Their supporters cheered and the Skeletons jeered. They were fined £5 or a months' prison. They all elected to go to prison including three sisters and a young blind organist. Many of them were replacement bandsmen shipped in from Brighton and Worthing. Only four out of the hundreds who a*ttacked* the parades appeared in court. One was fined 4 shillings and the other three were bound over to keep the peace. Later, when four boys aged between 7 and 10 were charged with willfully breaking windows at the Citadel their justification: "because Salvationists live there" drew laughter from the Bench.

The *Star* described the actions of the "Eastbourne bigots" as 'senseless prosecutions... the experience of other places like Torquay should teach them that it is about as hopeless to keep out the Salvationists as it was for Canute to drive back the tide. There are thousands of Salvationists ready to live in the county jail at the expense of the ratepayers'.[16]

The longer the dispute went on the more personal it seemed to become between the mayor and the Army. In June, a journalist and the publisher of the *Eastbourne Standard* were taken to court by the Army, accused of inciting a breach of the peace by suggesting the police should not protect Salvationists but should leave them to the mercy of the townspeople. It

---

15. *Eastbourne Gazette*, 15 July 1891.

16. *The War Cry*, 10 June 1891.

was tantamount to encouraging people to molest them. In addressing the Bench for the defence, Marshall Hall said 'General Booth was a man who stood out in this century as a perfect monument of the folly of the day, a man who stood out as a most ruthless instance of irresponsible and autocratic power, who had such power over this misguided minority of the country that he directed them whither and wherever he liked. Let him fight the authorities fairly and use legitimate means to repeal this private Act'.[17]

Although the case was dismissed there was embarrassment when it was revealed that part owner of the newspaper was none other than Mayor Morrison. According to Stephen Huggins, in *The Mob and The Mayor, Persecution of the Salvation Army at the Victorian Seaside* 'kindness and charity were his [Morrison's] hallmark' and he speculated why he was so much against the Army. Because of his higher social class did he take 'exception to the essentially working-class nature and ethos of the Army and those whom they sought to evangelise?' Did he feel his authority threatened and the town damaged by their presence or was he simply 'a bigot who abused the power and authority of his office?'[18] Whatever the motive, his unrelenting persecution of the Army prolonged and sustained the attacks.

Salvationists were not only being attacked on parades. James Blackman, wearing an ordinary coat but with his uniform trousers clearly visible was pounced on by a crowd outside the New Inn. They emptied a sack he was carrying and smashed and trampled on the musical instruments inside shouting "what price old brass, old chappy?' The police intervened and four men, including Mr Winchester, the Inn's owner, were later charged with assaulting Blackman and destroying the instruments. Laughably, in court Winchester claimed he had been trying to protect Blackman. The magistrates reluctantly fined him £5 for assault and awarded the Army £4 for the damaged instruments rather than the £9 it was requesting. In other cases, a Skeleton, James Moorton, who had led an attack, was only bound over to keep the peace and James Gibbs, who had violently attacked a police officer, had his case dismissed.

* * *

17. Ibid., 1 July 1891.

18. Huggins (2020) pp.28–30.

Whilst the first four jailed Salvationists languished in Lewes prison, other Salvationists gathered outside its gloomy walls. Some Hallelujah lasses brought their babies. Led by a local preacher, they sang, 'Glory to the Lamb', and offered up prayers for their comrades inside. Then with the order, 'Fix bayonets', raised their arms and singing, 'John Brown's Body', they marched down Lewes High Street. A crowd of 5,000 watched them, occasionally booing and jeering. At one point several Skeletons linked arms and stopped the progress of the band. This started a fight between two Salvationists and a jockey. The police arrested the latter. The Salvationists were bombarded with dirt all the way to the station. Later that evening Skeletons took to the streets singing, 'I Believe'.

When they were finally released, the four were met at the gates by comrades from Brighton, Eastbourne, Tunbridge Wells and Newhaven. Bell had lost several pounds in weight and his plank bed and wooden pillow had given him a sore shoulder. 'Sergeant' Baker, a bricklayer, said he had prayed for the mayor and also for the salvation of the prison chaplain who had 'done nothing but grumble and slammed the door as he left the cell'. He had called the Salvationists 'lazy loafers', frightened of doing a day's work and compared them to thieves and pickpockets. Loadsman, a painter, found his returned clothes so damp and mouldy he had to borrow clothes as soon as possible. The laundress, Louisa Clark, had found black beetles in the blankets and maggots in the food. She was released two hours after the others as punishment for making a mark on a prayer book. Afterwards, the prison martyrs were given a breakfast of ham and eggs at the home of a local sympathizer. Bread, gruel and water had been their prison fare. They all had shaky voices after their month of silence. After a few days' holiday in Brighton, they returned to Eastbourne. A *War Cry* reporter was sent to record their homecoming. He was in a poetic mood:

> The sea was a beautiful sight. There it lay like a great expanse of shot silk spread out in the dazzling glory of the King of the Morning. Lazily did the ripples – scarcely perceptible – roll on to the shingly beach, making a faint musical sound like the distant jingle of tambourine bells.[19]

19. 22 July 1891.

MOBS ATTACK THE CITADEL

Figure 20. Eastbourne mob attack on the 'Citadel'.

Figure 21. Salvationists welcome their comrades outside Lewes Gaol.

Bell and his comrades were given a tremendous welcome at the station by newspaper estimates of between 700 to 2,000 Salvationists, who had arrived via excursion trains from London, Brighton, Worthing and elsewhere. They were marshalled into ranks with bands and banners. The released prisoners were dressed in prison uniforms besprinkled with small broad arrows and placed in a 'war chariot', with covered wheels decorated to look like an ancient chariot. Over it was a banner with the inscription, 'Through Lewes Jail to Victory'. Others read: 'We claim the streets for God' and 'We are ready to suffer, but not to surrender.' Louisa Clark clutched a large bouquet of flowers as one of the bands struck up 'The Marseillaise'. Two other chariots contained Salvationists who had been convicted or summonsed.

The procession left the station, led by Herbert Booth on horseback, with mounted officers on either side. Conspicuous among the females were a number of 'slum sisters' from London, who had the word 'Slums' in red letters on their white aprons. The procession was followed and surrounded by a thousand friends and sympathizers. A well-known Skeleton tried to drive a four-wheeled vehicle through it but half a dozen people restrained him and told him to 'go to a lunatic asylum'.

In the afternoon, what was called a 'bombardment' – singing and band playing – was held at separate meetings. At the town hall, Herbert Booth spoke as 'the representative of the most powerful religious organisation in this country'. As more Salvationists were being imprisoned, he declared:

> the time has therefore arrived for us to fall back on reinforcements. . . . There were 250,000 'soldiers' in Britain and 5,000 had volunteered to come to Eastbourne. . . . 500 dossers, in connection with the Social operation in London, have volunteered their services. They say they are better used to this kind of thing than their comrades, and a month or two in jail won't make much difference to them. (Laughter) With such a force as this I think it will be advisable for the magistrates and the Town Council to take immediate steps for building a new goal. (Much laughter)

Herbert had received a telegram from 150 Dutch Salvationists offering to come if necessary. From London alone nearly 300 bandsmen had offered and one from Camberwell would be coming next week. He considered the Act to be contrary to the common law of England. The Army were 'law repealers', not law breakers. He complained about the leniency shown by the magistrates to the Skeletons who had either been fined or had their 'case dismissed'. He estimated they had only been fined a total of £6 whilst Salvationists had been fined £140. He concluded: 'we shall go on, and we shall win. God is on our side, of whom should we be afraid? (Loud cheers)'.[20]

In the evening, Salvationists returned to the station. *The War Cry* reporter, who had earlier predicted the Skeletons would wait until dark to attack, wrote:

> It was near the station that 'the tug of war' took place. Here a dense mass had congregated and seemed determined to wreak their vengeance on the home-going Salvationists. With wild yells the storm of fury burst; caps, helmets, bonnets and instruments were seized and their owners savagely attacked. The bravery and fine physique of the Salvationists as compared with the rowdies helped to counteract the overwhelming odds in point of numbers but it was a tremendous struggle to gain the station doors, and then a hard job to get through. . . . Miss Eva's [Booth] carriage was surrounded by a seething mob, but she was easily got through to safety, as did the others finally, with a few damaged instruments, lost headgear, and some cuts and bruises. . . . When the London trains steamed out of the station, they carried – a crest-fallen freight? – Not a bit of it, but a rejoicing, singing host, sure of victory![21]

Thousands took part and police batons had to be drawn. A letter from 'An Astonished Visitor' described what he saw:

> I have had considerable experience of riotous and disorderly crowds but never have I seen anything to equal the scene outside Eastbourne Railway Station at about 9pm. They were mercilessly assaulted on every hand, instruments broken and uniforms torn; women and men sharing in the rough treatment.[22]

20. 20 July 1891.

21. *The War Cry*, 22 July 1891.

22. *Eastbourne Gazette*, 15 July 1891.

Another eyewitness:

> saw free fighting going on in all directions outside the station and instruments flying about. One of the trombones was sent flying over to the new bank, and people had to lower their heads to avoid being struck with it. Every now and then the Salvationists raised their hands and blew their whistles – I suppose to indicate that they were safe. I saw several people enter the station with blood trickling down their necks. . . . Two or three of the women were in a fainting condition, and the children were crying and screaming.[23]

One Hallelujah Lass was thrown over a six-foot gate at the station and took weeks to recover from her injuries.

* * *

On one hand, the mistreatment of Salvationists was increasingly being criticized as counter-productive by residents. However, on the other, some shops had petitions against the Army for customers to sign and one had a large poster declaring:

NO MORE POPERY!
DOWN
WITH GENERAL
BOOTH!
STAND YOUR GROUND
BUT
KEEP YOUR TEMPER[24]

On the Sunday,19 July, during a parade, nine bandsmen[25] from Camberwell were arrested with their instruments near the Wish Tower on the seafront and taken to the town hall. The police said they had heard

---

23. Ibid.

24. *The War Cry*, 20 July 1891.

25. Four were clerks; two labourers; a waiter; a blacksmith and an accountant. This substantiates George Brick's contention that not many members were "from the gutter".

a 'note' and had arrested them for their own protection as they had been surrounded by a 1,500-strong crowd with sticks. They were committed for trial in December, charged with conspiracy and unlawful assembly.

One Salvationist, the concertina-playing, nineteen-year-old Walter Guy, whom the Skeletons tried to throw into a water trough, later wrote:

> To be in a rioting crowd was an unforgettable experience. People of all classes were in a sandwich like pack and were subject to the mood and rash swaying of the crowd. We were pressed up body to body, sometimes in more than one direction and could be lifted off your feet for several yards. The rioters put their arms on women and held them down. . . .
>
> Crowds came from London, Worthing and Rye for the fun. They came by road, bicycles, horse and trap, walking and by train. The leader was a tall bearded man and we nicknamed him 'the Goatee'. His real name was Groves. Another leader was a navvy in his working clothes, heavy hobnail boots, moleskin trousers . . . waistcoat with slops of beer, the dribble of tobacco juice from the corners of his mouth, a peaked cap and muffler round his neck. He had a horribly bloated face, eyes bleary and beastly to look at. Many of the Skeletonists were farm workers who carried sticks.[26]

Guy described how they would leave the Citadel and march at a snail's pace, quoting the scriptures and encouraging the crowd to convert. As most men carried walking sticks or canes, the pace made them easy targets. He remembered singing a particular chorus:

> *Oh the Love of Lords*
> *He loved me but I cannot tell why*
> *By and by we'll sing the King and crown him, lord and all*
> *No we never, never will give in, we mean to have victory for ever.*[27]

They were pelted with rotten eggs that had been placed in a hole in a dung pit for two weeks. As Guy remembered ruefully, they were 'the last word in smells'. In one of the worst attacks, he tried to protect the 'colour sergeant' Jack Elms from having the flag ripped off him. During the

---

26. Walter Guy, *Marching with Music*, pp.6–7.

27. Ibid.

Figure 22. Nineteen-year-old bandsman Walter Guy.

struggle Guy found himself 'very hot' at the bottom of a pile of bodies lying on the flag. As he lay there, he recalled hearing a strong woman's voice singing a song, written by William Booth's youngest daughter, Lucy:

Keep believing Jesus is near
Keep on believing there is nothing to fear
Keep on believing this is the way
Faith in the night as well as the day.[28]

When he eventually got up, the 'navvy' kicked him clean off his feet again but he scrambled up and managed to join his colleagues. On other occasions, he was kicked in the shins, almost suffocated and even lost consciousness. (*The War Cry* had declared that getting hit was a 'rare privilege'!) He was also arrested. His father told him, 'Walter, you have disgraced me.' Guy commented: 'He was afraid of the effect of my summons on his business which was with the gentry and tradesmen in the town.'[29]

Figure 23. The Eastbourne Salvation Army Band, 1891.

28. Ibid. p.8.

29. Ibid. p.9.

Guy recalled that the Skeletons regularly met in pubs to discuss tactics and that some locals did try to protect Salvationists as much as they could by mixing up in the mob. Thomas Boniface, his brother, Harry, and fellow fisherman, Jessie Huggett, formed themselves into a bodyguard and became known as the 'three musketeers'. Eventually they did become Salvationists – despite the objections of Tom's wife. He used to wear his Army jersey discreetly under his oilskins when fishing. A fishmonger bravely painted his pony and trap in Army colours.

* * *

A week after the arrest of the Camberwell bandsmen, Mayor Morrison swore in 101 local men as special constables, including two Salvationists. Many were members of the Skeleton Army. Huggins records one unfortunate outcome: 'While the "Specials" were held in reserve at the town hall they vandalized part of the building and spat over much of the floor. . . . Many got drunk having gone to the nearby New Inn Hotel.'[30]

The riots got bigger and bigger. On one occasion, there were allegedly 7,000 outside the Burlington Hotel on the seafront. With such a crowd it was difficult to hear the Army service or their band. When the mob caught sight of Morrison, they sang, 'For He's a Jolly Good Fellow' and also 'We'll Hang Old Booth from a Sour Apple Tree as We Go Rolling Home'. One man kicked a Salvationist drum and tried to put his head through it, whilst another struck a girl with her own tambourine.

By August 1891, 36 Salvationists out of 50 brought before the bench had been imprisoned. A prominent judge asked the town council whether, as a compromise, Salvationists could not be confined to one area. His proposal was rejected after a poll of residents who lived on the compromise route voted against it. By now the extra policing required on Sundays and the huge cost it entailed had made the Army even more unpopular. However, there was also a growing sympathy nationally for the bravery of the Salvationists and horror at the assaults on young Hallelujah lasses. In fact, Salvation Army headquarters tried to forbid women from attending open-air meetings. Louisa Clark told them to mind their own business.

It was not until September that the first Skeleton was properly punished. A cabman, Mason, described as 'a rough looking man with dark hair and a battered face'[31] was jailed for seven days with hard

30. Huggins (2020), pp.72–3.

31. *Eastbourne Gazette*, 2 September 1891.

labour without the option of a fine for attacking 'Lieutenant' Jackson, a shoemaker. Afterwards, the magistrate who jailed him had his windows broken. When Mason was released, there was talk of a public reception and procession but they were postponed. When he arrived back in town, he was dressed in a replica prison uniform accompanied by a man dressed as a prison warder. They visited several pubs and he was serenaded on his return with the song, 'Pudding and Beef'.

More and more Skeletons began to appear before the courts, although the magistrates still preferred fines to imprisonment. In September, Louisa Clark, during a parade, bent down to pick up a 'brother's' cap. William Hall, a carter, grabbed her around the collar, hit her on the face and knocked her down. She lost consciousness for two minutes. She had not been playing an instrument. Hall was fined £2 and costs or one month in prison. His fine was paid.

The town council still had strong public support from the established church. Herbert Henson, the vicar of Barking, backed the council's stance, saying that it was doing battle for civic rights. In a letter to *The Times*, Morrison declared that: 'the magistrates, and the Town Council have, and are doing, and will continue to do, their duty in endeavouring to maintain law and order and to prevent disturbances of the peace, and it is surely not too much to ask the Salvation Army to refrain from breaking the law'.[32] Several days later, Bramwell Booth, the Army's chief of staff, responded:

> The mayor had nothing to say about the thieves and rowdies, the prize fighters and boozers who have been allowed to gather together Sunday after Sunday, primed with liquor for the attack on inoffensive women and men, who are known never to return a blow, and who may, therefore, be struck by any coward.[33]

The Times commented that the Salvationists were 'disorderly champions of order' and deserved their punishments as lawbreakers.[34]

Feeling under pressure the council agreed that the Army could play two instruments on Sundays on private grounds but that it was not allowed to hold meetings in the street or pass down certain thoroughfares.

---

32. 7 September1891.

33. *Eastbourne Gazette*, 16 September 1891.

34. 7 September 1891.

Morrison and his supporters were aware that the riots were detrimental to the town's tourist trade and attracting roughs from the surrounding areas. However, much to their annoyance, the Army continued to form processions and import new bands to play music in the poorest parts of the town.

In October, William Booth suspended the parades on Sundays but the disorder seemed to increase. Salvationists accused police of letting Skeletons smash their cornets and drums to bits. They often tried to hide their appearance; fishermen would draw their oilskins over their faces. Others pulled their hats down and their coat collars up. *The War Cry* believed: 'there was every evidence of organization in the attacks. Whistles were blown for the purpose of rallying the roughs from various centres.'[35]

On 18 October, the cry went up, 'Shove them into the sea', as twelve Salvationists were pushed into a heap on the ground near the beach. Their caps were flung into the sea. One instrument was lost and two were seriously damaged. On the march back to their barracks, they alleged that the police grabbed them by the throat and seized their instruments. Five were then set upon by 100 roughs and their standard bearer was knocked to the ground.

Three days later, a crowd of 3,000–4,000 chased Salvationists back to the Citadel and pelted them with flour, paint, eggs, fish, dead cats and stones. Two women were dragged down onto the ground. Thirty windows were smashed as the terrified Army members took refuge inside. To get out in safety, officers dressed themselves in other peoples' clothing and passed out of the building in ones and twos. Only George Tobutt, a general dealer, was arrested for breaking windows. He was given bail and later acquitted at his trial, despite incriminating police evidence – after the jury had only been out for 20 minutes – to huge cheers and applause. His defence lawyer had cited the Salvation Army's own regulations in respect of smashed windows:

> until riotous spirit passed away, it would be very unwise to replace glass. Use wood instead. It would get more sympathy and effectively plead for the contributions which will be afterwards required to repair the breaches.[36]

---

35. 31 October 1891.

36. As reported in the *Sussex Agricultural Express,* 21 October 1891.

As 5 November approached, Army headquarters in London ordered that the Citadel should be closed and all windows boarded up. Skeletons appeared the day before and threw fireworks at the building. As police attempted to arrest the perpetrators, the crowd shouted, 'Down with the police' and 'Down with the Salvation Army protectors', and they were attacked as well. Eventually four Skeletons were arrested, including Charles Wadey, a licensed victualler, and Albert Philips, a printer's manager. Two were given one month's hard labour and the others, two weeks'.

In the municipal elections in November, no Salvation sympathizer was elected. Morrison was re-elected for the third time and 300 people attended a celebration at the Grand Hotel. He was undoubtedly a popular figure. However, the celebrations were dampened by the news that solicitors representing the Army were seeking to bring a private bill before Parliament for the repeal of the 1885 Eastbourne Improvement Act. In response the council started a petition to oppose any repeal. A testimonial fund was set up by the Reverend Crake of Eastbourne and Alderman Wallis, with the largest property owner in the town, the Duke of Devonshire, contributing funds and with the town's MP, Admiral Field, supporting the petition.

Morrison wrote to other councils seeking approval for his actions; asking them to introduce a similar byelaw. He asked whether the councils had had any complaints about 'processions in your towns'. He received little sympathy. A typical reaction was that of Stockport council, which passed a resolution condemning Eastbourne council as 'a lot of rich snobs who had it all their own way'. Edinburgh council declared that 'Eastbourne had become a name of infamy in England; by its barbarous, intolerable oppression of a few law-abiding citizens'.[37] Even Hastings council failed to endorse Eastbourne council's stance. Moreover, Worthing, which had seen the worst rioting so far, refused to offer any support – as did nearby Newhaven where the suggestion was made to throw Morrison's letter onto the fire. The only person who wished him 'good luck' was the mayor of a small town in Australia!

By the end of November, the Skeleton Army's own band was ready to join the fray. The *Eastbourne Express* reported that, 'what with the playing of the two "bands", the shouting, groaning and ribald singing of sections of the crowd, the din was deafening'.[38] At the latest clash the

---

37. *Eastbourne Gazette*, 2 March 1892.

38. 24 November 1891.

police forcibly stopped both bands from playing and also charged at the crowd, who had shouted, 'Down with the Salvation Army protectors'. Ironically, it was at this point that the Salvation band temporarily stopped playing and only carried their instruments.

During the same month, a four-page, crudely hand-written leaflet called *The Eastbourne Scorpion* was first published at one penny a copy. It was still being sold in April 1892. It was published by James Moorton, a Skeleton, who had previously been bound over to keep the peace. It attacked the Army with caricatures and insults:

> It is probable that every MP who supports the Booth Bill will be promised by Booth a free pass to Heaven. A promissory note, however, of which he is the maker, is more likely to be honoured in hell. And MPs need not hug themselves with the belief that by supporting this fraudulent organization they can wipe out as with a sponge their enormous sins and iniquities.[39]

The Skeletons who attacked the Army were not too dissimilar from the men who joined it. They were typically working men, bricklayers, grocers' assistants and so on. Their ages ranged from the mid-teens to the early thirties. They often knew each other. Later, at a Parliamentary inquiry,[40] 'Staff Captain' Chatterton described Eastbourne Skeletons as 'some young men, some elderly men, mostly well-dressed'. They were tacitly supported by the ratepayers, who, although they mainly confined their complaints to letters to the council and the press, in reality effectively worked in conjunction with the roughs. This resulted in Salvationists, rather than Skeletons, being imprisoned.

* * *

On 3 December, the trial began in London of the nine bandsmen from Camberwell arrested in July. According to Morrison, as soon as the bandsmen had put the instruments to their lips, the crowd of 1,500 had rushed them, shouting, 'Down with old Booth'. He said some bandsmen had struck out with their drumsticks at the crowd. Fearing a riot, he had ordered the police to arrest them and take them to the town hall.

---

39. Arch Wiggins (1964) vol 4 1886–1904 p.275.

40. Commons Hybrid Committee, May 1892. This was an inquiry into the passing of the Amendment Act in respect of the 1885 Eastbourne Improvement Act,.

The defence insisted that they had only beaten the drum once or twice and had played one or two notes. The jury acquitted the bandsmen of breaking the Act but found them guilty of unlawful assembly.

As news of the verdict filtered out, on his arrival from London, Morrison proceeded by carriage through the streets of Eastbourne to the town hall, where he addressed the public and asked them to stop attacking Salvationists and to leave the matter to the police to deal with. He had received many letters from Salvationist sympathizers hostile to the council. The wording was so similar he believed it to be an orchestrated campaign. In the evening, there was a torchlight procession to Morrison's house.

(The judgement against the Camberwell bandsmen turned out to be short-lived. Justice Hawkins refused to accept the verdict, claiming that they were only walking along carrying their instruments and that 'it would be impossible to conceive of a more peaceable body of men'. Several weeks later the high court quashed the conviction.)

The following day, the town council's Watch Committee, prompted by the mayor, decided to issue a temporary order forbidding open-air meetings of *any* kind on Sundays. Although aimed at Army meetings, the order backfired as other Nonconformist groups and the Wesleyans, who had been holding open-air meeting in Eastbourne on Sundays for 20 years, objected. They were determined to disobey the order and 'assert their rights'.

On Sunday, 13 December, the Army tried a new tactic of dividing into three sections and only combining for the march back to the Citadel. At the Wish Tower, as the Salvationists kneeled to pray, their women were dragged to their feet by police and thrown to the mob. The *Daily News* reported:

> As members of the Army were going up the slipway one of the police was seen to forcibly throw back one of the officers named Baker, apparently to prevent him following the others. Another constable was seen to take hold of the standard bearer, J. Elms, by the hair of his head and run him along to the delight of the crowd, he being so ill-used that he was in a fainting condition. Another constable was detected forcing the members along by means of jerks with his knee. This even the crowd resented. No attempt was made to play the instruments.[41]

---

41. 14 December 1891.

Figure 24. This headline from *The War Cry* (26/12/1891) was over optimistic. The worst rioting was to come.

Two days later, Salvationists met along the foreshore and the police intervened and scattered them in every direction. Some were almost forced over the sea wall into the sea. The police were cheered by the public on the upper parade. Flag-bearer Elms was again in the wars as his flag was snatched from him and he and two others had to take refuge in private houses. When they returned to the Citadel there was a double line of policemen to protect them. At the end of the year five Skeletons were fined £2 or fourteen days' hard labour. Their ages ranged from eighteen to 55.

In the New Year, on the afternoon of Sunday, 3 January 1892, 'Captain' Lynne and 60 Salvationists marched in one body to the Wish Tower beach. They had their names written on pieces of paper to save the police the trouble of writing them in their notebooks. Led by Lynne, they formed a ring, knelt down on their knees and started praying. Some of those watching on the upper and lower parades shouted at the police to move them on. Still kneeling, the Salvationists began singing, 'Forgive Them, Father, O Forgive, They Know Not that by Thee They Live". The thousand strong crowd began to get restless, clambered onto the beach and pushed up to the ring. The police ordered the Salvationists to stand up. They refused. "Pull 'em up," shouted the crowd to the 18 policemen, and "move them on". They got up by their own accord.

As the Salvationists linked arms and clung together, mounted police were called to disperse them on the beach. Horses plunged and scattered the shingle in all directions to the great cheers of the crowd. Several Hallelujah lasses were knocked down and had their clothes torn. Caps and bonnets were lost and one brass cornet was thrown into the sea and a trombone damaged. The Salvationists staggered off the beach. Their slow pace was hurried along by the police. Edith Maynard, a dressmaker, had her skirt torn off by a horse when the policeman dragged her up. Catherine Piper was kicked and assaulted by police and Jack Elms was almost thrown into the sea.

Afterwards, a sympathiser and ex-Councillor, Reuben Climpson, told Morrison "You and the police are a disgrace to the town". He had been assaulted and couldn't walk for two weeks. A letter in *The Times* from Army HQ – which had sent out 100,000 letters asking for assistance – echoed this feeling:

> The police have resorted to violence and terrorism by pushing, hustling and kicking the persons engaged in these services [religious] lifting bodily by ear when kneeling, riding them down, dragging them by the hair along the street, throwing them to the mob.[42]

Meanwhile, the Wesleyans and the Longstone Hall Mission were holding their own street meetings and the mounted police had to gallop from one point to another to disperse them. The crowds thought this was a huge joke. The Wesleyans were moved on and claimed to be attacked by the crowd and the police. They complained it was like Russia where you had to move on. The following day a local Wesleyan preacher, Felix Wilson was given a nominal fine of one shilling by the magistrates and warned to his future conduct. Subsequently, the Watch Committee withdrew the ban on Sunday open-air meetings as it was proving impossible to enforce.

Snow falling the following Sunday presented a new danger. Salvationists were bombarded with snowballs, often with stones inside. Police helmets also became a target. Walter Guy, exclaimed 'it was great fun to see the

42. 4 January 1892.

policeman's helmets sent over their eyes, on the side of their heads and down the back of their necks'. Although Salvationists were bringing their instruments along, they hadn't played for six weeks. But, on this occasion, when some of them tried to put instruments to their mouths, police knocked them from their lips. Louisa Clark fainted and had to be carried away by sympathizers as some of the crowd tried to hustle the Salvationists into the sea. This time police, under threat of legal action from the Army solicitors for not protecting their members, did summons seven of the mob including a married woman. Amongst the others were two luggage porters, two flower hawkers, a grocer's assistant and a cab driver. They all denied throwing snowballs with stones in them despite evidence the snowballs bounced! The magistrates let them all off with a caution including one of the flower hawkers who had struck "Captain" Lynne. The only punishment meted out was to the other flower hawker who had failed to answer the summons. He was fined 2s.6d.

Gradually, public opinion was turning against Morrison and the town council. The solicitor-general, Sir Edward Clarke, publicly stated that the processions were not a public nuisance and that, as soon as Torquay had repealed a similar act, there had been peace. The idea that Eastbourne had allowed mob rule to get the upper hand was gaining ground. Nevertheless, *The Times* continued to condemn William Booth for inciting his followers to break the law: 'The streets all over England are made hideous by the discordant din of big drums and bass instruments played out of tune at any hour day or night which was an intolerable nuisance'.[43] During the worst of the Eastbourne riots, Booth was on a six-month tour of India and Australasia.

* * *

One hundred and fifty ratepayers met to oppose the mayor in his opposition to the repeal of byelaw 169. They argued it was too expensive. In response, Morrison called his own meeting. The majority still supported him and over £500 had been raised to support the anti-repeal action. During a boisterous meeting one Army sympathizer shouted out," Is music a crime?" which drew the response, "Yes, when it is out of tune!" A poll of ratepayers was taken: 3,257 support the council and only 470 were opposed. According to an Army supporter, a Baptist minister, the Reverend John Turner, there had been widespread intimidation and 'terrorism".

43. 11 January 1892.

The Army's weekly Sunday battles continued unabated and became more bitter after the verdict against the Camberwell bandsmen was quashed in January. Joseph Rowntree, a Yorkshire MP staying at the Grand Hotel, thought that:

> There's great and general bitterness in the town still against the Army. The church-going people generally and many of the chapel-going people here have stood by and never uttered a word of protest against even the personal ill-treatment meted out to the Salvationists by the roughs.[44]

On Sunday 31 January one of the worst and prolonged struggles took place around the Wish Tower. Singing Salvationists with four carrying instruments, were escorted by 20 policemen. When they got to the beach, they found that 50 to 60 Skeletons had formed a ring where they usually stood and were singing, 'We never, never, never will give in', and were watched by thousands of bystanders. The Salvationists retired to a part of the beach with a high embankment of shingle on three sides. The Skeletons showered them and the police with shingle and rushed at them. 'Captain' Jackson and a local Wesleyan preacher had their hats knocked off and were pushed down an embankment. The four with instruments were stopped by the police and dispersed. The crowd then attacked. They threw instruments into gardens and Salvationists into mud. All the way down Grand Parade the disturbances continued. In front of the Burlington Hotel their banner was torn to shreds. The few policemen on duty were powerless to stop them.

The following month, as the Salvation Army solicitors had threatened, three policemen were accused in court of assaulting two female and one male Salvationist on Sunday, 3 January. Several witnesses testified that two mounted policemen had ridden through the Salvationists without touching the mob. Despite the police offering no evidence for the defence, the magistrates dismissed all the charges (with costs) on the grounds that the Salvationists were causing an obstruction and that the police had used minimal force. However, a few days later the magistrates did fine a policeman for attacking a youth outside the Citadel and another was fined £2 for assaulting James McCann, the blind organist imprisoned the previous year.

44. *Eastbourne Gazette*, 2 March 1892.

When William Booth arrived in Southampton after his successful tour of Australia, New Zealand and India, his steamer was met by a Salvation 'fleet': seven chartered steamers containing 3,000 officers[45] with thousands more surrounding the arrival dock. There was press criticism of the cost of this 'naval pageant'. *The Globe*, calling him 'King Booth', suggested imposing an extra week of self-denial upon the rank and file to pay for it and asked 'can people be deluded by this gigantic piece of Tomfoolery?'[46] The conservative *St James's Gazette* linked the event with Eastbourne: 'There is a fine division of labour in the Army. The "General" travels the world round in special trains and luxurious steamers; the "soldier" is sent down to have his head punched by a justly irritated mob.'[47] The *Brighton Gazette* complained about the Salvation martyrs feeding on water gruel in order to 'swell the coffers of William Booth'.[48]

The tour had been a big success, particularly in India where the red carpet had been laid out for him. There were huge torchlight processions and locals had thrown down their coats for him to walk upon. Instead of being pelted with stones and dead animals, he had been pelted with roses and his clothes showered with rich perfumes. On his return, Booth embarked on a twelve-day 'welcome home' party visiting eight cities. At the first stop, the Army blocked the traffic in central London for an hour and a half. The cost of the 'Salvation Circus' was criticised. However, his return was a huge boost to his beleaguered 'troops' on the south coast.

On the morning of Sunday, 6 March, a mob of 5,000 got the upper hand again. The Salvationists had no instruments with them – although it was rumoured that they had tin whistles in their pockets. They had not played any instruments since November 1891 and were attacked as they marched towards the beach. In the afternoon Salvationists left the Citadel and made their way through a volatile crowd. The chief constable told the Salvationists they could not go onto the beach. The

45. Some newspapers estimated eight steamers with 5,000 Salvationists on board.

46. 13 February 1892.

47. Idem.

48. *Brighton Gazette*, 27 January 1892.

crowd pushed them back towards the railings of the Cavendish hotel and six lasses were thrown down and trampled on; the men were left bruised and bleeding.

The police were overpowered and could not move one way or the other and lost control. Suddenly someone shouted, 'For God's sake keep back, there are women down! If you are men, have mercy on the women!' The crowd shouted back, 'They should stay at home!' The women were insulted, abused and had their clothes torn to pieces. Several were in a fainting condition and one, Ruth Parsons, aged nineteen, was carried by four men to the hospital in a semi-conscious state. Another had liquid blacking thrown at her. They eventually reached the Citadel in an exhausted condition. That evening 'Captain' Jackson sent a telegram to William Booth:

> Morning: Marched to waste land; five instruments; although lawful to play standing, the police withdrew until mob assaulted us: ring broken several times; insisted on holding meeting; quiet march back.
>
> Afternoon: no instruments; police refused to allow us on the beach and dispersed us; mob of thousands; individuals seized, 12 women knocked down; some repeatedly; one indecently assaulted. Scene beyond description . . . soldiers scattered in all directions . . . caps stolen . . . no proper processions . . . several women seriously injured, dr sent for, ordered one to hospital; unconscious when carried to cab; crowd cheered. Report from hospital still semi-unconscious state. . . . Soldiers and friends send love and loyalty to, and confidence in their general and say 'Never give in'.[49]

Booth told them to stop marching.

In a speech directly afterwards, Morrison claimed the reports had been exaggerated. He had seen two female Salvationists helped up off the ground after they had 'flopped down' and hospital staff told him Ruth Parsons was too ill to have taken part. He said it was the 'sweet lasses' doing all the shoving and pushing. He described the male Salvationists as 'animals with two legs'. He later called his description 'poetic'.

49. *Eastbourne Gazette*, 9 March 1892.

The next day in an unrelated court case, a stepmother who was a Salvationist, was accused in court of neglecting her husband's child who had died. As the parents left court, they were pelted by a thousand-strong mob with mud and stones and had to be escorted home. In the evening, police had to stop the mob from burning an effigy of her.

On 10 March, tension in the town reached fever pitch on the day of the Parliamentary vote on the repeal. Inside the Citadel, Salvationists were praying for victory. Meanwhile, Morrison and his supporters were confident of a good result. Local bands had been practising the music to 'Conquering Hero' for several weeks and a torchlight procession had been arranged through the town. When news arrived, it came as a blow to the town council. The House of Commons voted at Second Reading to amend the 1885 Eastbourne Improvement Act by 269 votes to 122 and declared that it had infringed the general freedom of the citizen. If the amendment passed through the Parliamentary committee stage, it would come into force in September. William Booth's tactic of writing to every MP had paid off.

Morrison returned from London and addressed a large crowd at the railway station. He still blamed the Army for the disturbances and warned the crowd to leave arrests to the police. Later, he and the council did try to propose a new byelaw but it was rejected by the home secretary.

At the end of it all, 59 Salvationists had been prepared to go to prison and the town's ratepayers had had to pay for the heavy policing and the legal expenses incurred by the council. William Booth sent the Eastbourne corps a message:

> Your comrades throughout the world, who have eagerly read from week to week the story of your devotion, and who have prayed God for the continuance of grace and strength to enable you to persevere, are rejoicing in the tidings of the victory which are now known to all, and will for years to come make the name of your town a watch-word and a stimulus in the defence of liberty to publish Christ and His salvation to the sons of men. And now, what next? There must be no exultation from any selfish or party feeling: on these grounds let there not be even an unfriendly reference to the past. As far as possible let the very memory of it be buried in oblivion. Let it not be forgotten for a moment that we have not been striving for mastery, or in any spirit of self-glorification, but solely for the liberty to spread the knowledge of that religion

> the essence of which is love, and the manifestation of which is only by deeds of mercy, making known the life and the work of the Christ who came to save.[50]

The *Daily News* called the repeal a 'triumph for the cause of civil and religious freedom'.[51] Nearby Hastings had little sympathy for Morrison: 'We have simply acted in our dealings with the local resident followers of General Booth on the give-and-take principle, and in return we have found them singularly reasonable. Eastbourne blundered. She was intolerant, partial and high-handed, and she has paid the penalty of her folly.'[52]

The Sunday following the parliamentary vote Salvationists wisely decided to stay in the Citadel. A crowd several thousand strong gathered outside and hooted, hissed and hustled them as they entered the building. They stood outside for several hours and clashed with the extra police brought in from Hove and Tunbridge Wells. The Army announced it would not be holding any open-air meetings or processions. As it only let the authorities know at the last minute, it was impossible for the town council to cancel the extra 50 policemen from outside the town coming to reinforce the 34 local policemen.

In May, during the Parliamentary inquiry into the amendment bill, according to one witness, Reuben Climpson, the police would walk behind the Salvationists and let the Skeletons attack them for five or six minutes before intervening. They would punch them in the neck and ribs and pinch the women's arms so they could not see who was attacking them. When the women last marched out on 6 March, Climpson saw the mayor talking to Skeletons outside the Citadel. Climpson shouted out: 'Are you giving the Skeleton leaders orders for the afternoon meeting?' He said it had been the roughest afternoon he could remember.

Rebecca Chatterton spoke of the 31 January riot near the Burlington Hotel: 'The women screamed and choked. There was a crowd of 2,000–3,000. We were attacked on other days as well [apart from Sundays]':

---

50. Arch Wiggins (1964), p.278.

51. Ibid.

52. *Hastings and St Leonard's Observer*, 7 May 1892.

> Emily Mills told how she had been beaten and sexually abused by a mob of about forty men who laughed and jeered at her pain and humiliation. She had consequently felt ashamed and unable to disclose to the police what had happened. To add to her suffering Emily said she had been sacked by her employer for attending Parliament that day to give evidence.[53]

The inquiry also interviewed chief constables from towns that had suffered serious disturbances. James Terry of Brighton said the riots there had only lasted two or three weeks and he had employed 70 to 80 policemen to put down the Skeletons. Five had been jailed in one day. The Army had given him notice every Sunday where it was going and he had placed 20 officers at each place where its bands were playing. Salvationists had also agreed to avoid the principal streets. Douglas Barber of Torquay said that most of the local mob were on the side of the Salvationists. Whilst Worthing's Captain Drummond, said 22 Skeletons had been arrested and tried and that no Salvationist had been imprisoned.

According to Chief Constable Fraser of Eastbourne, the Skeleton Army largely consisted of youths coming to the town for 'a lark or a spree'. The magistrates' clerk claimed no serious injury had been reported to them and that the Army had sent poor people into the street to pose as martyrs. He suggested that the fines should be paid by William Booth and that it was better to confiscate instruments rather than send Salvationists to prison. However, legally they couldn't as all the instruments were in Booth's name. A local doctor claimed that some of his patients had suffered from the disturbances. Local boatmen said they had lost business. One said the majority of the east end of the town were against the Army band because 'their horns blow like foghorns and the drums like a hundred-ton gun'. At the end of the inquiry, the repeal of the Act was confirmed.

With the change in the law due to come into force in September, Salvationists were last summonsed to court on 29 June. In the municipal elections, two candidates opposed to the Army easily won against two supporting it. By September, the Army band was playing unmolested every Sunday but limited its marches. When they played in one street, residents came out and made a noise with old tins and tea trays. Meanwhile, the finance committee of the council had produced figures on the financial cost of the disturbances between May 1891 and

53. Huggins (2020), p. 93.

September 1892. It estimated that the legal expenses of the prosecutions and opposition to the repeal bill amounted to the equivalent of almost a million pounds today. In conjunction with the loss of tourism, this represented a substantial cost to the town.

Despite the repeal, there were still strong feelings that the Army had desecrated quiet Sundays, injured trade and had brought the good name of the town into disrepute. Occasionally, this anger surfaced. On 5 November an effigy of Booth in a bonnet and skirt, tambourine in hand and dancing, was flung onto a bonfire. The Bonfire Boys[54] sang:

> *No, we never, never, never will give in*
> *No, we won't, for we mean to have the Army out of*
> *Eastbourne*

In a spirit of compromise, the band ceased playing after November till Christmas Day 1892. That day, after a short prayer meeting, 'Adjutant' Rankin said: 'Is everybody ready for the march? Band to the front!' There were fifteen in the band and 120 soldiers and lasses. They sang, 'Onward Christian Soldiers'. The streets were deserted but the first taps of the drums sounded the alarm and people came rushing from their homes. The opponents of the Army began pushing against the band and they were hustled back into the Citadel. The police had to intervene and restrain the attacking crowd.

The next day their open-air meetings and processions were attacked. Three Skeletons were arrested and fined. Subscriptions were raised to pay the fines. Fraser, the chief constable of Eastbourne, reported that the disturbances were recommencing again and the police themselves had received anonymous threatening letters. The magistrates warned that they would send Skeletons to prison without the option of a fine and this seemed to stop the disturbances.

In the end, the Army had won the right to proclaim the word of God on the streets. It is inconceivable that the disorder could have continued. It had been bad for business; holiday makers who came for peace and quiet had stopped coming. Even the bathing machine men had lost business. It had also attracted the wrong sort: the roughs from nearby towns. With such big crowds, watches and wallets had been stolen and the police had arrested at least one pickpocket from London.

54. *Eastbourne Gazette* (9 November 1892) reported that they hadn't been involved in the riots. That seems unlikely.

The ill feeling between the town council and the Army lingered on and, in December 1893, it was still refusing to let Salvationists hold meetings at the town hall. In December 1895, former Mayor Morrison died suddenly, aged only 52. Huggins believes his health had been broken by the stress of the disturbances and that he had been held in high regard by his fellow townsmen for his kindness and charity. His 'blind spot' had been his dealings with the Army. His funeral was attended by a huge congregation, including Salvationists.

The following year, the Citadel welcomed the new mayor, J.A. Skinner and other councillors, with a 'God Bless the Mayor' banner. They were serenaded by the brass band. Occasionally though, Salvationists were still sent to prison. In October 1898, Alfred Gatrell, an 'ensign', received fourteen days after 31 householders complained about him singing in their street.

For many years afterwards there was tension between pro- and anti-Salvationist supporters. Councillor Chambers, in his 1910 book *Eastbourne Memories of the Victorian Period, 1845–1901* was still bitter. He wrote:

> There were riotous scenes in the streets, brought about by the wicked misconduct of the Booth faction in defiance of the law and of the inhabitants at large. . .It was well understood at the time that the votes of the M.P.'s concerned would have been different, perhaps widely different, if a General Election had not been coming off in a few weeks, and many members were frightened by the threats of the Salvationists.[55]

* * *

The last known reference to the Skeleton Army in the UK was in Egham, Surrey in 1893. Before that there had been trouble in nearby villages like Sunninghill, where, on Whit Monday 1891, Salvationists had dirty water and rotten eggs thrown at them. One of the Skeletons, William Turner, a labourer, was sent to prison for one month. When he returned, Skeletons carried him though the village as the hero of the day. The sentence did not deter him as he was arrested again later on and fined for unlawful assembly.

---

55. Quoted in Arch Wiggins (1964) vol.4 p.268.

In September, a local artist took a photo of the local Skeleton Army: 'Some carried bottles, whilst others posed with rotten eggs held threateningly aloft.'[56] In November, Salvationists had their drum cut open and the men carrying it were thrown over a hedge. Surprisingly, as a result, 'Captain' Thomas and another Salvationist were sent to Windsor gaol for a week for obstruction after refusing to pay the fine. The following year three Skeleton leaders tied their legs together in the Salvation Hall and were only evicted with great difficulty. They were subsequently fined £3 or 21 days' hard labour. Skeleton activity quickly ceased in Sunninghill once it was reported that the local gentry were going to sack any employee who was a member.

The Army opened up at Egham – which lay halfway between Windsor and Kingston – on 20 July 1893. Led by 'Captain' Robins of Staines, their little band was subjected to sticks, stones and refuse of all kinds and several times the Salvationists were driven back over Staines Bridge. The police protected them as well as they could and arrested several Skeletons who were brought before the magistrates and fined. Disturbances went on for the next couple of months. Sometimes, there were up to 3,000–4,000 hostile people on the streets.

In September, ten Salvationists arrived at the railway station. Two hundred Skeletons walked in front of them ringing a bell, banging kettles and shouting. The Salvationists tried to have an open-air service in front of the parish church but were soon hemmed in on all sides. As it was getting dark, two Skeletons put their banner over the streetlamp and started to throw stones. Some hit policemen standing by. (During the clash one well-known tradesman was heard to offer a sovereign to anyone who hit a 'copper'.) Eventually, the Salvationists were escorted back to the station, followed by a jeering mob. Afterwards, ten Skeletons were charged with obstruction and fined. There were allegations, strongly denied, that the local constitutional club, particularly a churchwarden called Gardner, was raising money to pay their fines.

In October, Salvationists again had an open-air meeting in front of the parish church. When they tried to form a ring, the local Skeleton leader, James Collier, a labourer, broke it up and assaulted the bandmaster, William Saunders. He then made a speech to a crowd regretting the falling off of the Skeleton Army. He made a collection with a hat and

56. *Reading Observer*, 19 September 1891.

Figure 25. *The War Cry* (7/10/1893) declaring final victory in Egham.

tried to incite the crowd to attack. In court, Collier and his brother were fined. By this time disturbances had ceased because the chief constable brought in extra policemen. *The War Cry* announced:

> A Most Glorious Victory
>
> What changes we do see in this life! Egham, that has been so much disturbed by our meetings of late, has become comparatively quiet. The lion has lain down with the lamb. As we went along, we were agreeably surprised to find that opposing forces had stayed away. We were actually allowed to march up the street to our stand unmolested. They brought no banners. . . . We stood from three to four at the one stand, had a fine meeting. One dear old gentleman, who stated he belonged to some mission at Bermondsey and knew the General and Mrs Booth, advised the people of Egham not to oppose us, as we were sure to get victory, for we had the Lord

> on our side. The majority of the people listened attentively. They gave us a collection. One or two individuals were rather boisterous. Some of them said, 'Get a barracks; we will listen to you.' Perhaps they will help us?[57]

The following year when three drunken labourers were arrested in Chelmsford they were described in court as the 'remnants of the Skeleton Army'. Thereafter, the Skeletons were only mentioned in the memoirs of old Salvationists recounting their 'battle' experiences.

* * *

In the 1880s and 1890s, the Salvation Army had become a stock figure of fun in music halls, theatres and comic magazines. So had the Skeletons. Both armies were paraded in James Willing's play, *The Ruling Passion*, at the Standard Theatre in London, which included a scene with a Skeleton Army 'scrimmage'. The cockney music-hall king, Fred Lay used to dress in a red coat ornamented with skull and crossbones and imitate a Skeleton. Entertainers Fredericks and Drew toured with an act publicised as 'The Skeleton Army: Still the Rage!', which made fun of William Booth and his movement. *Punch* parodied a typical Skeleton soldier:

> **Umpire:** What do you represent?
>
> **Private:** I dunno, Sir. I'm carrying this 'ere flag.
>
> **Umpire:** Well you ought to know, you represent a company in extended order. Understand.
>
> **Private** (after deep cogitation)**:** And do I draw the beer for a company when I get to camp?[58]

Although there were still occasional attacks on the Army, and threats that the Skeleton Army might be resuscitated, they came to nothing. Not that criticism of their parades stopped. In August 1899, residents of Weymouth described the Salvationists singing, preaching and band

---

57. 2 October 1893.

58. *Hampshire Chronicle*, 29 September 1906.

playing as 'an intolerable nuisance'. The *Western Chronicle* suggested the council should ban parades and meetings within a hundred feet of the Esplanade walls. Tongue in cheek, the paper admitted that:

> there is probably plenty of good material in Weymouth for a Skeleton Army in the advent of a conflict between the Salvation Army and the local authority. But we have no desire to alarm our readers, and will not anticipate such a repetition of history.[59]

Before and during the Skeleton Army riots of 1881–93, Salvationists were attacked and imprisoned. Afterwards, they were rarely assaulted in Britain[60] – although still occasionally sent to prison, as in Hastings in 1910, when 'Adjutant' Slee was sentenced to 21 days for breaking a newly introduced byelaw. There do not appear to have been any prosecutions after the First World War.

---

59. 18 August 1899.

60. Some Salvationists were murdered abroad, innocent victims caught up in conflicts. Cf. *They Gave Their Lives*, Bateman, Alan (2008).

Conclusion

The Skeleton Army riots were a symptom of the rise of popular conservatism in the last decades of the nineteenth century. In places where they occurred, the Conservative Party – the party of the Establishment and Anglican church – often posed as the defender of working men's pleasures and 'their right to a pint of beer in the face of Liberal temperance fanatics'.[1] Certainly, the Worthing Liberal, George Head, felt he was being opposed for his political beliefs as much as religious. Moreover, the patriotic anthems of the Skeletons reflected Queen Victoria's increased popularity – public sympathy after eight assassination attempts helped – and the success of Disraeli's assertive foreign policy as the empire expanded.[2] Hence, when Salvationists decided not to attend the 1887 Jubilee celebrations in Chipping Norton, they were seen as unpatriotic.

Generally, the Skeletons were more likely to be supported by Conservatives than Liberals. It was said the Conservative government's 1874 Licensing Act – which introduced variable regulation – turned every pub into a recruiting ground for the party, while Liberals tended to sympathise with temperance reformers. In the last two decades of the century, the Conservatives experienced great electoral success before suffering a heavy defeat in 1906.

---

1. Roberts (2007) *Popular Conservatism in Britain 1832–1914,* p.400.
2. Martin Pugh has written: 'It was imperial conflicts and disasters that provided the most plentiful material for the apostles of popular conservatism'. *Popular Conservatism in Britain: Continuity and Change 1880–1987* p. 273. (1988).

Although Booth believed publicans and their friends were behind nearly all the Skeleton attacks, the reality was that opposition sprang from many sources. The early constant vilification and lampooning of Booth and his followers by the press also played a significant part. It built up a negative picture in the public mind. From the mid-Victorian period onwards, there was far more religious equality enshrined in law for Roman Catholics, Jews and non-Anglicans,[3] but the anti-Catholic Murphy riots of the late 1860s showed that religious intolerance was still alive and kicking. The Protestant rioters who attacked new Catholic missions and areas sang 'Rule Britannia' and used the tune of 'John Brown's Body', just as the Skeletons did when they attacked Salvationists in the 1880s and early 1890s. Both groups saw themselves as defending their communities and culture from changing circumstances. It was convenient for the Army to blame the Skeleton Army on the publicans but opposition was not solely down to them.

Chris Hare believes that, when the Skeletons (as Bonfire Boys did) sang, 'Rule Britannia' with its line, 'Britons never will be slaves', it was evocative of the popular sense of community and identity of their area. For this reason, initially, town authorities tended to turn a blind eye to Skeleton activity. This contrasted with the rioting in London, especially around the time of the Trafalgar Square riots of the late 1880s, when the unemployed attacked hotels and restaurants in the West End, which was seen as a threat to the social order. Rioting of any kind frightened the capital's authorities and was quickly stamped out.

In his excellent and comprehensive book about opposition to the Salvation Army, *Blood on the Flag*, Nigel Bovey, a Salvation Army officer, showed how in its early days it was opposed all over Britain. Organised Skeleton Army mobs, however, were largely a southern England phenomenon, although there were exceptions and copycat imitators. In 1883, *The War Cry* reported on the 'capture' of a Skeleton captain and a big drummer in Preston. Other examples were: Skeleton Armies in Alton (Staffordshire), Berwick, Oldham (where the Army band was disbanded and its instruments sold), Ripon and Rotherham; Skeleton deserters in Cannock; and even Skeletons operating in Sweden

3. 1858 – professing Jews allowed in Parliament; 1866 – abolition of special Parliamentary oaths for Roman Catholics; 1868 – the ending of the imposition of "church rates" upon non-Anglicans.

in 1887 where, on William Booth's first visit, they demanded an exit fee (from the hall) from Salvationists and plunged it into darkness by cutting off the gas.[4]

In the early 1880s Skeletons in Hereford attempted, almost successfully, to push Booth and his cab into the River Wye. There were also reports of minor Skeleton activity – mainly involving young boys and teenagers – in Arbroath, Edinburgh, Glasgow, Leith and Ross in Scotland. It is surprising that there was not more opposition in Edinburgh as Salvationists there were demanding all pubs be closed and turned into coffee shops or prayer rooms. They didn't usually demand what they should be turned into. (Bizarrely, in Stockport in August 1882, a Skeleton Army was formed to protect Salvationists from the roughs as they marched through the Irish quarter.) In Birkenhead, there was serious rioting in October 1883 after the Army marched through a Roman Catholic area. Four Salvationists were taken to hospital including one female who had been stabbed in the eye. With approximately 4,000–5,000 people on the streets, there was a violent clash between Skeletons and Salvationist sympathisers, who threw back the stones and brickbats that had been aimed at the Army. Eighteen Skeletons were taken to court and, later, two were sentenced to two months' hard labour for attacking a Salvationist, who had once been a Skeleton, at work.

Apart from these, few records exist of Skeleton activity in the Midlands and the North. Victor Bailey, who has written much about the rioting, puts this down to the fact that in those 'counties, the Salvationists found either sympathetic nonconformist support, or a culture that might oppose the Army without riot'. According to Bailey, 'the Army's assault on popular culture was most strongly resisted in those areas where working-class consciousness was weakest [i.e. the South] . . . the Salvation Army arrival was less disruptive in industrialized areas like Manchester because it posed less of a threat to their already modernized and moralized way of life'.[5] Glenn Horridge believes that: 'in the north of England interaction between geographically mobile individuals from various backgrounds gave rise and credence to new ideas on behaviour and respectability. The Army found a generally friendlier reception in the Midlands and the North compared to the South.'[6]

---

4. Information gleaned from The British Newspaper Archives.
5. Bailey (2014), *Order and Disorder in Modern Britain*, p.7.
6. Horridge (1993) p.125.

Whilst 'rough-musicking' was still strong in parts of the South, it had died out in the industrial towns and cities of the North. Horridge argues, that in the latter, industrialists wielded more local power in terms of sitting on the council and on the magistrates' bench, than the brewers and therefore were not so much against the temperance-supporting Salvationists.

In August 1882, the Army received its most public endorsement when a document signed by the mayor and sheriff of Newcastle-upon-Tyne, four MPs and twelve magistrates praised its marked success in the area. It may be significant that the Booths preached in nearby Gateshead in the early 1860s and were well known locally: 'The north-east became one of the strongest bastions of the early Army.'[7]

There may be another reason why there were fewer disturbances in the Midlands and the North. A perusal of the British Newspaper Archive shows that, on the whole, the Christian Mission had a much stronger and longer presence in those areas than in the areas where the worst Skeleton riots occurred. So, when its name changed to the Salvation Army, its entry was seen as less provocative than when it entered completely new towns. In places where the worst rioting occurred, only the East End – where it was short-lived – had any significant previous Christian Mission presence.

Bailey believes the 'working-class "mobbing" of Salvationists was most typical of the small southern town', where 'there was an "old culture", which in some ways was less inhibited and "non respectable", rudely rejecting the values of temperance and respectability, but was equally often deferential and jingoist'.[8] After the Worthing riots, the *Pall Mall Gazette* blamed the riots in 'miserable little towns in the South' on 'the weakness of the police and the connivance of the authorities'.[9]

Bailey claims that, between 1878 and 1892, there were riots in at least 60 towns and cities. One half of them took place in towns with a population of between 3,000 and 20,000. I agree with his conclusion that the Skeleton Army riots were no substantial threat to the social order and were similar in nature to the earlier Protestant mob attacks on

---

7. Larsson (2019), *Thirteen Astonishing Years that shaped The Salvation Army 1878–90*, p.26.
8. Bailey (2014), p.25.
9. 21 August 1884.

newly established Catholic missions. They were essentially conservative, protecting an outside challenge to the status quo; reactionary rather than revolutionary.

Of course, the personalities of the mayors, magistrates, local dignitaries and Army leaders also played a part in the development of the riots. It is not exactly clear why the Skeleton Army originated in Exeter. Peter Jackson, whilst admitting that sometimes it is difficult to identify factors which 'set off the crisis at that particular moment', believes:

> In the case of the tensions that contributed to the development of the Skeleton Army in Exeter one suspects that individual personalities may have been a major contributary factor. The fact that the mayor at the time was a publican and that the leadership of the Salvation Army in Exeter was in the hands of an individual who may well have been over-zealous might well have led to the focusing of conflict in the town on the Salvation Army and its crusade against the brewing industry. The existence of active bonfire societies in the city could then have provided the model for the particular form the protest took in the shape of the Skeleton Army.[10]

According to Asa Briggs, after the Bank Holidays Act 1871:

> It was in holiday resorts that the Salvationists could find perhaps their most accessible audiences, and it was against the background of public house, promenade, pier and beach that resistance could most obviously be expected, not least from holiday makers bent on amusement and with money to pay for it. . . . Brighton, as oldest of the resorts, with a long and varied history of offering entertainment to visitors of all classes, 'benefitted' most from the invasion of holiday makers, but there were more quiet 'resorts' which set out to meet the demands of the 'respectable' and to keep out the 'rough'.[11]

---

10. Peter Jackson, retired Senior History lecturer, Brighton University, email 23 June 2021.

11. Briggs (1981), *The Salvation Army in Sussex 1883–1892* p.190.

The worst rioting occurred in Eastbourne, arguably the most conservative town of them all and probably the last resort in Britain to allow a fish and chip shop on its seafront. Any change was resisted. After the Poor Law Amendment Act of 1834, a serious attempt was made to burn down its workhouse. The 'No Popery' poster in the Eastbourne shop window, seeking to connect Salvationists with Catholicism, is another example of the town's antipathy to a new religious movement. Catholic children on their way to school in the town were still being pelted with stones in the 1920s and 1930s.[12] Whilst the riots there and in Worthing were amongst the worst, it is surprising that the town sandwiched between the two – Brighton – got off so lightly. Its much larger size, the local elite's greater tolerance, the quick, decisive action of the police and the longer presence of the Army (having first established itself as the Christian Mission) in the town might explain this.

In many ways, Eastbourne was the Skeleton Army's dramatic last stand. However, it was fighting against the tide. The misogynist attacks on Hallelujah lasses proved to be completely counter-productive and upset decent Victorian society. Moreover, unlike other towns who had witnessed riots, it received little or no support from other authorities. After Eastbourne, Skeleton activity petered out and was confined to a couple of Surrey villages. As Bovey writes, 'after thirteen years, the Skeleton Army had run out of recruits, allies and ammunition'.[13]

Why did the Skeleton Army surface so strongly in small to medium-sized towns in the late nineteenth century during a time of great social and economic changes? Telephones were spreading across the country; bicycles were giving people greater independence; and compulsory schooling brought with it greater literacy. With improved sanitation and living conditions, people were living longer and far more children were surviving past infancy. However, some places in England sought stubbornly to resist change: for example, close-knit, inward-looking towns like Worthing and Eastbourne in which social deference, the status quo and tradition ruled. If given the discreet nod of approval by their social betters, it more than encouraged the mob; a fact often pointed out by local newspapers: 'Town councillors [in Hastings] would do well to avoid encouraging the Skeleton Army by uncalled

12. As told to me by an elderly town resident.

13. Bovey (2015), p.368.

denunciation of the Salvation Army and by covert hints that the mob are not so bad as the disciples of William Booth.'[14] In September 1884 in Hastings, a councillor and publican was fined for throwing a firework into a parade.

The worst disturbances occurred in places where there was an informal, unofficial alliance between the Skeletons and an unsympathetic local authority and its middle-class property owners. The riots were an attempt to uphold 'a traditional conception of order against the disruptive challenge of militant methodism'.[15] In these towns, disturbances could be sustained over a long period of time because they gave tacit support to the Skeletons. (In London where there was no such alliance, the riots were sporadic and short lived.) Often the authorities would hope the mobs would force Salvationists off the streets and back into their halls. If that failed, they used local byelaws and fines in the hope that these would stop Salvationists. Ironically, Bramwell Booth claimed that: 'magistrates who had imposed fines that our comrades, on principle, refused to pay, and so were put in prison, rushed off to pay the fines themselves! We refused. Sometimes they wanted to bring the Salvationists quietly out in the night.[16] According to William Booth, in Torquay some of the fines were paid by MPs.[17]

Horridge conducted a case study of the Honiton riots, which confirmed:

> that the organized and worst riots occurred in the small and medium-sized towns of southern England, where the conservative social ties sustained local rather than national loyalties, that is to the successors of the town squire; that the Skeleton Army was directed at the Salvation Army and its supporters within towns by important tradesmen with connections on the council; and that the Army was often considered to be the initial perpetrator of the violence by actually being there.[18]

* * *

14. *Hastings & St Leonards Observer,* 18 October 1884.
15. Bailey (2014), p.3.
16. Bramwell Booth (1925), ch.4 p. 26.
17. *The Times*, 25 May 1888.
18. Horridge (1993), p.168.

Booth's success was bound to cause resentment from other religious groups, especially his ability to raise funds; another reason why in small towns the Army may not have been welcomed with open arms. Important charities such as the Christian Organisation of Charity (COS) – nicknamed 'Cringe or Starve' by its critics – were very much against what they saw as the Army's practice of indiscriminate charity. COS believed that it deterred the poor from helping themselves. Also, initially, many Anglicans feared the Army were social revolutionaries trying to destabilise the 'natural order' of society: 'An Army containing reformed drunkards and former "fallen women" was inevitably at odds with polite, Anglican society.'[19] Respectable opinion was scandalised to see female 'captains' leading Salvation Army corps through the streets and addressing meetings. Almost half the Army's officers were women. Catherine Booth epitomised this new, independent woman who provoked reaction. Hare writes:

> The Salvation Army was not only something new and alarming in religious terms, it also gave equal rights to women. Women speaking in public was still regarded as unseemly, even unnatural by some – but women in uniform commanding male soldiers – what had the world come to? These young women should be getting married and having children not in the middle of a street war. Interestingly, in the years leading up to the First World War, many of the towns that saw Skeleton Armies saw attacks on Suffragettes, including Worthing in February 1913.[20]

Contemporaries were shocked to see young girls sent to dens of vice and drink and set up new corps all over the country. Hallelujah lasses tended to be both religious and adventurous and the Salvation Army was an exciting prospect. Their persecution received the most press coverage. Although Catherine Booth believed women should not forsake their wifely duties in the home, there is little doubt that the Army played a part in their eventual emancipation in the twentieth century.

---

19. Kneale (2018), p.86.
20. Chris Hare, email 24 July 2020.

When the Army came marching into town, 'what critics reviled as blasphemous carnival the Salvationists believed was the reason for their success'.[21] Pamela J. Walker, in her book *Pulling the Devil's Kingdom Down*, writes:

> Salvationists responded to verbal and physical attacks by proclaiming that they were the champions of the people, engaged in hand-to-hand combat with a repressive state, a corrupt church, and the vicious drink trade, which enslaved working people. The crowds were, Salvationists argued, not a genuine part of the neighbourhood but rather deluded men lured by publicans into acting on behalf of a corrupt world.[22]

The Salvationists' fiery rhetoric and zealous proclamations disturbed local authorities and communities and paid little homage to established religious custom. Their high-profile advocacy of total abstinence created a strong opposition from elements of the working class, the local elites and the drinks trade. When they invaded the poorest areas, it was like a red rag to a bull. On another level, noisy Salvation marches with drums, tambourines and trumpets could be perceived to be a public nuisance, especially on a Sunday. Not only for their discordant noise (in the early days) but also for blocking roads and impeding traffic. Moreover, they were sometimes accused of marching out at seven in the morning banging a big bass drum; something few would find acceptable today.

There is perhaps another reason why there was so much resistance. Before the Army's arrival in a town, local newspapers would already have been full of national newspapers' reports highlighting its fanaticism, noisy processions and its verbal attacks on working-class institutions and pastimes and also about its undercutting the labour market in London. Such stories would at the very least have produced a certain amount of apprehension, even though they were often exaggerated. Once their processions started, the smaller the town, the more likely Salvationists would be passing and repassing the same streets several times a day: a genuine nuisance, especially on a Sunday. When they invaded small villages, they were often followed by the Skeleton Army, which led to private property being damaged. One inhabitant of a small village near

---

21. Pamela Walker (2001), *Pulling Down the Kingdom* p.212.

22. Ibid., p.232.

Stowmarket suggested that 'this eccentric body [the Salvation Army] should pay some of the bills'.[23] Another grievance of church and chapel-goers on a Sunday was that they would be just settling down to hear the service when they were disturbed by a noisy band outside.

Other strong temperance movements, such as the Blue Ribbon Army, were rarely physically attacked like the Army. The former was once opposed by a Skeleton Army in Yarmouth, whose banner had a skull and crossbones on one side and a mug of ale and bottle drawn on the other, but it was not attacked. The same was true of the Church Army. When 300 Skeletons marched past its parade in Westminster in January 1883 with staves and stones, they left its followers untouched. It was the attention-seeking activities of the Army which provoked so much anger and the perception that they were religious fanatics. It was not just seen as a temperance movement but as an organisation that attacked working-class pleasures and pastimes. Lyon comments that: 'The issue of temperance alone was not sufficient to rouse the wrath of inhabitants',[24] especially in the East End.

Who formed the Skeleton Army? The generic name gave an identity to the Army's attackers as it spread.[25] Calling themselves an army in order to oppose another army seemed natural. In February 1883, the *Pall Mall Gazette* described them as 'the hoodlums and larrikins of the street. . . . For the most part they indulge in rough and riotous behaviour solely for the love of mischief and the opportunity of having a little fun.'[26] Based as it was in London, the *Gazette* was probably accurately describing the London Skeletons. Their attacks were often spontaneous and less organised than those in small towns and 'it is entirely possible that members of the working-class communities [in London] were in fact acting of their own volition'[27] rather than being sponsored by publicans. This is also argued in the letter 'From A Sinner's Point of View' in Chapter Five. In fact, he denied there was a Skeleton Army in the East End; just poor working men trying to make their voices heard.

---

23. *Ipswich Journal*, 2 March 1886.
24. Lyon (2018), p.29.
25. In very rare cases, as in Guildford, the roughs there were known as The Red-Nose Army. They carried a red flag and wore red ribbons.
26. 9 February 1883.
27. Lyon (2018), p.26.

Outside London, Skeletons were an organised bunch of roughs often financially aided and supported by publicans and local elites. In Sussex, particularly Worthing, there was often a strong correlation between them and the local bonfire societies. Effigies of William Booth and Hallelujah lasses carrying copies of *The War Cry* were regularly burnt on Guy Fawkes Night and, certainly, it was dangerous for Salvationists to risk appearing in public that day. It cannot be a coincidence that some of the worst riots occurred in Sussex, Surrey, Essex and Devon where the 'Bonfire Boys' were strongest. Predominantly young male manual workers, they could also be supplemented by respectable tradesmen. There is no record of female Skeletons being arrested and their role seems to have been a supportive one. They collected stones and so on for their menfolk to throw. Intriguingly though, the *Pall Mall Gazette* reported that at a demonstration in Trafalgar Square in 1883, the life of the female chief of the Skeleton Army was being sold for one penny.[28]

Although there was evidence of communication between Skeleton Armies, particularly in Sussex and Devon coastal towns and villages, unlike the Salvation Army, Skeletons had no headquarters or national strategy and no single, unified army. As their violence got out of hand, few respectable people would openly admit to supporting them. Neither did they have any particular beliefs other than to get rid of the Army. On the other hand, Salvationists had an almost fanatical belief in their cause. In 1884 alone, William Booth claimed that more than 600 Salvationists had been imprisoned. By 1893, the figure was probably in the low thousands. ('The historian, David Jones, lists Salvationists as the "fourth highest number of people taken into custody on a charge of riot" in the nineteenth century').[29] It should not be forgotten that sometimes 'soldiers' lost their jobs and accommodation whilst in prison. It was always going to be an unequal battle.

Many of the Skeletons, living in towns and villages where there was not much to do (in their free time), were no doubt attracted by the excitement of being in a mob and attacking 'outsiders'. It also gave them a chance to have a go at the police. At their worst, Skeletons were as violent as the football hooligans of the 1970s and 1980s. At their best, they were more like bonfire night rowdies or the mods and rockers of the 1960s. They were against Salvationists for what they stood for,

---

28. 15 February 1883.

29. N.H. Murdoch,' Salvation Army Disturbances in Liverpool, England, 1879–87', *Journal of Social History*, vol 25, issue 3, Spring 1992 p. 579.

not for who they were and their riots posed no enduring threat to the social order. Harassing teetotal Salvationists and assertive Hallelujah lasses was almost a sport. Moreover, just as Salvationists were treated as heroes when they left prison, so too were Skeletons. When one returned to Tunbridge Wells railway station in February 1886 after completing his sentence, he was carried by supporters up the hill in triumph.

Reading now about the Skeleton Army with their turnip-throwing practices and loutish attacks, they can appear to be quite comical. (Canadian Salvationists allegedly made omelettes out of the eggs thrown at them in Canada!) They were experts at devising ways of intimidation and humiliation. However, there was a serious side to these attacks. It could be particularly terrifying for young Hallelujah lasses. It took real courage to march though a screaming, taunting, armed mob with just a tambourine in hand. It was nothing short of a miracle that more people were not killed[30] or that more did not suffer serious injuries because the riots could involve thousands concentrated in narrow thoroughfares. Small-town police forces were unprepared to deal with such large-scale disturbances and gave Salvationists little protection.

Salvationists could divide communities and families. Those who were 'saved' were often resented by those who kept up their normal way of life. The riots often pitted working class against working class, labourer against labourer. Tradesmen who supported the Army were boycotted and could be put out of business. In extreme cases, employers threatened employees with the sack if they got saved. Ironically, once the Skeleton Army became perceived as a menace, membership of it too became a disadvantage when trying to get a job. Court records show that often male Salvationists had a similar occupational and class background to the Skeletons opposing them. They sometimes swapped sides, often from Skeleton to Salvationist – although Tom Stocker, a butcher's boy, a witness to a riot in Romsey, admitted in court that he marched with both groups depending on how he felt![31] It is also probable that some

30. Nigel Bovey, after his extensive research, concluded 'The Salvation Army did not – and does not consider Susannah Beatty and Sarah Broadhurst, who died a few years after their injuries, as martyrs'. Email, 17 June 2021. But there were certainly 'collateral' deaths due to the opposing parades such as that of the bricklayer, Isaac Buckingham, in Chapter Five. Also, *The Times*, 20 March 1885, reported that a sixteen-year-old boy died at Wyke when a horse took fright at a Salvation parade and went into the crowd.

31. *Salisbury Times*, 24 March 1883.

hooliganism/vandalism was carried out by people (using the 'cloak' of the Skeleton Army) for reasons of personal vendettas – especially in small communities – and had nothing to do with the Salvation Army itself.

Bailey believes that the Salvation Army was an expression of independent, working-class cultural development, not an agency of middle-class domination and that 'it was the beneficiary of an emerging working-class consciousness',[32] similar to the temperance bands, trade unions and co-operative society branches. Sometimes Skeleton Armies too demonstrated an independence from their middle-class masters by continuing to attack Salvationists against their wishes, as was the case in Worthing.

The Skeleton attacks were in the end counter-productive. The tactic of passive resistance and unjust imprisonment, so successful when later used by Gandhi in India and Matin Luther King in America, attracted huge sympathy for Booth's Army. Although they occasionally did physically fight back, on the whole they did not, which made their attackers look like cowards, especially for their assaults on defenceless females. Salvationists linked the persecution they suffered to the persecution of Protestants under Queen "Bloody" Mary Tudor and the attacks on other religious groups like the Quakers. They were placing themselves in a long tradition of struggle for religious and political liberty. Furthermore, by being despised and persecuted, they could readily identify with the suffering of their Lord. Consequently, there was never ever a shortage of martyrs for the cause. Whilst in prison, they were often comforted by the sound of an Army band parading round it, as at Maidstone in 1888 when the local band sang, 'Our Comrades in the Cold Dark Cell'.

Ultimately, the Skeleton Army and their backers were less defeated on the streets than in Parliament and in the law courts. Booth's use of the legal system – often hiring top London barristers like Thomas Sutherst, who went up and down the country on his behalf, charging paltry fees – was exemplary. He also gradually attracted support from important political and Establishment figures in late Victorian Britain. Local petty-minded magistrates and councillors were no match for them. Also, harsher sentences meted out to Skeletons, such as the sentence of eighteen months' hard labour given to one in Tunbridge Wells in April 1886, were a deterrent. Skeleton Armies usually disbanded after

32. Bailey (2014), p.70.

heavy sentencing, although Luton council had a rather unique way of dealing with the Skeletons. They swore in their leaders and 200 roughs as special constables and kept them in the town hall with refreshments and beer whilst the Army paraded!

In 1909, Booth's second in command, George Scott Railton, admitted that the Army in Britain had faced more violence than in any so-called 'heathen' land. One of the ironies of the Skeleton attacks is that, according to some commentators, they actually significantly helped the Salvation Army to survive and prosper. The famous Victorian journalist and Army supporter, W.T. Stead, who died in the sinking of the *Titanic*, wrote:

> Much as the Salvation Army has been helped by its friends, it would have been at a comparative standstill but for its enemies. They have enabled it to pose as the champion of liberty of speech and liberty of procession; they have furnished it with a noble company of officers whose university has been the jail, and who have been tempered in the furnace of tribulation before they have been called to the ministry of love for the salvation of the lost. . .[33]

As Bovey comments, 'it is a moot point as to what would have happened without such opposition'.[34]

33. Arch Wiggins (1964) vol 4 1886–1904 ch. 2 p. 279.

34. Email, 16 June 2021.

Epilogue

Within two years, Booth's *Darkest England* scheme, which was originally given a warm welcome by substantial sections of the trades union and Socialist press, came under severe criticism. As donation cheques had to be made out to him personally, there were accusations that the money was benefitting his family and financing his foreign tours and that the whole scheme was flawed. Despite reports[1] proving that all the money donated went towards the scheme and not to him or his family, it suffered from the adverse publicity. It ultimately proved to be a failure and the annual funds needed to sustain it never materialised. A 3,000-acre colony had been acquired at Hadleigh in Essex but its mixed farming and brick manufacturing made financial losses. In the Army's city shelters, the level of hygiene was criticised and its workshops – 'elevators' – accused of undercutting wages. It also failed to acquire the overseas colonies intended and instead sponsored emigration abroad. By 1905, the London Trades' Council was denouncing the emigration of good workers needed at home. There was also a racial aspect to it: numerically increasing the number of white men in the colonies. However, the *Darkest England* scheme did, in the long run, enhance the Salvation Army's reputation. No other religious organisation had attempted to do anything like it on such a massive scale.

1. *The Truth about the Salvation Army Finances* by the journalist Arnold White. His report blew away the fallacy that the Army was enriching the Booth family. The Lord Onslow Committee of Enquiry (19 December 1892) was led by an eminent lawyer Sir Henry James and recommended Booth appoint trustees to run the "In Darkest England" fund. He refused.

When the Army gave food to strikers' families during the early trade union struggles of the 1880s and 1890s, it was heralded as Salvation Socialism. (Indeed, the 1889 Christmas edition of *The War Cry* had a supplement entitled *Salvation Socialism.*) Bailey has written how Salvationism and Socialism: 'swept through areas like a new religion. Salvationists and Socialists alike sought not only their own spiritual and social welfare, but also the deliverance of their neighbourhoods and workmates from personal vices and denigrating social conditions.'[2] Both groups were united in their determination to establish the right to hold open-air meetings and processions. Nonetheless, it was the Army's dogmatic insistence that sin was the authentic source of poverty, that drunkenness caused unemployment, and its non-political stance, which made the labour movement gradually distance itself from Booth.

By concentrating on social work, the Army could publicise how many poor people they were helping materially rather than how few heathens they were saving. It no longer concentrated on militant evangelism in urban areas. In fact, between 1883 and 1890 membership had been in decline – weekly sales of *The War Cry* had gone down by at least 60,000[3] – and some have argued that the concentration on practical social work reversed this decline and helped to make the Army accepted and respectable. When Queen Victoria addressed him as General Booth (without the inverted commas) in a telegram in 1897 in response to his Diamond Jubilee congratulations, William exclaimed, 'Now I am a General beyond dispute!'[4] In 1903, the *Tower Hamlets and East End Local Advertiser* declared that 'the Army owes its popularity to its social work'.[5] By then, Charles Booth's *London Poverty Maps* had concluded that unemployment, under-employment and low wages were the chief causes of poverty rather than indulgence in alcohol.

---

2. Bailey (2014), p.67.
3. *The War Cry*, 17 May 1890. From 350,000 to under 290,000.
4. In his article, *Religion in an Age of Empire: The Salvation Army and British Imperialism, 1878–1914*, Andrew Eason has argued persuasively that the Army began to "embrace the monarchy enthusiastically. In the wake of the Darkest England social scheme, which solicited support from governments at home and abroad, the organisation began to view royal occasions as opportunities to express fidelity and imperial pride". (p.108)
5. 14 February 1903.

By 1899, the Army had 6,822 corps in 45 different countries, with 14,441 male and female officers. The Social Wing had thirteen social farms, 92 rescue homes, 53 workshops, shelters for 13,288 people, 112 food depots and supplied 6,207,733 meals during the year. *The War Cry* was translated into 21 languages.[6] Later on, such was their impact in the area of welfare, it was mooted the government might ask it to run the workhouses. Even then, however, its concentration on social work was not entirely welcomed by other churches. One clergyman claimed that it brought tramps to the London bridges and embankments in order to raise money. Bramwell Booth wrote, 'it was the deans and vicars who went about making statements we were after the poor people's money and that presently we should be off "to America!"' There was also criticism from the East End. In December 1895, *The Times* reported on a demonstration of unemployed men of Poplar with a band. Its banner read:

> As we see them. Our motto is 'Blood and Gold'. The Salvation Army Limited.
> General Bill Booth.
> Notice! Only Good willing Christian Slaves need apply.
> Notice! Unemployed wanted to work. Sixpence a week.
> No work-shirkers need apply. Gold is Good.[7]

* * *

In his later years Booth became obsessed with the number of people his corps were saving. If the figures were low, he would berate the local officers for not praying enough! Sadly, he also fell out with three of his children – Ballington, Kate and Herbert, all holding leading positions overseas – who resented being moved arbitrarily to new locations and left the Army. Booth did not want his officers to stay too long in one place lest they sink into the relationship of pastor and flock; an idea he inherited from traditional Methodism. Moving on was Army policy and Booth made no exceptions.[8] The Salvation Army was 'his family'

6. Information from the *Pall Mall Gazette*, 21 August 1912.
7. Ibid., 14 December 1895.
8. He allowed Ballington Booth and his wife a three-year-extension in the United States beyond the normal five-year "moving on period", but Ballington still left. Neither he nor his brother, Herbert and sister, Kate, ever saw their father again after leaving.

and he refused to have any contact with his children who left. This may account for his sad-looking eyes in old age. However, he was also worn out by his work. As long ago as 1887, whilst giving a talk in his home town of Nottingham, he was described as being prematurely old by a reporter, who felt 'we were in the presence of a weird wilderness prophet burdened with an unearthly presence'.[9]

In truth, in the early days Booth's nepotism towards his family had been crucial: 'Notwithstanding their capabilities, Booth children were placed in positions of considerable authority at very young ages, often replacing more seasoned officers in the process.'[10] However, it had bred an atmosphere of unquestioning obedience, so important in the Army's early development, and had given it a solid foundation.

In 1906, Douglas Beven, in his *Startling Revelation: Eight Years' Experience in the Salvation Army*, complained about Army headquarters taking too much money from corps and the fact that the musical instruments had to be obtained from the trading department rather than cheaper sources elsewhere. More seriously for Booth was the critical memoir of one of his most senior former officers, *General Booth and the Salvation Army* (1910) by Alex Nicol who had been a 'Colonel', an editor of *The War Cry* and a close confidant for 30 years. He claimed that the Army paid more attention to the financial than to the spiritual and that it had underpaid its skilled workers. He criticised it for meeting criticism with silence, a point illustrated by its response to Brick's speech at Chipping Norton.

In May 1908, Booth was the *London Daily News* 'Man of the week'. The reporter who interviewed him wrote: 'You went in to meet a saint and a visionary. You came out having met the astutest man in the city. You feel that if the tradesman's son of Nottingham had applied himself to winning wealth instead of souls he would have been the Rockefeller of England.'[11] His business mind had managed to finance a world-wide movement using entrepreneurial techniques, although he himself lived a spartan lifestyle,[12] only ever claiming travel expenses.

After having travelled the world – including five times to the United States and Canada and three times to South Africa and Australasia – he spent his last few years travelling around Britain in a chauffeur-driven car visiting villages and towns, drawing great crowds wherever he went

9. *Nottingham Journal*, 28 December 1887.
10. Eason (2003), p.148.
11. 30 May 1908.
12. It was said an apple was his greatest luxury.

and greeted like a conquering hero. His hero, John Wesley had done the same by horse. Booth visited workhouses and prisons and even prayed outside their gates on execution days. With his long, white beard he looked like a biblical prophet of an ancient people. He had become a living saint, his career a religious romance, fêted by the rich and powerful, meeting kings, queens and political leaders and presidents, even opening the Senate in the United States. Newspapers declared he was the most popular man in England and a great social reformer. He had become 'respectable', something he had always resisted. However, he never forgot his purpose as an apostle of the poor. Whenever he saw a homeless person he would say, 'These are our people!'

In 1910, he commissioned the famous novelist of romantic fiction, H. Rider Haggard, to write a report on the Army's social work. The result was *Regeneration.* In a balanced report, he reported favourably on its activities and how many people it was helping and the self-sacrifice of its members. He concluded that: 'Love is its watchword, the spirit of love is its spirit, love arrayed in the garments of charity.' That same year when the Conservative Party lost the general election with their 'Vote Tory for cheaper beer and bacca' slogan, it would have reminded Booth of the old Skeleton Army banners.

Shortly before his death he spoke at the Royal Albert Hall to an audience of 9,000:

> He stood there, a tall, frail old man in black, swaying a little as though the gusts of applause that rose in waves of noise about him, actually stirred his body to and fro, as an old tree bends to the wind. His face was almost as white as his great mane, and as the long white beard, which flowed upon his black coat, but his eyes burnt with some of their old fire. His soul seemed to light them up, though his first words were a confession that he could not see a face in all that sea of faces, and stood in the blaze of lights as an impenetrable darkness.
>
> Then the voice that came as a faint, clear whisper through the great hall, where otherwise there was a deep long silence, he told the tale of his life, of his ideals, of his failures, of his achievements, of his hopes. It was a familiar story to everyone there, a story of continual self-sacrifice.[13]

---

13. *The Midlothian Journal*, 23 August 1912 (extract from an article by Philip Gibbs in the *Daily Chronicle*).

He had once said: 'I'd stand on my head at the top of the dome of St Paul's Cathedral if I thought I could help anybody by doing so.'[14] It is estimated in his lifetime that he preached between 50,000 and 60,000 sermons. He had outlived in turn ridicule, hostility and suspicion. For so long he had been looked upon as a self-advertising humbug and his Army as a money-making machine. However, he had lived down the criticism. As years went by, the good work of the Army had gradually worked itself into the public mind.

When he died in August 1912, totally blind after a failed cataract operation, his organisation was all over the world. The overwhelming press reaction was that he was the greatest evangelist since John Wesley and the 'saint of the nineteenth century'. The *Pall Mall Gazette* called him 'one of the most astounding men of modern Britain'.[15] The *Daily Chronicle*: 'one of the supermen of the age'.[16] The Archbishop of Canterbury declared that: 'he had done the scavenging work of the Church'.[17] There was even a memorial service for him in Eastbourne. The *Bath Chronicle* spoke for many when it declared: 'We can join in regretting his loss and honouring the memory of a man who was consumed by love of his fellow-creatures, and by an intensity of faith which could kindle faith in others and call forth self-sacrifice in an age when selfish materialism is rife.'[18]

Only *The Times*, of the national newspapers – who described Booth as having the 'temperament of the Prophet and Evangelist of old'[19] – was still putting 'General' in inverted commas and doubting the survival of the Army without him. Nevertheless, it praised his 'prodigious strength of character, his genius for seeing what would appeal to a large number of humble folk' and admitted 'there is much to be learnt from the Salvation Army and from the earnest, strenuous, and resourceful personality of the man who made it'.

Of the national newspapers, only the new Socialist *Daily Herald* printed any major criticism, declaring that: 'An extremely interesting charlatan has passed away' and denounced him as a quack doctor'.[20] The same paper published a stout defence the following week from the writer, Miss Gertrude E. Shaw:

---

14. *Derby Telegraph*, 21 August 1912.
15. 21 August 1912.
16. Idem.
17. *Brighton Gazette*, 28 August 1912.
18. 24 August 1912.
19. Idem.
20. *Daily Herald*, "Reflections", 23 August 1912.

'In Defence of General Booth'

The contemptible effort to belittle and vilify a man whose long and arduous life was spent in uplifting and redeeming the most degraded and miserable of mankind comes strangely from the columns of a journal representing the interest of the working classes, among whom the Salvation Army has done so wonderful a work all over the world. General Booth needs no defence from us – his work spoke for him, and will call out admiration and reverence in every heart that truly loves its fellows – but we are deeply concerned to make it clear that sympathy with the Labour Party does not imply, as this incident might lead some to believe, a contemptible spirit of jealousy and detraction towards those who accomplish miracles of reform by other than political means, inability to recognize the heroic, and blindness to the great spiritual forces which make for the regeneration of mankind.[21]

There was a mixed reaction in the East End. The *East London Observer* predicted that the Army would die out, 'perhaps more quickly than most people think. . . . Meeting places are empty and the red flag at street corners no longer draw the passers-by.'[22] It called for an enquiry into its 'character, position and work. . . . Any benefit received from the Salvation Army generally has to be paid for, and it is difficult to see where the philanthropy comes in.' Whilst the *Shoreditch Observer* declared that: 'in the dark places of the earth the Salvation Army has been a more powerful agency for good than all the other religious bodies put together. He [Booth] had to stand a fire of criticism and misrepresentation.'[23]

The most stinging criticism of Booth was in *Justice*, the small weekly radical organ of the socialist Social Democratic Federation:

'The Passing of a Successful Charlatan'

But for Booth's pernicious 'social' schemes the Army would have been defunct years ago. Money flowed to him for his religio-philanthropic quackery by which he professed to

21. Ibid., 28 August 1912.
22. 24 August1912.
23. Idem.

> be able to raise the submerged tenth without harming the capitalist order of society. The submerged tenth are still here, and curse him and all his works; his wretched soup, and his sweating 'elevators' that do not elevate. . . . Whatever his motives were, and of them we say nothing, his career for evil is finished.[24]

The criticism was extremely harsh but not surprising as some on the political left believed the Army, directly or indirectly, supported an unfair capitalist system in its repression of the poor. The transition from originally being perceived as an anti-Establishment organisation to being perceived as part of it caused resentment. However, if a man is to be judged by his legacy, then Booth's is overwhelmingly positive.

In the annals of faith there does not appear to be anything comparable to the Salvation Army. Uniquely, William Booth, starting from a humble little cottage in Nottingham, is probably the only man to have founded a giant religious organisation. Moreover, even though his *Darkest England* scheme failed, he had set out to fight poverty on a massive scale. By doing so, he raised new awareness of social conditions, forcing the problem of destitution on to the national conscience and had provoked a new desire for social reform. (Surely it was an achievement that, by the time of his death, the Army was going into pubs selling *The War Cry* and collecting money?) As the famous historian, E.P. Thompson, said of another great nineteenth century 'William', 'he is one of those men whom history will never overtake'.[25]

Prior to his funeral, 150,000 visited his lying-in-state at the Salvation Army Congress Hall before his coffin was transported to Olympia on the eve of his funeral pageant. A glass plate on the coffin permitted a view of his face and upper body, as had been the case with his wife:

> Many touching scenes were witnessed, and it was noticed that those who appeared most distressed were those who bore the most obvious traces of poverty. . . . A long line of poorly-dressed, unkempt working men approached the coffin with timid footstep, and stood gazing at the features, while charwomen,

24. 24 August 1912.

25. *William Morris, Romantic to Revolutionary*, (1955), Laurence and Wishart.

> cabmen, tram-car conductors, chauffeurs and policemen were also among the strangely assorted and unending procession.... There was an officer stationed to lift the children up.[26]

His daughter, Eva, who was by now head of the Army in the United States, arrived too late to see him before he died. At news of his death, she had had a nervous breakdown. At the funeral she stood silently with tears rolling down her cheeks. When it was her turn to speak, she cried, 'He was everything to me', before bursting into heart-rending sobs. She had to be assisted back to her seat by her sister. The funeral can still be seen on *YouTube*.

* * *

Bramwell, his eldest son, who henceforth referred to his father as 'The Founder',[27] attempted to sum him up:

> A vein of hardness in him ran side by side with a vein of exquisite tenderness. . . . His heart was a bottomless well of compassion, and it was for this reason principally that, although more widely and persistently abused than any other figure of his time, he was even more widely and tenaciously loved. . . . He really set out to do good to all men.[28]

It was no surprise that, when the envelope naming his successor was opened, it bore the name Bramwell. He already had a high profile because of his assistance to W.T. Stead, the editor of the *Pall Mall Gazette*, in exposing child prostitution and helping to raise the age of consent from thirteen to sixteen. Although some of those involved in the exposure were taken to court and received short prison sentences,[29] Bramwell was

---

26. *Yorkshire Evening Post*, 23 August 1912.
27. Catherine Booth's role has been increasingly recognised. John Larsson, the seventeenth General of the Army, in his recent book, *Thirteen Astonishing Years that Shaped the Salvation Army*, referred to her as the 'co-founder'.
28. Bramwell Booth, *Echoes and Memories*, ch. 1.
29. Stead, Rebecca Jarrett (a converted brothel keeper), Booth and another woman were all accused of the abduction of thirteen-year-old Eliza Armstrong, without her father's permission, in the attempt to prove that young girls were being trafficked to the Continent. It later turned out that the man claiming to be Eliza's father was not.

Figure 26. This image of William Booth preaching in Aylesbury Prison was part of a pictorial memorial to him in the *Daily Mirror* (21/8/1912).

Figure 27. William Booth's final journey.

acquitted but had had to face hostile mobs when going to and from the Old Bailey in 1885. At his father's death, newspapers queried whether the Army would divide up and become a sect or survive at all. In reality, Bramwell had been the organising force since Catherine Booth's death in 1890.

In an interview in *The War Cry* (May 1919), he said that the Skeleton Army had originated in Whitechapel, as 'Charrington' had claimed, and that, once the name had appeared in the press, the name had been taken up in other places. However, the *first* press mention of it came in Exeter in October 1881. During the First World War in 1915, to boost the morale of his 'soldiers', Bramwell, tongue-in-cheek, wondered whether the appearance of another Skeleton Army would help.

Bramwell led the movement until his death in 1929, by which time senior officers had decided his successor was to be voted in rather than secretly nominated. Eva, the daughter who had fought the Skeleton Army in Torquay and Eastbourne, eventually became the fourth 'General' of the Salvation Army in 1934.

The Army was ultimately successful as a movement because it had a simple understandable message and involved all its converts in its work. Those that joined felt part of something bigger than themselves and it gave meaning and an identity to their lives. It never succeeded in converting the working class as a whole though.[30] Indeed, in terms of saving souls, some observers in the East End felt it was the least successful organisation. It may not be a coincidence that today there is no corps in Bethnal Green or Hackney. Attempts to save slum-dwellers' souls proved to be a notable failure and many who joined the Army came from other religious bodies rather than the submerged masses. It never attempted to bring the culture of the educated classes to the poor. As Catherine Booth said shortly before she died, 'Christ came to save the world, not civilize it.'[31] It was a movement to oppose the staid complacency of other Christians and non-believers. In this, it was hugely successful.

Today, the Salvation Army works in virtually every corner of the world; it has a presence in more than 130 countries and a membership of 1.7 million. No one now remembers the Skeleton Army. Remnants of

---

30. With a membership of 200,000 by 1900, 'the Primitive Methodists were the most successful of all nineteenth-century denominations in reaching the working-class'. Horridge, *The Salvation Army*, p. 4.

31. *The War Cry*, 18 October 1890.

the disturbances in the shape of a bent cornet and blood-stained tattered flag can still be seen at the Citadel in Eastbourne. However, they had been a real threat. In a pawnbroker's shop in Exeter in 1903, a silver cup was discovered bearing the following inscription:

Presented to
Edward Williams
For stopping
The Salvation Army
From Assembly
Upon Angel Hill Tiverton
May 6th 1886.[32]

32. *Western Times*, 17 March 1903.

Bibliography

Books

Bailey, Victor, *Order and Disorder in Modern Britain: Essays on Riot, Crime, Policing and Punishment* (London: Breviary Stuff Publications, 2014)

Batchelor, Mary, *Catherine Bramwell-Booth* (London: Lion Books, 1986)

Bateman, Alan, *They Gave Their Lives* (London: Salvation Books, 2008)

Benge, Janet, and Geoff Benge, *William Booth: Soup, Soap and Salvation* (Edmonds, WA: YWAM Publishing, 2002)

Booth, Bramwell, *Echoes and Memories* (New York: G.H. Doran Co., 1925)

Booth, William, *In Darkest England and the Way Out* (London: Funk & Wagnalls, 1890)

Bovey, Nigel, *Blood on the Flag* (London: Shield Books, 2015)

Bramwell-Booth, Catherine, *Catherine Booth: The Story of Her Loves* (London: Hodder & Stoughton, 1970)

Chambers, George, *Eastbourne Memories of the Victorian Period, 1845–1901* (Eastbourne: V.T. Sumfield, 1910)

Clarke, Bob, *The Basingstoke Riots: Massagainians v The Salvation Army 1880–1883* (Basingstoke: Basingstoke Archaeological & Historical Society, 2010)

Claughton, Lilian, *Charles H. Jeffries: From 'Skeleton' to Salvationist leader* (London: Salvationist Publishing, 1946)

Collier, Richard, *The General Next to God: The Story of William Booth and the Salvation Army* (London: Collins, 1965)

Cox, Gordon, *The Musical Salvationist: The World of Richard Slater (1854–1939)* (Woodbridge: Boydell Press, 2011)

Eason, Andrew, *Women in God's Army: Gender and Equality in the Early Salvation Army* (Waterloo, Ontario: Wilfrid Laurier University Press, 2003)

Farthing, Peter, *1865: The Year that Made the Salvation Army* (London: Salvation Army Books, 2010)

Foote, George W., *Salvation Syrup: Or, Light on Darkest England: A Reply to General Booth* (London: Progressive Pub. Co., 1891)

Guy, Walter, *Marching with Music* (Eastbourne, Eastbourne Citadel Corps, 1964). It can be found at The Salvation Army International Heritage Centre.
Haggard, Sir H. Rider, *Regeneration: Being an Account of the Social Work of the Salvation Army in Great Britain* (London: Longmans, Green & Co., 1910)
Hare, Chris, *Historic Worthing: The Untold Story* (London: Cassell, 1991)
———, *The Secret Shore: Tales of Folklore and Smuggling from Sussex and Hampshire* (Pulborough: South Down Society, 2016)
Hattersley, Roy, *Blood and Fire: William and Catherine Booth and Their Salvation Army* (London: Little, Brown & Co., 1999)
Haw, George, *From Workhouse to Westminster: The Life Story of Will Crooks, M.P.* (London: Cassell & Co., 1907)
Horridge, Glenn K., *The Salvation Army: Origins and Early Days: 1865–1900* (Godalming: Ammonite, 1993)
Huggins, Stephen, *The Mob and the Mayor: Persecution of the Salvation Army at the Victorian Seaside* (Eastbourne: Sussex Academic Press, 2020)
Huxley, Thomas H., *Social Diseases and Worse Remedies* (London: Macmillan, 1891)
Inglis, K.S., *Churches and the Working Classes in Victorian England* (London: Routledge & Kegan Paul, 1963)
Jones, David, *Crime, Protest, Community and Police in Nineteenth-Century Britain* (London: Routledge & Kegan Paul, 1982)
Lamb, Edwin, *The Social Work of the Salvation Army* (New York: 1909)
Lansbury, George, *My Life* (London: Constable & Co. Ltd, 1928)
Larsson, John, *Thirteen Astonishing Years that shaped The Salvation Army, 1878–1890* (London: Salvation Books, 2019)
Longmate, Norman, *The Waterdrinkers: A History of Temperance* (London: Hamish Hamilton, 1968)
Manson, John, *The Salvation Army and the Public: A Religious, Social, and Financial Study* (London: Routledge, 1908)
McLeod, Hugh, *Religion and the Working Class in Nineteenth-Century Britain* (London: Macmillan, 1984)
Neville, Graham, *Religion and Society in Eastbourne 1735–1920* (Eastbourne Local History Society, 1982)
Nicol, Alex M., *General Booth and the Salvation Army* (London: Herbert & Daniel, 1910)
Railton, George S., *The Authoritative Life of General Booth, Founder of the Salvation Army* (New York: George H. Doran Co., 1912)
Report of the Committee of Inquiry upon the Darkest England Scheme, 19 December 1892 (London: Harrison & Sons, 1892) (A copy of the report is held in the Salvation Army Rare Pamphlet Collection, Pam/R.7)
Sandall, Robert, *The History of the Salvation Army 1865–78*, 7 vols (London: Nelson, 1947), vols 2 and 3
Search, Pamela, *Happy Warriors: The Story of the Social Work of the Salvation Army* (London: Arco, 1956)

Sims, George R., *How the Poor Live: and Horrible London* (London: Chatto & Windus, 1889)
Storch, R.D., *Popular Culture and Custom in Nineteenth-Century England* (London: Croom Helm, 1982)
Travis, John F., *The Rise of the Devon Seaside Resorts, 1750–1900* (Exeter: University of Exeter Press, 1993)
Walker, Pamela J., *Pulling the Devil's Kingdom Down: The Salvation Army in Victorian Britain* (Berkeley: University of California Press, 2001)
Wiggins, Arch R., *The History of the Salvation Army: Volume IV: 1886–1904* (London: Thomas Nelson & Sons, 1964)
Wilson, P.W., *General Evangeline Booth of the Salvation Army* (New York: Scribner's Sons, 1948)
Winston, Diane, *Red-Hot and Righteous: The Urban Religion of the Salvation Army* (Cambridge, MA: Harvard University Press, 1999)

Articles and pamphlets/periodicals

Arnstein, Walter, 'The Murphy Riots: A Victorian Dilemma', *Victorian Studies* 19, no. 1 (1975), pp. 55–71
Bailey, Victor, '"In Darkest England and the Way Out": The Salvation Army, Social Reform and the Labour Movement, 1885–1910', *International Review of Social History* 29, no. 2 (1984), pp. 133–71
———, 'Salvation Army Riots: The "Skeleton Army" and Legal Authority in the Provincial Town', in Tony Donajgrodzki (ed.), *Social Control in Nineteenth Century Britain* (London: Croom Helm, 1977), pp. 231–53
Briggs, Asa, 'The Salvation Army in Sussex, 1883–1892', in M.J. Kitch (ed.), *Studies in Sussex Church History* (Falmer: Leopard's Head Press, 1981)
Eason, Andrew, 'Religion in an Age of Empire: The Salvation Army and British Imperialism, 1878–1914', *Journal of Religious History* 45, no.1 (2021), pp. 91–111
Hare, Chris, 'The Skeleton Army and the Bonfire Boys, Worthing, 1884', *Folklore* 99, no. 2 (1988), pp. 221–31
———, 'Worthing in the Bad Old Days: Riot, Beer, and the Word of God: The Trials and Tribulations of the Rev. Francis Cruse', *Worthing Village Voices* (April 2021), - a community heritage website available at: https://worthingvillagevoices.org.uk/worthing-in-the-bad-old-days/ (accessed 11 October 2021)
Kneale, James, 'The Battle of Torquay: The Late Victorian Resort as Social Experiment', in Matthew Ingleby and Matthew P.M. Kerr (eds), *Coastal Cultures of the Long Nineteenth Century* (Edinburgh: Edinburgh University Press, 2018), pp. 79–97
Lyon, Edmund, '"An avalanche of wrathful violence": Physical Opposition to the Salvation Army, 1881–83', *Hackney History* 18, pp. 27–36
Murdoch, N.H., 'Salvation Army Disturbances in Liverpool, England, 1879–1887', *Journal of Social History vol* 25 issue 3, Spring 1992, pp.575–593

Pugh, Martin, 'Popular Conservatism in Britain: Continuity and Change 1880–1987',
Journal of British Studies 27, no. 3 (1988), pp. 254–82
Roberts, 'Brigadier' John, *The Battle of Torquay and One Month's Experience in the Devon County Prison*, Salvation Army Rare Pamphlets Collection, Pam/R.29, available at: https://www.salvationarmy.org.uk/about-us/international-heritage-centre/international-heritage-centre-resources/digital-collections/rare-pamphlets (accessed 15 October 2021).
Roberts, Matthew, 'Popular Conservatism in Britain, 1832–1914', *Parliamentary History* 26, issue 3 (2008), pp. 387–410
Spencer, Steven, '"The Fatal Gaze of this Moral Basilisk": The Salvation Army's War on Drink in Victorian Britain', *The Social History of Alcohol and Drugs* 33, no. 2 (2019), pp. 230–56
Swift, Roger, 'Guy Fawkes Celebrations in Victorian Exeter', History Today 31, no. 11 (1981), pp. 5–9
The General, *Orders and Regulations for Field Officers*, (London 1886)
The Salvation Army, *The Officers' Review May-June 1947*, (Salvation Army International Heritage Centre)
Turner, E.S., 'Hallelujah Lasses', *London Review of Books* 23, no. 10 (24 May 2001)

Websites

Exeter Memories: The Salvation Army in Exeter
The Skeleton Army, Tug Wilson
The Skeleton Army, Sunny Worthing

National Archives

In the search engine of the National Archives, under Home Office:
HO 45/9711/A51220, 'Disturbances: Salvation Army bands.'
HO 45/9960/X2676, 'Disturbances: Worthing, Sussex. Demonstrations against the Salvation Army.'
HO 45/9605/A1775 'Disturbances in Salisbury.'
HO 45/9607/A2886, 'Disturbances: Salvation Army meetings and processions at Basingstoke.'
HO 45/9613/A9275, 'Disturbances: Law Officers's Opinion 690 as to suppression of disturbances and instructions to Local Authorities . . .'
HO 45/9630/A23941, 'Disturbances: Salvation Army processions at Folkestone.'
HO 45/9636/A30742, 'Disturbances: Salvation Army disturbances at Luton.'
HO 45/9965/X18313, 'Meetings and Processions (See also Disturbances): Torquay Salvation Army.'
HO 45/9619/A15220, 'Disturbances: Salvation Army riots at Weston-super-Mare.'

HO 45/9666/A46170, 'Disturbances: Street processions of Salvation Army.'
HO 144/481/X32743 and
HO 144/482/X32743A, 'Disturbances: Salvation Army Disturbances at Eastbourne.'

Media

William Booth, recording of him preaching, available via YouTube at: https://www.youtube.com/watch?v=dSth5dpE6L4
Ann Feloy, The Just Cause: Worthing Community Play (2014)
Chris Hare, Worthing and the Skeleton Army (YouTube)
Riot Film Group, Marching to Music (2012)
The Sussex Book Club, 'Dare to be a Daniel': The Salvation Army Riots in Eastbourne. An audio recording from BBC Radio Sussex made, according to its producer, David Arscott, in the mid to late 1980s.

Newspapers

All national and local newspapers cited in the text

Index

Printed and bound by CPI Group (UK) Ltd, Croydon, CR0 4YY

24/08/2026

14947957-0004